NADIA AND LILI BOULANGER

Nadia and Lili Boulanger

CAROLINE POTTER
Kingston University, UK

ASHGATE

Published by

Ashgate Publishing Limited
Gower House
Croft Road
Aldershot
Hants GU11 3HR
England

Ashgate Publishing Company
Suite 420
101 Cherry Street
Burlington, VT 05401-4405
USA

Ashgate website: http://www.ashgate.com

British Library Cataloguing in Publication Data
Potter, Caroline
   Nadia and Lili Boulanger.
   1. Boulanger, Nadia 2. Boulanger, Lili, 1893–1918 3. Boulanger, Nadia – Criticism and interpretation 4. Boulanger, Lili, 1893–1918 – Criticism and interpretation 5. Women music teachers – France – Biography 6. Music teachers – France – Biography 7. Women composers – France – Biography 8. Composers – France – Biography
   I. Title
   780.9'22

Library of Congress Cataloging-in-Publication Data
Potter, Caroline
   Nadia and Lili Boulanger / by Caroline Potter.
     p. cm.
   Includes catalogue of Nadia's works (p. 165), catalogue of Lili's works (p. 174), and bibliographical references (p. 183).
   ISBN 0-7546-0472-1 (alk. paper)
   1. Boulanger, Nadia – Biography. 2. Boulanger, Lili, 1893–1918 – Biography. 3. Women music teachers – France – Biography. 4. Women composers – France – Biography. 5. Music – France – 20th century – History and criticism. I. Title.

   ML385.P75 2006
   780.92'2—dc22

2006002003

ISBN–13: 978–0–7546–0472–3
ISBN–10: 0–7546–0472–1

Printed on acid-free paper

Typeset in Garamond by Express Typesetters Ltd, Farnham

Printed and bound in Great Britain by MPG Books, Bodmin, Cornwall

Contents

List of Music Examples

Preface and Acknowledgements

Nadia (1887–1979) and Lili Boulanger (1893–1918) were pioneers in their fields and are two of the best-known women in music in the twentieth century. Their careers were closely linked during Lili Boulanger's short life, and there are several fascinating connections between their musical works. However, much of the existing literature on the sisters focuses on their (admittedly intriguing) lives rather than their musical achievements. The published studies by the American writer Léonie Rosenstiel on Nadia Boulanger (1982, reprinted as a paperback in 1998) and Lili Boulanger (1978) are based on a wealth of documentary evidence and supported by interviews with Nadia Boulanger and many people close to her. However, these books feature little critical appraisal of source material, a number of significant inaccuracies and little music analysis worthy of the name (none in the Nadia Boulanger book). Clearly, theirs is a 'good story': an attractive, talented but mortally ill young woman (Lili) achieves a certain amount of success as a composer, while her talented but plainer sister (Nadia) becomes one of the leading teachers of her generation and one of the first professional woman conductors, but allegedly gives up composing following the death of her sister, preferring to dedicate herself to teaching and to the promotion of her sister's works.

This popular view is true only up to a point. Nadia Boulanger's composing activities were more extensive than is generally known, and she did her best to conceal the real person and musician behind her carefully cultivated image. Moreover, surprisingly little of substance is known about her teaching methods, though I have studied some material at Lyon Conservatoire that sheds much light on this topic, and there is other documentary evidence available in the form of interviews with some of her surviving pupils. The most important book on Nadia Boulanger, by Bruno Monsaingeon, consists essentially of valuable interviews about her teaching activities, and Jeanice Brooks's articles on Nadia Boulanger's conducting career and connections with the Princesse de Polignac are essential reading for anyone interested in her long and varied career. Also, volumes of correspondence and the diaries of both sisters are housed in the Bibliothèque Nationale de France (BN), though a suitcase of material donated to the library after Nadia Boulanger's death in 1979 is subject to a thirty-year embargo. Some writers have speculated about the contents of the suitcase, some believing that letters or even missing musical works by Lili Boulanger may be stored here, but of course it will be impossible to prove or disprove these rumours until 2009.

Jérôme Spycket's book, *A la recherche de Lili Boulanger*, published in French in 2004, is largely based on the original manuscript sources in the BN. While this book uses many of the same sources (notably in Chapter 1), much of this material is published here in English for the first time and, again, Spycket's book focuses on the life rather than music of the composer. Lili Boulanger's diary is a particularly rich source for biographers (unlike her sister's, which is largely limited to lists of letters received and sent). By turns a diligent student and professional who is justifiably proud of her achievements, a lively young woman who loved parties and socializing, an invalid in pain or a typical teenager agonizing over her close relationships, Lili Boulanger reveals in her diaries an instantly likeable and very human character. Though she was often portrayed after her tragically early death as a saintly figure, it should come as no surprise that she was a far more complex and indeed touching human being than early hagiographies suggest.

Although Lili Boulanger's reputation as a composer is growing, her elder sister remains better known as one of the most important composition teachers of the twentieth century than as a creative artist in her own right. Yet, Nadia Boulanger helped prepare the ground, musically speaking, for her younger sister; she set a text, *Les sirènes*, for chorus and orchestra in 1905 that was set by Lili six years later, and, perhaps not surprisingly, they had many musical interests and influences in common. They sometimes set the same poets (and, on one occasion, the same text), and they shared a passionate interest in the contemporary French composers of their day, especially Debussy. The two sisters were both influenced by Debussy, and it appears they had similar literary tastes to the elder composer. Both sisters set poems by Maurice Maeterlinck, who was of course the author of the play *Pelléas et Mélisande*, and also of *La princesse Maleine*; in February 1916, Maeterlinck authorized Lili Boulanger to set the latter play as an opera. Some sources assert that she had almost completed the opera before her death, though there is little concrete evidence backing this up: only the short score of Act I, scene ii, two versions of the libretto and a sketchbook have survived.[1] Moreover, Nadia Boulanger's opera, *La ville morte*, written in collaboration with Raoul Pugno, was a setting of a play by another man who had worked with Debussy, Gabriele d'Annunzio. Contrary to received opinion, this four-act opera was completed before Pugno's death on

---

1 See Annegret Fauser (1997), 'Lili Boulanger's *La princesse Maleine*', *Journal of the Royal Musical Association* 122: 70. According to Fauser, three sketchbooks containing the *particelle* of the opera are lost. This splendid article, together with Fauser's work on women and the Prix de Rome, were important sources for the present book.

3 January 1914; a complete vocal score is now housed in the BN, as are the orchestrated versions of Acts I and III. But Pugno's death, coupled with the events leading up to the First World War, meant that the planned production of *La ville morte* at the Opéra-Comique never came to fruition. I have analysed their musical styles, highlighting similarities and differences and their places in French musical history.

Both sisters first came to public attention when they entered the Prix de Rome, the most important composition prize for Paris Conservatoire students, and much of their apprentice period as composers focused on preparation for this competition. Chapter 2 concentrates on their early development as composers and their entries in this competition. Both reached the final round of the Prix de Rome; Nadia Boulanger's best placing was the second prize she won in 1908, and many commentators believe that sexual discrimination prevented her from winning outright. In 1913, Lili Boulanger became the first woman to win the prize; arguably, she 'could' win because, as she was unlikely to live long, she would not be a professional threat to her male peers.

The gender issue cannot be avoided in any discussion of the sisters' musical activities. The sisters would simply not have had the educational opportunities that they did if they had not been born into an exceptionally musical family. But, despite this unusually privileged upbringing, the sisters exemplify the struggle women experienced when attempting to enter the professional musical world. But Lili Boulanger's approach to her career was outwardly more 'professional' than that of her sister; she was confident in handling large-scale genres (especially the choral work with orchestra), received many important commissions and signed a contract with a publisher. Nadia Boulanger, on the other hand, focused on the song and piano piece, genres which were traditionally associated with the lady amateur composer writing for domestic entertainment. Her most significant large-scale works were written in collaboration with her mentor, Raoul Pugno; his death in 1914 was arguably far more significant in her abandonment of her composing career than her sister's death four years later.

Both sisters (but especially Nadia Boulanger) suffered from critical hostility based on their gender. Although Nadia Boulanger refused to discuss the possibility that she had suffered discrimination (and she had a very traditional view of the proper roles of women and men), it is essential to examine the careers of both sisters in the light of the sexist comments they often encountered.

Since the primary focus of this book is the work of the two sisters and the impact they had on each other's careers, the long life of Nadia Boulanger after her younger sister's death is not investigated chronologically or comprehensively. However, as her teaching career is a central element of her reputation, Chapter 5 is devoted to this topic. In this chapter (which is partially based on a chapter, 'Nadia Boulanger: The Teacher in the Marketplace', published by Liverpool University Press in 2001), I aimed to collate information about her teaching methods and the content of her classes. As she never published any of her teaching materials (despite several solicitations from publishers), the archive at Lyon Conservatoire, together with the recollections of some of her pupils, was a significant source of information. In the final chapter, I investigate Nadia Boulanger's reputation in her own time and assess the impact of both sisters on the twentieth-century musical scene. Nadia Boulanger was a pioneer as a conductor and a tireless promoter of the music of her younger sister – though not of her own music.

Some parts of Chapters 2 and 3 were previously published in my *Musical Quarterly* and *Opera Quarterly* articles referenced in the bibliography. I am very grateful to Alexandra Laederich, of the Fondation Nadia et Lili Boulanger, for her encouragement; I was not, however, given access to the archives of the Fondation. I would also like to thank Edwin Roxburgh, Lucette Mansuy, Michel Crichton, Christel and Otfrid Nies, Peter O'Hagan and particularly Professor Robert Orledge for assistance of various sorts. Dr Tazul Tajuddin has been a source of constant support and has also helped with typesetting music examples.

Finally, I have attempted throughout this book to refer to the two sisters as Nadia Boulanger and Lili Boulanger rather than by first name alone; while this practice is not followed entirely consistently, it was abandoned only occasionally and then because the repetition of the surname would have been clumsy.

List of Abbreviations

BN	Bibliothèque Nationale de France, Paris
CNSM de Lyon	Conservatoire National Supérieur de Musique de Lyon
JAMS	*Journal of the American Musicological Society*
JRMA	*Journal of the Royal Musical Association*
OS	orchestral score
prem.	premiere
VS	vocal score

Dedicated to Tazul

CHAPTER 1

The Sisters and their Composing Careers

In the nineteenth and early twentieth centuries, the 9th arrondissement of Paris was by far the most popular residential area of the city with musicians. Berlioz moved to the area known as Nouvelle Athènes in 1834, and Liszt lived in the same area. Opera composers including Rossini, Massenet, Offenbach and Ambroise Thomas all lived in the area, and Verdi stayed there during his lengthy visits to the French capital. In the mid-nineteenth century, Pauline Viardot's Thursday salon at her 9th arrondissement home, 50 rue de Douai, was one of the most celebrated artistic meeting places in the city; her regular guests included Fauré, and the house was the venue for a performance of *Tristan and Isolde* in May 1860 with Viardot as Isolde and the composer singing Tristan.[1] Ravel was brought up in the 9th arrondissement, living there until he left the Paris Conservatoire in 1905, and later both Honegger and Milhaud lived in the area.[2]

The Boulanger sisters were born into a musical family (Juliette Nadia on 16 September 1887, Marie-Juliette Olga, always known as Lili, on 21 August 1893), the only two survivors of four daughters.[3] Nadia was born when the family lived in a flat at 36 rue Maubeuge in the 9th arrondissement; they moved to 30 rue La Bruyère (near the church Notre-Dame de Lorette)[4] before Lili's birth, and finally to 36 rue Ballu in the same arrondissement in 1904. The intersection of rue Ballu and rue de Vintimille, near this house, was named place Lili-Boulanger in 1970.

Their father, Ernest Boulanger (1815–1900) was a composer and former student of Berlioz's teacher François Lesueur at the Paris Conservatoire. He had some success as an opera composer after winning the Prix de Rome in 1836 and ended his long career as a singing teacher at the Paris Conservatoire and at the private Cours Gasset, where his colleagues included the pianist Raoul Pugno. His mother, Marie-Julie Hallinger, was a

---

[1] Nigel Simeone (1999), *Paris: A Musical Gazetteer* (New Haven: Yale), p. 144.

[2] Much of this information is taken from Nigel Simeone's fascinating book (ibid.). Pages 270–4 list properties in the 9th arrondissement occupied by musicians – a far longer list than for any other arrondissement.

[3] The other two daughters born to the couple were Ernestine Mina Juliette (born on 16 January 1885, who died 19 months later, possibly as a result of a fall) and Léa Marie Louise (born on 24 March 1898, died 18 August that year).

[4] This church was the site of Cavaillé-Coll's first organ in Paris (Simeone (1999), p. 156).

well-known singer who appeared regularly at the Opéra-Comique, and his father, Frédéric Boulanger, was a cellist in the Chapelle Royale. Frédéric Boulanger deserted the family when his son was still a child, but Ernest was devoted to his mother and lived with her until her death in 1850. His first three daughters were given the name Juliette in her honour.

One of Ernest Boulanger's last pupils was the Russian-born Raïssa Myschetsky. They may have met in 1874, while Ernest was conducting a concert in her home town, St Petersburg; Raïssa later claimed that she fell madly in love with him and vowed to follow him to Paris. She was around forty years his junior and always used the title 'Princesse', although there is no evidence to suggest that she was entitled to do so. There is some uncertainty over her year of birth, her real name (she also used the name Rosa or Rose in Russia) and social background. Some reports suggest she was a governess, and she definitely obtained a teaching certificate. It is also possible that she married while still in Russia, as she also used the surname Shuvalov. This was perhaps a proxy marriage which would enable her to leave the country, as a young woman would have required her husband's or father's permission to leave.[5] However, Raïssa married Ernest in 1878 and no more was heard of M. Shuvalov; indeed, Nadia Boulanger recalled that her mother was reluctant to talk about her early life in Russia.

Raïssa Boulanger was the dominant figure in the sisters' lives, particularly after her husband's death in 1900. She took charge of their education, forced Nadia to work very long hours even as a child, and was a constant presence alongside her daughters, even on occasions (such as Conservatoire classes) when this was not expected. She also instilled the importance of correct social, moral and religious behaviour into her children, though her religion, like so much else about her, remains a mystery. While Raïssa attended Mass and Nadia Boulanger always claimed that she and her mother were both born into the Catholic faith, there is no evidence that Nadia was baptized as a child.[6]

The sisters' family background was, to say the least, propitious for future musicians. Friends of the family included Charles Gounod and Gabriel Fauré; indeed, according to Léonie Rosenstiel, 'At the age of six, [Lili] had already read at sight Fauré's *Une Prière*, with the composer at the piano.'[7] When they moved to 36 rue Ballu in 1904, their neighbours in the building included Paul Vidal, the conductor and professor of composition at the Conservatoire; a frequent dinner guest who the girls knew as 'Popaul'.

---

[5] Léonie Rosenstiel's books on the sisters feature detailed biographical information about the Boulanger family.

[6] Léonie Rosenstiel (1998), *Nadia Boulanger: A Life in Music* (New York and London: Norton), p. 39. Nadia did, however, receive her First Communion in May 1899.

[7] Léonie Rosenstiel (1978), *The Life and Works of Lili Boulanger* (Cranbury, NJ: Associated University Presses), p. 37.

Georges Caussade, a counterpoint teacher at the same institution who played a major role in Lili Boulanger's musical development, also lived locally.

In addition, their mother was supposedly aristocratic though not wealthy. Their mother's hypothetical aristocratic background meant that it would have been unseemly for her to work to support the family, so this responsibility fell to Nadia when their elderly father died. At Lili's birth, their father had asked Nadia to vow that she would always take care of her sister, and throughout her life, Nadia kept her word, feeling her responsibility all the more because Lili never fully recovered from a bout of bronchial pneumonia contracted at the age of 2. In Léonie Rosenstiel's words, 'Raïssa Boulanger had carefully trained her elder daughter to take responsibility and duty very seriously indeed. To ignore either was a terrible transgression. Nadia remembered vividly the change in her life that this occasion [the birth of Lili] brought with it. "I walked into my mother's room a carefree child," she used to say, "and I left it an adult."'[8]

Lili developed intestinal tuberculosis (which would nowadays have been diagnosed as Crohn's disease) when she was only 3. At the time, this was incurable, though the family often took her to spas in the vain hope of some respite. Her life, and that of her mother and sister, was overshadowed by her illness.

Although Nadia hated music as a small child, an incident while her mother was pregnant with Lili changed everything; she claimed 'One day I heard a fire bell. Instead of crying out and hiding, I rushed to the piano and tried to reproduce the sounds. My parents were amazed.'[9] Aged only 5, she began to study music seriously, making up for what her parents considered was lost time. Initially, she studied with her father, singing to his piano accompaniment, and from 1895 she studied solfège and piano with Mlle Laure Donne, who was considered to be one of the leading teachers in Paris. She also took organ lessons and quickly revealed a talent for the instrument which her family encouraged. There was a harmonium in the flat in rue La Bruyère, where they lived at this time, but when they moved to rue Ballu they installed a full-size Cavaillé-Coll organ for Nadia. Monsieur and Madame Boulanger wanted Nadia to enrol at the Paris Conservatoire and eventually pursue a musical career.

The Paris Conservatoire was founded in 1792 as a school for military music, but by the early twentieth century its *raison d'être* was to be a school which trained students who would enter a branch of the music profession. The training it provided was, above all, systematic. All students began by studying solfège (aural training), moving on to harmony and practical

---

[8] Rosenstiel (1998), p. 30.

[9] Ibid., p. 34.

instrumental or vocal studies. In the Boulanger sisters' day, only those students who successfully passed their harmony exams could move on to a composition class. Counterpoint and fugue were the disciplines a would-be composer had to master before proceeding to freer styles of composition. Jane Fulcher notes, however, that 'counterpoint … carried clerical associations that were considered threatening in a Republican institution and was thus systematically deemphasised'.[10] The secular and vocational slant of Conservatoire teaching meant that composers were essentially trained to write for the lyric theatre; vocal studies also focused on the nineteenth-century repertoire which was the staple diet of these theatres.

From 1896 to 1905, the Conservatoire was directed by Théodore Dubois, a conservative musician and a family friend of the Boulangers who had promised Ernest that he would oversee Nadia's musical education. Instrumental music was not the primary focus of student composers, and music history was not on their curriculum at all. The aims of the Schola Cantorum were quite different; at this institution, which was founded in 1897 at the beginning of Nadia Boulanger's student days, the French musical tradition, church music, instrumental music and music history were all central to the student experience. Gabriel Fauré – another family friend, as we have noted – assumed the directorship of the Conservatoire in 1905 (following the scandal of his pupil Maurice Ravel's failure to be admitted to the preliminary round of the Prix de Rome) introducing reforms which resulted in a wider repertoire being studied and the introduction of music history as a compulsory subject.

The Paris Conservatoire was also in most senses a meritocratic institution, where success was based on winning prizes in end-of-year competitions. However, women were barred from some classes, including fugue and composition, until the end of the nineteenth century, even though women had enrolled on other Conservatoire courses since the earliest days of the institution. Indeed, a Mlle Félicité Lebrun won a second prize in violin in 1797 (the inaugural year of the Conservatoire), and a first prize the year after.[11] But in the Boulanger sisters' day, male and female students were taught solfège and harmony separately, and there were separate syllabuses for the violin and piano classes for the two sexes, the women playing less demanding repertory.

Nadia Boulanger entered the Conservatoire at the age of 9, though she audited classes unofficially when she was only 7 years old, two years below the minimum age for enrolment. The school address until 1911 was 2 rue

---

[10] Jane F. Fulcher (1999), *French Cultural Politics and Music from the Dreyfus Affair to the First World War* (Oxford: Oxford University Press), p. 27.

[11] *Le ménestrel* (10 September 1910); this fact is mentioned in the journal in a review of a book entitled *Les femmes compositeurs* by an American author, Otto Ebel.

Bergère in the 9th arrondissement, conveniently close to the family home.[12] Even at this age, Nadia was impatient to complete her studies and launch herself into a career. She took the end-of-year competition in elementary musicianship at the end of the year, but according to Rosenstiel, 'The accumulated burden of preparation and tension exhausted her, and after having been locked in her private cubicle to complete the evening portion of the examination, the young girl fell asleep, a lapse of which she was ashamed for the rest of her life.'[13]

Students who had reached the required standard were awarded one of four distinctions, which were, in ascending order of merit: accessit; premier accessit; deuxième prix; premier prix. These prizes were announced in the weekly music journal *Le ménestrel*, and the Prix de Rome was the subject of intense media interest, however surprising this may seem nowadays. A large number of first prizes (premier prix) was the recognized guarantee of quality for musicians, and Nadia Boulanger's aim was to win as many as possible in the shortest possible time. In 1897, she was placed third out of 55 female candidates for the solfège examination (when she was by far the youngest student in the class), and in 1898 she won a first prize. She was admitted to Paul Dukas's piano accompaniment class in 1900; a misleading title as students did not simply accompany others at the piano, but studied disciplines including figured bass and score reading.

In 1903, she won a first prize in harmony, as a student of Dupuis, following this in 1904 (before her seventeenth birthday) with first prizes in organ, fugue and piano accompaniment. These Conservatoire prizes were of crucial importance to her future career, being guarantees of her ability and status as a teacher. She also enrolled in Fauré's composition class in 1904. Fauré was at this time very much a Conservatoire outsider, having trained at the Ecole Niedermeyer, a small Parisian school which focused on training church musicians. He was therefore ineligible to compete in the Prix de Rome, and was not interested in the operatic career that was the traditional destiny of Conservatoire composition students. Despite his reputation as a composer of songs, piano works and chamber music of great originality and quality, he was not employed by the Conservatoire until 1896, and even then he was only narrowly preferred to Charles Lefebvre, a composer of far less importance. Jean-Michel Nectoux writes that 'Fauré's class attracted the Conservatoire's most original talents, and reports from many of these people lead us to believe that the class was more what we would now call a seminar, rather than the traditional Conservatoire composition class, which was essentially conceived by some as the transmission of good recipes for preparation for the sacrosanct Prix de

---

12 It moved to 14 rue Madrid – on the border of the 8th and 9th arrondissements – in 1911.
13 Rosenstiel (1998), p. 37.

Rome cantata'.[14] The composer Jean Roger-Ducasse recalls that the harmonization of chorales was a favourite teaching tool of Fauré's, and that 'We did not approach musical forms in chronological order (which was rather unusual). The students gradually absorbed the work, and he reminded us of the rules … of forms ranging from a motet to a song, from a quartet movement to a fantasy, from the slow movement of a symphony to a genre piece, always illustrating his thoughts with examples taken from the masters.'[15] Nadia Boulanger surely drew many ideas for her own composition classes from Fauré.

At the same time, according to Rosenstiel, 'Lili was learning informally in months what it had taken her elder sister years to master'.[16] Lili Boulanger was a precocious musical talent; she learned violin, piano, voice and harp, making her public debut on the violin on 5 September 1901, during a Mass in Trouville, where the family spent their summers until 1904. She studied piano with a Mme Chaumont, and performed as a pianist in the Salle Erard in Paris as early as 1904 (when she played Beethoven's Sonata in C sharp minor as part of a class performance). Intriguingly, she shared a piano programme at the same venue with Juliette Toutain on 26 March 1905;[17] Toutain was one of the first women to compete in the Prix de Rome, which Lili would eventually win. When her health permitted, Lili would occasionally accompany her elder sister to her Conservatoire classes.

One of the judges for Nadia Boulanger's piano accompaniment examination in 1904 was Raoul Pugno, who became a crucially important figure in her musical career. Pugno (1852–1914) had studied at the Ecole Niedermeyer and the Paris Conservatoire, though as an Italian citizen he was ineligible to compete for the Prix de Rome. He later taught at the Conservatoire, being professor of harmony from 1892 to 1896 and professor of piano from 1896 to 1901. As a composer, he concentrated on salon pieces and other lighter genres, though his compositional activity decreased after 1893, when he decided to focus once more on performing. One of the leading pianists of his age, he gave recitals with Eugène Ysaÿe from 1896 and, on 6 May 1893, provided a two-piano

---

[14] 'Tous écoutent la parole du maître: Gabriel Fauré et ses élèves', in Anne Bongrain and Alain Poirier (eds) (1999), *Le conservatoire de Paris: deux cents ans de pédagogie, 1795–1995*, p. 348: 'la classe de Fauré attira les talents les plus originaux de l'établissement, et les témoignages nombreux que l'on possède laissent à penser qu'elle tenait peut-être davantage du séminaire au sens où nous l'entendons aujourd'hui, que de ce que l'on entendait alors par classe de composition, conçue essentiellement par certains comme la transmission des bonnes recettes pour la préparation de la sacro-sainte cantate pour le prix de Rome.'

[15] Cited ibid.: 'On n'abordait pas chronologiquement, si je peux dire (et cela est un peu particulier), les différentes formes. Au fur et à mesure des travaux des élèves, il rappelait les règles … d'un motet à une mélodie, d'un mouvement de quatuor à une fantaisie, d'un adagio de symphonie à un morceau de genre, affirmées par des exemples toujours demandés aux maîtres.'

[16] Ibid., p. 39.

[17] Programmes reproduced in Rosenstiel (1978), p. 36.

accompaniment with Debussy for a celebrated performance of *Das Rheingold*. In 1903, he made a recording for the Gramophone and Typewriter Company in Paris.[18] He was well-known both for his Mozart interpretations and for his vast size; one contemporary cartoon shows his rotund frame surrounded by a semicircular piano designed to accommodate his girth.[19]

Although in a long-term relationship and the father of a daughter, he was also a notorious womanizer, and his close friendship and collaboration with Nadia Boulanger led to gossip and damaging publicity for the young woman. Léonie Rosenstiel, who interviewed her in her declining years, claimed that 'In the end, the old memories would surface and, in her later years, Nadia could not refrain from crying when she thought of Pugno and how much she had wanted to have a child',[20] though if this had indeed happened, the scandal would have been immensely damaging for Nadia Boulanger and her family. From 1904, the Boulanger family spent the summer in Hanneucourt, a hamlet near Gargenville, where Pugno also had a home. They bought their own property, Les Maisonnettes (which faced Maison Blanche, Pugno's house) in 1908.

Nadia Boulanger started teaching privately once she had obtained all her first prizes, and also launched herself as a performer on the piano and organ. On 4 February 1905, her mother hosted a concert in their home during which Pugno, Vierne and Nadia Boulanger all performed; this was an opportunity to show off their new organ to influential Parisian musicians, many of whom attended the concert. Nadia's public début took place on 16 March that year, in a concert dedicated to the works of the family's friend and neighbour, Paul Vidal.[21] In what little spare time she had, Nadia Boulanger attended concerts in Paris, often benefiting from free tickets from influential friends, including Fauré.

Although her studies were now officially over, Pugno recommended that she audit Charles-Marie Widor's composition class. She did this for the next four years, a decision which saddened Fauré, as she never explained to him why she left his class. Although it is not clear why she changed teachers, it is reasonable to assume that Fauré's lack of interest in the Prix de Rome was a decisive factor. Her continued association with Widor, a Conservatoire professor who, unlike Fauré, was an experienced and successful teacher of Prix de Rome finalists, enabled her to enter the prestigious competition and therefore follow in her father's footsteps. She

---

[18] Guy Bourligueux (2000), 'Pugno, (Stéphane) Raoul' in www.grovemusic.com.

[19] Amazingly, this may just possibly have been a real instrument rather than a joke; the excellent musical instrument museum in Brussels possesses a piano of this design dating from the late nineteenth century.

[20] Rosenstiel (1998), p. 63.

[21] Ibid., p. 55.

reached the final round of the Prix de Rome for the first time in 1907,[22] though her cantata *Selma* failed to win a prize.

However, the following year she was placed second with her cantata *La sirène*, although she created a stir in the preliminary round when she wrote an instrumental fugue instead of the vocal fugue demanded by the judges. Lili Boulanger records the incident in a diary entry on 2 May 1908: 'Nadia wrote a fugue for instruments and a really lovely chorus. The instrumental fugue wasn't permitted to be judged according to the Conservatoire – Saint-Saëns didn't want Nadia's work to be heard, but the jury overruled him and allowed it to go forward.'[23] No doubt because of this complication, the departure of the six top contenders for the final cantata round in Compiègne was delayed from 15 August to 19 August.[24]

Nadia Boulanger attracted a good deal of press attention after this success, including a gushing interview with Camille de Sainte-Croix, a journalist with *La petite république*, which is worth quoting at length. For his article, entitled 'Une jeune fille moderne', Sainte-Croix met the Boulanger family in Gargenville. He says that Mme Boulanger 'lives there from July to October, with her two daughters, Mlles Nadia and Lili, in the constant company of their gracious friend and neighbour, Mlle [Renée] Pugno' – and, one imagines, her father Raoul Pugno, though it was certainly more politic to assume that the young women were close to the daughter rather than the father. He continues: 'Lili, the younger daughter, is at most fifteen years old [he was right]. Very tall, slim, supple, her gestures are delicate and lively, and her distracted and wandering eyes are nonchalant and dreamy. Scarcely recovered from a long illness, she is resting in the country, awaiting a full return to good health, so she can allow her surprising gifts to blossom.' Lili is therefore presented as a budding musician, though first and foremost she is an attractive young 'femme fragile'.

But Nadia was the main focus of this interview: 'The elder, Nadia, is the attractive and serious child who, in the past three or four years, has drawn the attention of the musical world and who, the other month, made the Institut chatter. ... In 1908, she has just won the Second Grand Prix [de Rome] and is therefore, with Mlle Hélène Fleury, the only woman who, for a century, has appeared at this level in the order of merit.' Sainte-Croix predicted that Boulanger would go one better than Fleury, and win the first prize: 'Nadia Boulanger, a loyal and energetic 20-year-old, will not fail to do this. She will also not fail to have a splendid career as a great composer. ... Oh! Nadia Boulanger is so much a woman of these times! She is so much

---

[22] She entered the competition for the first time in 1906, but failed to progress beyond the first round.

[23] 'Nadia fait une fugue instrumental et un choeur tout-à-fait joli. La fugue instrumentale n'est pas permis au jugement du Conservatoire – Saint-Saëns ne veut pas qu'on entende l'oeuvre de Nadia, mais le jury passe par-dessus et l'admet quand même.'

[24] Also recorded by Lili in a diary entry on 15 May 1908.

one of these fine people, born in the last years of the nineteenth century, whose talent and education combine with genuine feminine charm, and a beneficiary of those moral victories made by other brave ladies over we men!'[25] Camille de Sainte-Croix clearly believed that women's time had come, and that nothing would prevent Nadia Boulanger from fulfilling her promise as a creative artist. His references to the physical appearance and feminine charms of both sisters show that, whether they liked it or not, their gender would play a major part in the way their work was received by the public.

In the same year, 1908, Nadia Boulanger began the teaching career that lasted until shortly before her death in 1979. Although she again reached the final round of the Prix de Rome in 1909, and her cantata *Roussalka* was considered by *Le courrier musical* to be 'the most expert and original composition',[26] she failed to win a prize. She therefore decided to rewrite the cantata under a new title, *Dnégouchka*, complete with a reworked text by Georges Delaquys, Pugno's son-in-law. Unusually (and irregularly) for a Prix de Rome competition failure, this work was performed in Paris on 13 May 1909 in the Concerts Colonne series.

Socializing was very important to the Boulanger family. Wednesday afternoon was Raïssa Boulanger's 'at home' day, as it was usual for someone of her background to welcome guests for tea and conversation at a regular time each week. She also frequently invited friends to dinner, often before or after a theatre or concert outing, and hosted chamber concerts. While many middle-class Parisian families hosted musical evenings *en famille*, few had friends of such renown to grace the event.

Lili Boulanger's earliest surviving diary – from 1908 – reveals how much she relished these occasions. On 16 January, she wrote: 'Amazing crowd – probably 100 people. Evening at home, Pugno and Hoffman play …

---

25 In *La petite république* (22 July 1908): 'Mme Boulanger habite là de juillet à octobre, avec ses deux filles, Mlles Nadia et Lili, en la constante compagnie de leur gracieuse amie et voisine, Mlle Pugno. … Lili, la cadette, compte, au plus, quinze ans. Très grande, mince, souple, elle a des gestes légers et vifs, qui démontent la nonchalance rêveuse d'un joli regard vague et distrait. A peine quitte de longue maladie, elle attend, en ce repos de campagne, le plein rétablissement de santé, pour reprendre le cours d'éclosion de ses dons suprenants, un moment arrêtés.' … L'aînée, Nadia, c'est cette belle et grave enfant qui, depuis trois ou quatre ans, retient l'attention du monde musical et qui, l'autre mois, mit l'Institut en rumeur. … En 1908, elle vient de gagner le second grand prix et se trouve, par ce fait, avec Mlle Hélène Fleury, la seule musicienne qui, depuis un siècle, soit montée si haut dans l'ordre des récompenses. … Nadia Boulanger, elle, dans la foi et l'énergie de ses vingt ans, ne le ratera pas. Ce qu'elle ne ratera pas non plus, c'est une magnifique carrière de grand compositeur. … Oh! Qu'elle est bien de son moment, Nadia Boulanger! Comme elle est bien une de ces fines personnes, nées dans les dernières lustres du 19e siècle et dont la vocation tout autant que l'Education allient aux charmes féminines les plus sincères, le bénéfice des conquêtes morales effectuées, dans ce même temps, par leur sexe justement enhardi, sur notre humanité masculine!'

26 Cited in Rosenstiel (1978), p. 83.

Dupeyron and Madame Bérizat sing.'[27] Lili's favourite expression in this
diary is undoubtedly 'monde fou' (amazing crowd); although she frequently
mentions that she was ill, when she was well she loved nothing more than
being surrounded by crowds of people and going out. The family went to
concerts on 18, 20, 21, 22 and 23 February, a schedule which was not
unusual. The first of these was a Pugno recital at the Salle Pleyel followed,
in Lili's words, with 'supper at Welper [she surely means Wepler, the well-
known seafood restaurant] Bd de Clichy, about 17 people'. Pugno
performed again on 22 February (a concert which also featured Nadia
Boulanger as piano accompanist to the flautist Philippe Gaubert) and yet
again on 23 February, this time in the Concerts Colonne series. Lili does
not give details of the programme or the performances, evidently being
more interested to write that 14 people came to dinner afterwards on the
23rd.

Nadia Boulanger often said that her mother was the primary influence
on her life and work; her mother taught her the importance of applying the
highest possible standards to herself and, by extension, to others. Also,
Boulanger's refusal to waste a minute of time – exemplified by her very
busy teaching schedule – can be ascribed to her mother's influence. Her
teaching day often began at 8 a.m. and continued until the early hours of
the morning. For as long as she was able, she worked six days per week.
She would often invite students to lunch or dinner and continue a class
during the meal. Finally, her mother constantly stressed the importance of
doing one's duty and, as a teacher, Boulanger dedicated her life to her
students.

At first, she taught solfège, harmony, counterpoint, fugue, piano and
organ privately. Many of her students for these subjects came to her
through word-of-mouth recommendation, often via family connections.
The family's reputation as fine musicians must have provided her with many
advantages when setting herself up as a music teacher. But at the same time,
it was not considered desirable for a young lady of her social background
to solicit work through advertisements.

Lili Boulanger was one of her first pupils, studying fugue with her sister
from 3 July to 11 October 1911[28] as an adjunct to her Conservatoire classes
and private lessons with Georges Caussade. She had begun studying with
Caussade on 10 December 1909 (a diary entry on 10 December 1911 states
'2 ans que je prends des leçons avec Caussade'), and his impact on Lili is
comparable to that of Pugno on her elder sister. He taught Lili up to three

---

[27] Her extant diaries are now housed in the Bibliothèque Nationale de France, Paris. 'Monde fou –
probable 100 personnes. Soirée à la maison Pugno et Hoffman jouent … Soirée très amusante –
Dupeyron et Mme Bérizat chantent.'

[28] Rosenstiel (1978), p. 49.

times a week, though her fragile health, and the family's travels to Gargenville and other places, meant that these lessons often took the form of correspondence classes. For example, from 10 April to 11 May 1911, she travelled to Nice with her mother for a series of therapeutic baths, and to stay with her new friend Miki Piré, who shared her Franco-Russian origins, was a former piano pupil of Pugno's and became Lili's closest friend. Her only diary entries during this period reveal her bathing schedule and the fact that she sent five pieces of work to Caussade. The work he set included fugues and the setting of texts which had been prescribed for past Prix de Rome competitions (the surviving works will be discussed in Chapter 2). Lili notes all their classes in her diary and records Caussade's remarks on her work; it is clear that his opinion mattered a great deal to her.

She worked extremely hard, especially from 1912 when she made the decision to enter the Prix de Rome. On 27 March 1912, Lili records that the family went to Gargenville for a short stay, and that she will be working on a chorus, *Soir d'été* (the chorus used in the 1911 competition) and a fugue with a subject by Caussade (which had previously been used for the Conservatoire organ competition). She worked on the chorus on 28 and 29 March, and on the fugue for the next two days. On 1 April, she wrote: 'It's snowing – it's wonderful to see this white curtain in front of my window. Received telegram from Caussade – I'm working a lot, progressing more. In the night of Monday to Tuesday [1–2 April] I copy the fugue until I go to sleep and do the orchestration. I feel very ill.'[29] But on the next day, she was determined to continue: 'Return from Gargenville – I cry and am ill, have nearly finished – haven't slept since Monday morning. 6 p.m. lesson with Caussade [she notes that this is her 81st lesson with him] – I'm exhausted.'

Lili also circles St George's Day in her diary, and writes far more about Caussade than any other person in her diaries from 1910 to 1913. She may well have had a normal teenage crush on him, and was disappointed that he did not say anything when she brought him a bunch of lily of the valley, a traditional seasonal gift, on 1 May 1912. On the second anniversary of the beginning of her lessons with him, she wrote in her diary: 'At 2 p.m., I showed him the test chorus [formerly used in the Prix de Rome] *Les sirènes* – very happy. At 5.30 p.m. I showed the second test chorus, *Renouveau*, and my first fugue (in F minor), and *Les sirènes* to Pugno at his home – he is happy with it and more than kind. Charming dinner at home [she lists the guests] – I am touched to see the exquisite way Caussade talks about me to Pugno – it's touching to see a teacher being interested in a pupil like

<hr>

29 'Il neige – c'est splendide de voir ce rideau blanc devant ma fenêtre. Reçois dépêche de Caussade – travaille beaucoup, avance plus. D[an]s la nuit de lundi à mardi copie fugue jusqu'au repos et fais l'orchestre. Je suis très souffrante.' … 'Reviens de Gargenville – pleure et suis malade, ai presque fini – je n'ai pas dormi depuis lundi matin. 6 h[eures] Caussade – suis éreintée.'

that.'[30] (It is interesting that the chorus texts used at the Conservatoire are numbered, revealing that they must have been set texts for Prix de Rome hopefuls.)

Lili Boulanger passed the entrance examination to Paul Vidal's composition class in January 1912, a move which would enable her to enter the Prix de Rome in her turn. Her motto at this stage in her life could well have been 'work hard, play hard'; she went out to concerts and dinners frequently. She enjoyed going to a ball on 10 February 1912 (arriving home at 2.45 the following morning) and danced with several young men, and her reactions to these men are completely typical of an inexperienced 18-year-old. She wrote in her diary: 'I was dressed as Isabeau de Bavière – very successful, even too much! My dancing partner intimidated me so much that I was scared.'[31]

Another momentous occasion early that year was the first concert featuring her works; Lili devotes much diary space to a report of this occasion. Naturally, she notes that 21 people dined with the family after this concert, which was another event at 36 rue Ballu featuring well-known performers who were also family friends. Pugno and Nadia Boulanger played works for two pianos by Saint-Saëns and Nicolaieff, and Jane Bathori performed songs by Debussy (accompanying herself) and Ravel (accompanied by the composer, who also stayed to dinner). But for Lili, the most important thing was that, in her words: 'For the first time, things by me were played – the chorus *Les sirènes* (the Engel-Bathori choir conducted by Aubert) – and *Renouveau* as a vocal quartet, with Mlles Berthier et Sanderson, M. Pollet and Tordo [her singing teacher] – this number was encored – everyone was very kind – Caussade came – completely overwhelmed.'[32]

She entered the Prix de Rome for the first time that year, telling Caussade (according to her diary) that she wanted to enter the competition as a 'pupil of Caussade and Vidal', but he persuaded her that this was a politically inadvisable move.[33] While she reached the final, her poor health meant that

---

[30] Entry on 10 December 1911: 'A 2 h[eures] lui montre "Les Sirènes" choeur d'essai (4e) – très content. A 5h30 – montre à Pugno chez lui Renouveau (2e) choeur d'essai ma 1er fugue (en fa min[eur]) et Les Sirènes – il est plus que gentil et content. Dîner charmant à la maison … – je suis émue de voir la façon si exquis dont Caussade parle de moi avec Pugno – c'est touchant de voir un professeur s'intéresser à une élève comme cela.'

[31] 'Suis déguisée en Isabeau de Bavière – beaucoup de succès, même trop! Mon danseur m'a tellement intimidé que j'ai eu peur.'

[32] Written at the beginning of her 1912 diary; 'On joue pour la 1re fois des choses de moi – 1 choeur Les Sirènes (les choeurs Engel-Bathori sous la direction de Aubert) – et Renouveau en quatuor vocal – Mlles Berthier et Sanderson, M. Pollet et Tordo – ce dernier est bissé – tout le monde a été très aimable – Caussade est venue – tout-à-fait emballé.'

[33] Entry on 29 April 1912; 'Je voulais faire mettre élève de P[aul] Vidal et de Georges Caussade – il m'a dit que cela me ferait du tort auprès de Vidal – mais il a compris le sentiment de la connaissance qui m'a inspiré l'idée.'

she had to withdraw from the competition a week into the composition of her cantata. On her return home from Compiègne, Lili wrote that 'Caussade has been so exquisitely considerate about this, and he has never said that there is a lesson to be learned from it'[34] – leaving one to imagine that this was her mother's response (Lili notes that they had had 'a scene' that day).

Lili Boulanger was an ambitious student, as a letter to Fernand Bourgeat, the chief administrator of the Conservatoire and a family friend, reveals. She wrote pleading her case for winning a Conservatoire composition prize: 'Admit it, I don't bother you much – so do me a favour for once and make a big effort to oblige your old Lili. I'm submitting a chorus and a vocal quartet to the examiners; intervene with those members of the jury with whom you are friends and ask them to perform the two things and beg them, if they find my work as good as people say it is, to give me the Prix Lepaul and allow my works to be played in the orchestra class.' The familiar tone of the letter (she uses the 'tu' form) and her unashamed attempt to use a personal contact to gain advantage over other students belie the traditional image of her as a weak, unworldly individual.[35] And her strategy worked: *Le ménestrel* announced on 8 February 1913 that she won the prize with her choral works *Pour les funérailles d'un soldat* and *Printemps*. The article also announced that she would enter the Prix de Rome that year.

In 1913, Lili Boulanger was placed second in the preliminary round of the Prix de Rome (with the chorus *Soir sur la plaine* and a fugue) and was therefore admitted to the final. She mentions this result in her diary on 13 May, adding that Pugno came round for dinner that evening and 'Mother teased me so much that I cried.'[36] Lili went one step further than her elder sister, winning the Prix de Rome with her cantata *Faust et Hélène*. The judgement was on 5 July 1913, and Lili was the overwhelming victor, receiving 31 out of 36 votes. Significantly, the cantata was not dedicated to her Conservatoire composition teacher, as was traditional, but to Nadia. But as Nadia was away on a concert tour (and perhaps because she did not want to detract from her sister's success), Lili performed the traditional courtesy visits to members of the Institut with her friend Renée de Marquein.

The cantata was performed several times in Lili Boulanger's lifetime, including a gala performance at a Presidential ball at the Elysée Palace on 2 March 1914. Its first orchestral performance took place during the official

---

34 Entry of 15 May 1912: 'Caussade plus qu'adorable – il ne veut à aucun prix considérer ce temps comme une leçon.'

35 Letter sold by Drouot in June 1987 and quoted in Fauser (1998), p. 107; 'Je ne te rase pas souvent, avoue-le – laisse-toi donc faire pour une fois et mets-toi en quatre pour obliger ta vieille Lili. Je montre à l'examen 1 choeur et 1 quatuor vocal – interviens auprès de ces membres du Jury que tu trouves particulièrement de ton amitié afin qu'il fasse exécuter les deux choses et prie-les, s'ils trouvent mon travail aussi bien qu'on le dit, de m'octroyer le Prix Lepaul et qu'on me joue à la classe d'orchestre.'

36 'Maman me tacquine [*sic*] tant que j'en pleure.'

awards ceremony at the Académie des Beaux-Arts on 8 November 1913, conducted by Henri Busser, an old friend of the Boulanger family. Busser had been the assistant conductor for the first performance of Debussy's *Pelléas et Mélisande* in 1902, and Debussy himself reviewed a Concerts Colonne performance of *Faust et Hélène* which took place a week after the prize-giving ceremony. Debussy wrote in *S.I.M.* on 1 December 1913:

> Lili Boulanger ... is only nineteen years old. Her experience of the techniques of writing music is far greater, however! Certainly, here and there we hear those little strings with which one knots the ends of phrases in this type of work, but Mlle L. Boulanger adds fine workmanship to them. The entry of Hélène, on otherworldly pulsations of divided violins, sways gracefully. But as soon as she comes on the scene, Hélène, interpreted by Mme [Claire] Croiza, has the timbre of a daughter of Zeus, overwhelmed by so many conflicting destinies. Faust is intoned by the pretty voice of M. David Devriès.
>
> If the character of Mephistopheles and the inevitable trio are a little conventional, we should not forget the conditions under which one writes a cantata, which are most unfavourable.[37]

Lili Boulanger's Prix de Rome success led to a contract from the publisher Ricordi which assured her of a fixed yearly stipend, enabling her to devote herself to composition and giving her the regular income that Nadia Boulanger had always sought for herself. This contract was signed on 1 August 1913.[38]

In the summer of 1913, Nadia Boulanger and Raoul Pugno embarked on a concert tour of French spa towns which had the dual function of publicizing Nadia Boulanger as a performer and enabling Pugno to undergo various treatments for a kidney condition. Despite his precarious health, they also arranged to travel to Russia for concerts later that year. They were to share programmes with the soprano Marie de Wieniawska, who had been the soloist for a performance of Boulanger and Pugno's jointly composed song cycle *Les heures claires* in the Salle des Agriculteurs on 4 May 1912, accompanied by Pugno. After a long journey, which was extended by an unscheduled stop in Berlin as Pugno went down with bronchitis, they arrived in Moscow on 22 December 1913. They were due to give their first

---

[37] Review reprinted in François Lesure (ed.) (1987), *Monsieur Croche et autres écrits* (Paris: Gallimard), pp. 252–3: 'Lili Boulanger ... n'a que dix-neuf ans. Son expérience des diverses manières d'écrire la musique en a bien davantage! Il y a bien, ça et là, des petites ficelles avec lesquelles on noue les fins de phrases dans ce genre d'ouvrage, seulement Mlle L. Boulanger y met plus de fine rouerie. L'arrivée d'Hélène sur des battements aériens de violons divisés, ondule avec grâce. Mais à peine arrivée, Hélène, par la voix de Mme Croiza, prend l'accent qui convient à une fille de Zeus, accablée par tant de destins contraires. Cependant que Faust susurre par la jolie voix de M. David Devriès. Si le personnage de Méphistophélès, l'inévitable trio, sont un peu conventionnels, il ne faut pas oublier les conditions dans lesquelles on écrit une cantate. Ils sont nettement défavorables.'

[38] Rosenstiel (1978), pp. 112–13.

concert that evening, but as Pugno was in no fit state to play, Wieniawska's husband contacted Serge Rachmaninov and asked whether he would be able to replace Pugno as Wieniawska's accompanist and play two short solo items of his choice. But, in Léonie Rosenstiel's words, 'Rachmaninov lived in morbid fear of germs and sudden death' after his daughters' recent bouts of typhoid in Italy. He refused to replace Pugno, and the concert was therefore cancelled.[39]

Pugno did not recover from this illness, and died on 3 January 1914. This was a severe blow to the Boulanger family and to Nadia in particular. As Léonie Rosenstiel succinctly wrote, 'Pugno's name alone had helped to generate public interest in Nadia's concerts and recitals. Now he was gone.'[40] Rosenstiel also claims that Nadia Boulanger detested Rachmaninov for the rest of her life for not agreeing to replace Pugno on their arrival in Moscow, and indeed the Russian composer was heavily criticized in the local press for not assisting Pugno and the other members of his party.[41] Nadia had to deal with the return of his body to Paris, and was obliged to ask Miki Piré to send money urgently to enable her to cover all necessary expenses.[42] Pugno was buried on 14 January in Gargenville after a service in La Trinité, the largest church in the 9th arrondissement; Lili regretted that her poor health meant that she could only attend the service and not the burial.[43]

Like Debussy, Lili Boulanger arrived in Rome quite some time after her competition success, and later than she was expected. She was supposed to arrive by the end of January 1914, but she submitted a doctor's note stating she was unfit to travel. However, many Villa officials did not believe she was indeed ill, and this misunderstanding created problems for the composer during her first stint in Rome. Lili Boulanger and her mother left Paris on 20 February 1914, and according to her diary 'about twenty friends' saw them off. They arrived in Nice the following day, staying with Miki Piré and her family until 2 March; Boulanger started composing the song cycle *Clairières dans le ciel* during this visit, having been introduced to Francis Jammes's book of poems, *Tristesses*, by her friend. The Boulangers then took an overnight train to Florence (where they had to register with the police), and finally travelled to Rome, arriving on 9 March, an unfortunate time to arrive as no taxis were available at the station due to a strike.

Her late arrival, and the fact that she was accompanied by her mother, displeased the director of the Villa Medici, Albert Besnard,[44] although her

[39] Rosenstiel (1998), p. 116.
[40] Ibid., p. 118.
[41] Ibid., p. 116–17.
[42] Ibid., p. 117.
[43] Diary entry, 14 January 1914.
[44] Albert Besnard (1849–1934) was a French painter who won the Prix de Rome in 1874. He became

mother moved into the Imperial Hotel on 12 March. Boulanger also had great difficulty sanctioning approval for a lady's maid, rather than a male servant, to attend to her, and it appears that Besnard did not appreciate how serious her illness was. Inmates of the Villa Medici were expected to take their meals together, but when she was ill, Boulanger was unable to leave her room. Her diary entry of 18 May both hints at the problems she had with Besnard and shows that she was far from reluctant to get involved in student life: 'Trouble with Besnard who called me to his office – he's really nasty. Send a telegram to the Institut on the advice of [Pierre] Bodard, [Jean] Dupas etc. [two fellow Villa residents] – they are kind – we go out to dinner at the Concordia and then to the cinema before returning.'[45]

Lili Boulanger was immediately popular with her fellow Villa residents. Bodard started a portrait of her on 3 April and showed it to her on the 30th, according to her diary, and despite visits from a doctor three days in succession from 1 May, she mentions an 'evening at the cinema with Bodard, Dupas, Martial, [Louis] Lejeune, [Jacques] Debat-Ponsau – ice-cream afterwards at Faraglia' in an entry dated 3 May.[46] She also had her sister to keep her company in Rome from 4 April until 23 May, though the only other time Nadia is mentioned in her diary is on 26 April, when the sisters attended a concert of two Beethoven symphonies, conducted by Mengelberg, with Dupas. On 5 June, she sent Nadia a letter, enclosing a piano piece in B major which is probably a work now housed in the Bibliothèque Nationale (though its texture is often unsympathetic to the piano, and only its final bars are in that key).

Lili composed a short piece, *Cortège*, from 4 to 5 June, originally for piano and then arranged for violin and piano; the latter version is dedicated to the violinist Yvonne Astruc. Her few diary entries for this month show how much fun she was having in the Villa. On the 9th, she writes 'we shut Bénard in the bell tower'; this unfortunate young man had a argument with Lejeune two days later, but Lili acted as peacemaker by speaking to both friends and, not least, by sending them two bottles of Asti. On the 13th, 'after lunch we threw water on Dupas who sprayed all of us – I'm working (copying my piece) – after dinner, we broke plates while having fun. We wanted to kill the lizards on the ceiling of the loggia, but we didn't manage it.'[47] In the remaining entries, she suggests that she is tired of her mother

---

director of the Villa Medici in 1914, shortly before Lili Boulanger's arrival.

45 'Ennuis avec Besnard qui me fait appeler chez lui – il est vraiment méchant. Envoie, sur le conseil de Bodard, Dupas etc. télégramme Institut – ils sont touchants – allons dîner au Concordia, puis au cinéma – et rentrons.'

46 'Soir cinema avec Bodard, Dupas, Martial, Lejeune, Debat-Ponsau – glaces après chez Faraglia.'

47 'Après déj[euner] on arrose Dupas qui en arrose tous – je travaille (copie de mon morceau) – après dîner, on casse des assiette en jouant. [On] veut tuer des salamandres au plafond de la loggia – on n'y arrive pas.'

accompanying her everywhere: 'Maman [Cyrillic characters] – in the morning, the afternoon – she's also coming tonight – id[em].'[48]

While Nadia Boulanger was visiting her mother and sister in Rome, the female intermediate-level piano students at the Paris Conservatoire wrestled with the difficult sight-reading piece that she had been commissioned to write for the 1914 end-of-year exams. A critic writing in *Le ménestrel* said that the 31 students found the exercise far too challenging and modern.

The First World War and the Comité Franco-Américain

Lili Boulanger left the Villa without having obtained the necessary approval of the director on 1 July, first going to Miki Piré's home in Nice (where she finished *Clairières dans le ciel*) and then to Gargenville. However, her stay in the Villa Medici, and that of everyone else, was curtailed by the outbreak of the First World War on 1 August 1914. Almost immediately, she started a voluminous correspondence with her Villa friends which soon expanded into a support network for musicians on active service. Her aim was to keep spirits up by forwarding mail and arranging for food, clothing and money to be sent to soldiers.

Nadia Boulanger became involved in this work, and the two sisters contacted American artists and diplomats in search of practical support. Their organization became known as the Comité Franco-Américain du Conservatoire National de Musique et de Déclamation, and the American architect Whitney Warren (a corresponding member of the Académie des Beaux-Arts) was its patron; he had already been involved with a similar initiative for former students of the Ecole des Beaux-Arts, the leading art school in Paris. Warren's principal role was to go to the United States to raise funds from charity dinners and concerts.

On 23 September, the sisters wrote to Widor, Saint-Saëns, Fauré, Charpentier, Paladilhe and Vidal, asking whether they would consent to being honorary committee members. These composers responded with enthusiastic declarations of support for the cause, with one notable exception: Saint-Saëns. Perhaps because he had not forgiven Nadia Boulanger for the 'affaire fugue' of 1908, Saint-Saëns replied on 29 September that he was often asked to be an honorary member of various committees and 'I have not responded to such requests for some time now. I do not really trust the charity you talk about, but cannot refuse you or M. Whitney Warren. So, use my name and do what you want with it.'[49] The

---

[48] Entry on 26 June 1914: 'Maman [Cyrillic characters] – le matin, d[an]s l'après-midi – elle vient aussi le soir – id.'

[49] Letter housed in the BN: 'depuis quelque temps je ne réponds plus à ces demandes. Je n'ai pas

Conservatoire professors Widor and Vidal were named Vice-Presidents, an astute move as the sisters wanted to use the Conservatoire as the primary contact address for the Gazette they planned to send to their comrades.

An American composer and diplomat, Blair Fairchild,[50] acted as Treasurer, and the Boulanger sisters were the founding secretaries,[51] thus playing a typically female, supportive role during the First World War. Unlike their fellow Conservatoire graduates, they were not called up; this left them free to help soldiers keep in touch with their friends and families. Their unique position as elite female Conservatoire graduates gave them the contacts to fulfil this role successfully, and Lili in particular had a winning personality which easily persuaded everyone to assist her in any venture she undertook. The sisters' wartime activity also proved decisive for Nadia Boulanger's future career, as the Conservatoire Américain, which was central to her teaching activities and the reason why she gained a reputation as a teacher of American students, evolved after the war thanks to contacts she made through her committee work.

Lili Boulanger's very busy composing schedule and bad health did not prevent her spending time involved in committee work for her Franco-American organization and other war-related causes. Almost every day in January 1916, she notes a committee meeting in her diary; on 3 January, her mother and sister visited their friend Loulou Gonet while she stayed at home, occupied with paperwork. By the 6th, she admits: 'I am lying down, being exhausted from this tiring committee work and those concerts in December',[52] though even being confined to bed did not prevent her from doing her committee work and keeping up a vast correspondence.

Lili Boulanger's fragmentary diary of 1915 also hints at fascinating developments in her personal life. Frustratingly, only five tiny monthly diaries (for the months of January, February, March, April and June) survive in the Bibliothèque Nationale collection, but this extant material documents a close relationship with Jean Bouwens, the son of her guardians Marthe and Richard Bouwens van der Boijen. She wrote to Jean on 1 January, telegraphed him on the 2nd and in the second half of February and early in March, they saw each other almost every day. On 6 April, she noted that he was leaving for Bourges, and on the following day she wrote in red ink

---

grand confiance dans l'oeuvre dont vous me parlez, mais à vous et à M. Whitney Warren je ne puis rien refuser. Prenez donc mon nom et faites-en ce que vous voudrez.'

[50] Born in 1877, Fairchild had read politics and music at Harvard before entering the diplomatic service. He abandoned this career in 1901 on moving to Paris to study with Widor, in whose class he stayed until 1903. See Jérôme Spycket (2004), *A la recherche de Lili Boulanger* (Paris: Fayard), pp. 270–1.

[51] Rosenstiel (1998), p. 125.

[52] 'Moi, étant éreintée, de toutes les fatigues du Comité et des concerts en décembre, je reste couchée.'

(not the pencil of the other diary entries): 'Richard came after dinner to talk – we had a serious conversation – I told him our decision.'[53]

Jean came to see her again on 16 April; he brought her some carnations and they each kept a white flower, and an enigmatic note in her diary '4 mois – f. – J.B. L.B.' reveals that this was a significant anniversary for them. Indeed, Jérôme Spycket believes they could have become secretly engaged (the 'f' would then stand for 'fiançailles' – engagement).[54] Other entries in the April diary suggest she was commemorating other significant days: on 27 April she wrote 'It's 8 months since our trip to Gargenville. The last day before <u>Nadia, Jean and I</u> leave for Nice', and on 30 April a still more intriguing '<u>9 months since the conversation in my office in Gargenville</u>'.[55]

Spycket's researches explain the intriguing list of numbers at the end of this diary: '268 + 281 = 549 (550 jours le 7 avril – 79 semaines le 4 avril)'. Lili Boulanger was partial to these precise calculations; we have already seen that she kept a careful record of the number of classes she had taken with Caussade, for instance. The date of 7 April was her 'serious' discussion with Jean's father, and the date 550 days after this is 8 October 1916 – Jean Bouwens' twenty-first birthday. Spycket therefore determined that the couple became secretly engaged on 4 April and were awaiting Jean's coming of age to announce it officially.[56] If they were indeed engaged, it must have been broken off fairly rapidly as there are no references at all to Jean in the surviving 1916 and 1917 diaries, though Lili Boulanger did continue to see his parents regularly.

Lili Boulanger therefore had her mind on Jean and her composition work as well as her wartime committee activities in this very busy period. The sisters edited a *Gazette des classes de composition du Conservatoire* to distribute to mobilized students; the first number had a print run of 300 copies and was sent out in December 1915. They had received news from 54 Conservatoire graduates and teachers for this number, and were seeking contact details for a further 136 people. André Caplet wrote ruefully to the *Gazette*: 'I have just returned from the trenches, where for a week I have had all the time in the world to undertake a study of the pitch of those sounds known as "war noises". It's tiring for the ear and dangerous for the health.'[57] Indeed, Caplet's health was broken during the war as the result of a gas attack. While the composer Charles Koechlin was not mobilized because of his

---

[53] 'Richard vient après diner parler – n[ou]s discutons gravement tous les deux – je lui dis notre décision.'

[54] Spycket (2004), p. 265.

[55] 'Il y a aujourd'hui 8 mois de notre séjour à Garg[enville]. Le dernier avant dép. p[ou]r Nice <u>Nadia, Jean et moi</u>'; '9 mois de la convers[ation] à Garg[enville] d[an]s mon bureau.'

[56] Spycket (2004), p. 264.

[57] *Gazette* no. 1: 9; 'Je reviens des tranchées où pendant 8 jours j'ai pu tout à loisir faire des études sur la hauteur des sons: des "Bruits de guerre". C'est assez fatigant pour le tympan et dangereux pour la santé.'

age, he was characteristically a regular correspondent and passed on some startling news: 'I saw [Maurice] Delage the other day, who told me that Ravel (who had asked to enlist in the aviation section as a bomb-thrower) is still a lorry driver in Vaugirard.'[58]

The second number of the *Gazette* was printed in February 1916, and headed by a warning from censors that it was strictly forbidden to send copies of the journal to people in neutral countries. It is also clear from this warning that the editors should not, as they had done in the first number, mention the regiment or location of any of the soldiers, for security reasons. This number appeared after a serious dispute with the pianist Alfred Cortot which jeopardized the future of the *Gazette*. Nadia Boulanger sent a draft of a response to Cortot to Blair Fairchild in January 1916, and from the contents of her letter, it is possible to deduce that Cortot had objected to the 'Franco-American' designation of the Committee; to their using Conservatoire premises as an office; and, fundamentally, to the very existence of their charitable organization, not least because he was involved with an organization with similar aims, the Association Nationale. While there is no detail about Cortot's attempts to undermine the Comité Franco-Américain in Lili Boulanger's diary, she noted on 11 February that she had met Cortot at the Conservatoire at 1.30 p.m.

Blair Fairchild expressed his anger and frustration with Cortot's attitude far more openly than Nadia Boulanger. The sisters left for Rome in late February, as it was considered safe for Prix de Rome winners to return to the Villa Medici, but Fairchild kept them in touch with events by letter. He wrote to Nadia Boulanger on 21 February 1916: 'I have seen Cortot – and was most displeased by what he said, though we were very polite when we left each other. To start with, he was very unpleasant ... and he told me that, in brief, our Committee does not exist as it was not officially declared, and that he has the right to cause us a lot of trouble about that. I told him that I was unaware of that (and actually I thought you were going to sort that out before leaving) and I begged him not to do anything before you come back so we can put everything in order – and he promised he would do that. If necessary I can sort things out with Widor's help.'[59] During the

---

58 Ibid., 16; 'Delage que j'ai rencontré l'autre jour m'a dit que Ravel (qui avait demandé à passer dans l'aviation comme lance-bombes) continue à faire fonction de camionneur de poids lourds automobiles, à Vaugirard.'

59 Letters now housed in the BN. 'J'ai vu Cortot – et ce qu'il m'a dit m'a beaucoup déplu – quoique nous nous sommes quittés en très aimable façon. Pour commencer il a été très désagréable ... et il m'a fait remarquer qu'en somme notre Comité n'existe pas – n'ayant été déclaré – et qu'il avait le droit de nous ennuyer beaucoup là-dessus. Je lui ai dit que je ne le savais pas (et en effet je croyais que vous alliez le faire avant de vous en aller) et je le priais de ne rien faire à ce sujet avant que vous ne reveniez et que nous puissions nous mettre en règle – ce qu'il m'a promis. Au besoin je peux le faire avec l'aide de Widor.'

sisters' absence, their friend Renée de Marquein assisted Fairchild by acting as a general administrative assistant, a task she fulfilled more than competently; Fairchild described her in a postscript to the above letter as 'truly admirably devoted and of outstanding character'.[60]

Fairchild's efforts to placate Cortot worked. Cortot wrote in a letter to Fairchild on 24 February that he would not take any action until he had heard from Nadia Boulanger and consulted the Committee, and insisted that 'we will do nothing to hinder Whitney Warren's generous initiative'.[61] Warren's contribution certainly was generous; Fairchild mentioned in the letter to Nadia Boulanger cited above that he had given 50 000 francs to the cause. Cortot met members of the Association Nationale early in March 1916, and this Association voted not to do anything to harm the Comité Franco-Américain. It appears that they decided it was not worth offending Whitney Warren, who had made such a generous contribution.[62] Nadia Boulanger wrote to Blair Fairchild about the Cortot incident on 1 May 1916 (from Rome, where her sister was still unwell); she believed that 'he will <u>never</u> forgive us for simply wishing to bring Conservatoire pupils together, with no personal motive involved. We are too naïve – and that worries him!'[63]

The Comité Franco-Américain helped many musicians by sending them parcels of food, clothes and other items (Roussel, Ibert, Schmitt and Ravel all received parcels on the front), and many musicians or their needy relatives were sent a small monthly income. They received many letters suggesting suitable candidates for help, including some sympathetic letters from Vincent d'Indy seeking support for Schola Cantorum students in need. D'Indy stated the case for each individual in a manner which showed his detailed knowledge of the circumstances of each person and a genuine concern for the well-being of these former students who were in dire financial straits. He also wrote a jingoistic editorial for the *Gazette*, which he enclosed with a letter written on 24 September 1916. This was published in the third issue of the *Gazette*, which at only 17 pages long was about half the length of the previous number. On the first page, d'Indy wrote: 'You are fulfilling a noble task, because, besides even the material defence of our country under attack, you, artists, have the admirable mission of ridding our Latin art from the pernicious influence of fake German culture. It will not be a small victory to revive our Music with the flame of our traditional French qualities: <u>clarity</u>, <u>concision</u>, <u>a sense of proportions</u>.'[64] Though

---

[60] 'absolument admirable de dévouement et de caractère'.

[61] 'nous ne ferons rien pour entraver en quoi que soit l'initiative généreuse de M. Whitney Warren.'

[62] Letter from Blair Fairchild to Nadia Boulanger, 8 March 1916.

[63] Letter housed in the BN; 'il ne nous pardonnera jamais d'avoir cherché tout simplement à réunir les élèves du Conservatoire, sans même un but personnel. Nous sommes trop naïfs – et cela l'inquiète!'

[64] 'Vous remplissez une noble tâche, car, en dehors même de ce défense matérielle de notre pays attaqué, vous, artistes, vous avez l'admirable mission de débarrasser notre art latin de la pernicieuse

d'Indy's intemperate attacks on German art, and still more his anti-Semitic views, paint an unflattering picture of the composer, he had a far more humane side which he also revealed to the Comité Franco-Américain.

It is not possible here to list every recipient of aid from the Comité Franco-Américain; the Boulanger sisters kept up an enormous correspondence, ensuring that money and food reached the recipient, recording letters of thanks from soldiers and their families, and following up any problems. Offers of financial and practical help often had to be handled sensitively, as Nadia Boulanger realized when she wrote to Blair Fairchild in March 1916. She had received a letter from one of her former teachers, the organist and composer Louis Vierne, 'who is losing his sight, it's an appalling tragedy and he's completely alone. Judge for yourself what we can afford to do for him, but I beg you, don't tell anyone [underlined three times] that we are helping him in his dreadful hour of need, we would hurt him so much that nothing could console him. Please, in the account book, in your conversations and even in front of the Committee, do not name him. I will tell you face to face just how important this is [underlined three times].'[65] The singer Jane Bathori wrote to Blair Fairchild seeking support for 'our friend Erik Satie who is going through a difficult time – like many others besides'; a second letter, written in 1918, asks 'I wonder whether you could send him another package in a few days' time; it will be very necessary.'[66] On 9 April 1916, Nadia Boulanger received a letter from Saint-Saëns, who was clearly still not fully supportive of the Committee: 'I was a bit surprised to read the report of the treasurer of the Comité Franco-Américain: having received 31062.20 francs, only 6671.75 have been spent.'[67] However, as Fairchild noted in his response, the Committee had undertaken to support around 200 people with regular monthly payments, and this considerable buffer enabled them to plan for the future and honour their many commitments.

Bathori also gave a concert in aid of the Committee's work, though most of their funds were raised in the United States. Walter Damrosch was one of the principal fundraisers, and Nadia Boulanger was anxious that French

---

influence de la pseudo-kultur-allemande. Et ce ne sera pas un mince résultat que de reviver notre Musique à la flamme de nos vieilles qualités françaises: clarté, concision, sentiment des proportions.'

65 'qui est en train de perdre la vue, c'est un drame atroce et il est complètement seul. Jugez vous-même de ce que peut faire la caisse pour lui, mais je vous en prie, ne dites à personne que nous l'aidons dans sa grande et profonde détresse, nous le peinerions alors tant, que rien ne peut le soulager. Veuillez donc dans le livre, dans vos rapports et même vis-à-vis du "Comité", ne pas le nommer. Je vous dirai de vive voix à quel point c'est important.'

66 Two undated letters, now housed in the BN (the library suggests a date of 1918 for the second letter); 'notre ami Erik Satie qui traverse un moment bien difficile – comme beaucoup d'autres du reste'; 'Je crois que si vous pouvez renouveler un envoi d'ici quelque jours, cela lui sera très nécessaire.'

67 Letter housed in the BN: 'Je suis un peu surpris en lisant le rapport du trésorier du Comité Franco-Américain, qu'en ayant reçu 31062,20 [francs] on n'a utilisé que 6671,75 en secours!'

musicians should show their appreciation to him. She sketched a letter on Committee headed notepaper: 'Mr Walter Damrosch, the conductor of the Symphony Society of New York and president of the organization "American Friends of French Musicians", which allows us to continue our work and which supports all current musical activities, is now in Paris. He let me know that he is sorry not to be able to say hello, he so wanted to see you during his stay in Paris.'[68] This (undated) letter would presumably have been addressed to the members of the honorary committee; she concluded by hoping that the addressees would send a message to Damrosch via her.

Lili Boulanger's decline and death

While the Comité Franco-Américain was being set up early in 1916, Lili Boulanger was also thinking about her opera project based on Maeterlinck's *La princesse Maleine*. On 20 January, she had lunch with the Bouwens, when they discussed Maeterlinck (and Zeppelins flew overhead at 10 a.m.). By February, it was considered safe for her to return to the Villa Medici, and she set off from Paris on 13 February. Lili, Nadia and their mother broke the journey in Nice, where they stayed with Miki Piré and her mother, and they met Maeterlinck on 15 and 16 February. Lili wrote in her diary on the 15th: 'Saw Maeterlinck – we have an understanding about Princesse Maleine. I am very, very happy. Visited Maeterlinck in the morning who gave me Princesse Maleine; we go out in a car with Lejeune who is waiting for us.'[69] They continued their journey to Rome, via Genoa and, on the 18th, Milan, where Tito Ricordi met them at the station. Lili had lunch with him on the 19th, when they discussed business matters relating to her opera project, and the following day she went to Lake Como and had dinner with Ricordi's wife. She arrived at the Villa Medici on 22 February.

Nadia stayed with Lili in the Villa, keeping her company when she was ill (Lili wrote on 24 May: 'Still in bed because of my leg. Nadia doesn't go out – I'm happy about that').[70] She tried to participate in Villa activities as much as possible, and posed for a bust by the sculptor, and fellow Villa resident, Lucienne Heuvelmans shortly after her return to Rome. Most of her diary entries record her state of health or her occasional outings, and

---

68 'Mr Walter Damrosch, le chef d'orchestre de la Symphony Society de New-York et president des "Amis Américains des musiciens français", société qui nous permet de continuer notre tâche, et qui soutient toutes les organisations musicales actuelles, est en ce moment à Paris. Il nous a dit son regret de ne pouvoir vous saluer, il désirait tant vous voir pendant son séjour à Paris.'

69 'Vu Maëterlinck – entendu p[ou]r Princesse Maleine. Suis bien, bien heureuse. Visite le matin chez Maët.[erlinck] qui me donne la P[rincesse] M[aleine] y allons en voiture avec Lejeune qui n[ou]s attend.'

70 'Toujours couchée à cause de ma jambe. Nadia ne sort pas – j'en suis contente.'

many show how worried she was about the war. On 2 March she wrote: 'Am in anguish about this German attack on Verdun – so much more unhappiness – I think of those who will not return and my heart aches.'[71] A second German attack on 7 March also concerned her.

It is against this backdrop that she started composing her opera – she announced in her diary on 2 May that she had composed Hjalmar's theme – and Annegret Fauser is surely right to emphasize the contemporary appeal of *La princesse Maleine*, a play with a bloody war at its centre. However, Lili rarely writes about her music in her diary, though she does mention on 12 May that she went to the piano and found the beginning of a sonata for piano and violin.[72] While a fragment which is presumably these introductory bars can be found in one of her notebooks, she does not appear to have had time to pursue this project further.

By the end of 1916, Lili was very weak, but she still took pleasure in Nature. She writes on 20 December that 'the snow still hasn't melted and the sight of this great white plain gives me much pleasure.'[73] She had developed a great interest in geography in 1916, and as a substitute for the journeys she dreamed of making, she read travel books and looked at maps for hours; her favourite Christmas present in 1916 was an atlas from Marthe Bouwens.[74] But by the 29th, she wrote: 'I am so tired that I can't get up – I knit lying down – I read a bit. When will I finally be <u>cured</u> – I am so ill I can hardly eat,'[75] though however bad her state of health, she did not lose her gift for a surprising expression. On 30 December 1916, she wrote 'I am shivering all over – my blood is jumping and bounding in my veins like a motorbike starting up.'[76]

Lili Boulanger's final extant diary, for 1917, features entries which are almost all in her sister's hand. She was in severe pain, which was not alleviated, as hoped, by an appendectomy performed on 30 July 1917. Rather than insights into her state of mind, the diary records lists of people who wrote letters to Lili or visited Gargenville or the rue Ballu flat. From 15 July, Nadia lists gifts of flowers and food that have been sent. Lili received a further blow on 3 September 1917, when her 5-year-old goddaughter (and Pugno's granddaughter) Madeleine Delaquys died of meningitis.

---

[71] 'Suis très tourmentée de cette offensive allemande contre Verdun – que de tristesses encore – je pense à tous ceux qui ne reviendront pas et mon coeur souffre.'

[72] 'Vais au piano – trouve comm[encemen]t sonate piano et violon.'

[73] 'La neige n'est pas encore fondue et la vue de cette grande plaine blanche m'est un vrai plaisir.'

[74] Diary entry, 25 December 1916.

[75] 'Je me sens si lasse que je n'arrive pas à me lever – je tricote, couchée – je lis un peu. Quand, donc, serais-je enfin <u>guérie</u> – je ne puis presque pas manger, tant j'ai mal.'

[76] 'Des frissons me parcourent – mon sang bond et saute d[an]s mes veines comme une motocyclette qui se met en marche.'

In early 1918, when Paris was bombarded by the Germans and it was clear that Lili did not have much longer to live, the family moved temporarily to Mézy, a quiet village north-east of Paris which was closer to the capital than their home in Gargenville. Miki Piré was at Lili's bedside, often in the absence of Nadia who had to work. Miki also attended the premiere of *Clairières dans le ciel* in Paris on 8 March – one week before Lili died peacefully in Mézy. Miki Piré and Lili's fellow composer Roger-Ducasse were with Nadia Boulanger at her sister's deathbed. For her funeral at the Trinité on 19 March and burial in Montmartre, she was dressed in the velvet dress she had worn for the Institut performance of *Faust et Hélène* in November 1913.[77]

Nadia Boulanger's composing and performing careers declined after Pugno's death. She wrote a few short instrumental works after 1914, some of which were commissioned, and briefly regained enthusiasm for composing in 1922. In this year, she set four texts by the music critic and author Camille Mauclair. Mauclair was a politically active figure who was no stranger to controversy. He was a socialist, supporter of Dreyfus in the early years of the twentieth century, and ex-anarchist who believed that music should have a social purpose. He praised Gustave Charpentier's realist opera *Louise*, mainly because it featured working-class characters, and wrote several articles criticizing the formulaic teaching at the Conservatoire. Boulanger, who was essentially a political conservative, a woman who believed her mother was descended from Russian royalty, and very much a product of the Conservatoire, appears on the surface to have little in common with Mauclair. But for a time she enthusiastically supported various political causes he espoused, no doubt in an attempt to win his favour. The poems of his she set are popular in flavour, in keeping with Mauclair's belief that French art should draw on indigenous, plebeian sources. She wrote her final song soon after her collaboration with Mauclair; a setting of a poem by her friend Renée de Marquein (writing under the pseudonym François de Bourguignon) whose text includes, appropriately enough, 'J'ai frappé sur des portes closes' (I have knocked on closed doors). In contrast to her sister, though, Nadia Boulanger's most significant contribution to music was as a teacher rather than as a creative artist.

---

[77] Rosenstiel (1978), p. 133.

CHAPTER 2

Towards the Prix de Rome

Nadia Boulanger's first extant composition, a setting of Victor Hugo's *Extase* for voice and piano, is dated '16 septembre 1901' – her fourteenth birthday. Most of her early works are songs for voice and piano, predominantly settings of major poets including Paul Verlaine and Heinrich Heine. Some of these were composed for composition classes at the Conservatoire. Fauré was her composition teacher from 1904, and in June that year he described her as 'talented, a regular attender and hard-working'.[1]

Her setting of Verlaine's *Ecoutez la chanson bien douce* (from the collection *Sagesse*) was, according to the manuscript, written from October to December 1905. Very much in late Romantic style, its emotional breadth ranges from intimacy to a grandiose, quasi-operatic manner, and there are many changes of tempo in this song. Boulanger's frequent performance directions to the singer (the voice is not specified, though a mezzo-soprano seems most suitable) make the emotional mood of the song even more explicit; markings such as 'découragé' and 'avec chaleur' heighten the Romantic atmosphere.

The setting is also quintessentially French in style, not least in the eight-bar piano introduction (Ex. 2.1). The multi-layered texture featuring a dominant pedal, and the chain of chords spanning a tenth in bars 5–8, are both absolutely typical of French music of this period.

It is also, already, very much typical of Nadia Boulanger's musical language, in that it is tonal though with occasional chromaticism and dissonances. Just before the second verse, there is an enharmonic change of key from chord V in E flat major to chord Ib in F sharp major (Ex. 2.2), a device which Boulanger may have absorbed from Fauré. Her use of parallel seventh chords in the third verse is also characteristically French.

However, Boulanger's choice of poem, which is both pious and sentimental and certainly not Verlaine at his best, is questionable. Perhaps she, like Fauré, considered literary merit to be unimportant when selecting poems to set, or perhaps this type of poem was assumed to be suitable for young women composers. The 18-year-old composer orchestrated her

---

[1] Cited in Jean-Michel Nectoux, 'Tous écoutent la parole du maître: Gabriel Fauré et ses élèves', in Anne Bongrain and Alain Poirier (eds) (1999), *Le conservatoire de Paris, deux cents ans de pédagogie, 1795–1995* (Paris: Buchet/Chastel), p. 359; 'bien douée, assidue et laborieuse'.

Ex. 2.1   Nadia Boulanger, *Écoutez la chanson bien douce*: bars 1–8

Ex. 2.2   Nadia Boulanger, *Écoutez la chanson bien douce*: bars 20–1

setting, either as a useful exercise or perhaps because she was hoping it could be performed during an orchestral concert series in Paris. Finally, this song is interesting because it was published by Hanneucourt in 1905 and is therefore her earliest published work.

More interesting is her first orchestral work, simply titled *Allegro*, an unpublished work whose manuscript is dated 17 January 1905. This 82-page work, written for double woodwind (plus piccolo and cor anglais), four horns, two trumpets plus two cornets, three trombones, tuba, timpani and strings, reveals that the young Nadia Boulanger was confident when handling these large forces. The work is in B flat major and is essentially in sonata form, with a varied recapitulation of the opening material from p. 57 of the score. The opening bars with their characteristic dotted rhythm (Ex. 2.3) are an assertive beginning to the work, and a contrasting idea, an instrumental dialogue, is heard on p. 9 (Ex. 2.4).

This figure moves through several keys, and therefore has a developmental character rather than that of a conventional sonata form second subject. The true second subject, a flute melody which often recurs, is introduced on p. 16 (Ex. 2.5) with an unusual *sur la touche* string accompaniment.

Ex. 2.3   Nadia Boulanger, *Allegro*: bars 1–4

Ex. 2.4   Nadia Boulanger, *Allegro*: OS p. 9, instrumental dialogue

Ex. 2.5   Nadia Boulanger, *Allegro*: OS p. 16, flute

The restless modulations of Nadia Boulanger's *Allegro* are already typical of her style; the confidence of the writing, however, was less apparent only a few years later. There are very few additions or crossings-out in the manuscript – only the timpani part seems to have been added at a later date – and the elaborate title page and the flourish of her signature betray her pride in this work. There is no evidence it was ever performed, even though Fauré wrote in a report on his student that she was a 'remarkable pupil. I would be happy if her Allegro were judged worthy of being tried out by an orchestra.'[2]

Some of her early songs were performed in public, including another Verlaine setting, *Soleils couchants*. Rather shorter than *Ecoutez la chanson bien douce* – it only has two verses – Boulanger provides an oscillating accompaniment for the first verse, and a multi-layered accompaniment featuring pedal notes for the second. The song begins in B flat major, but moves to the relative minor in the last few bars. It was premiered on 21 March 1907 by the soprano Fernande Reboul at the prestigious Salle Pleyel

---

[2] Cited ibid.: 'remarquable élève. Je serais heureux si son "allegro" était jugé digne d'être essayé à l'orchestre.'

in Paris, together with her *Elégie*, a setting of Albert Samain, a poet who would surely now be forgotten had many composers, including Fauré, not set his verses.

Composed, according to her manuscript, on 21 April 1906, this song was frequently performed in the years Nadia Boulanger actively promoted her music. Like many of her songs, *Elégie* has a prelude which is harmonically and texturally straightforward, but the music soon becomes more dramatic and complex before returning to the opening texture for the closing bars. Both the sentimental poem and the accompaniment, which is largely based on pounding chords, are rather old-fashioned; only the occasional chromatic descending sequence lifts the setting above mediocrity.

The orchestrated versions of *Soleils couchants* and *Elégie* were also premiered together, in January 1909. They were conducted by Camille Chevillard as part of the Concerts Lamoureux season. On 30 January, a review of this concert by Amédée Boutarel appeared in *Le ménestrel*. He wrote: 'The first of these features a very simple musical idea, the expression of which is precise and very sincere. A high tremolo accompaniment, played by muted violins, neither lacks distinction, nor a somewhat descriptive poetic feeling. The second work is also dreamy in character. The author does not destroy its charm by trying to create effects. The work ends as it began: sad, serious and solemn. These are two attractive impressions of an artistic soul.'[3] While this is certainly an encouraging review, it is also clear that the writer views her as a modest talent rather than an outstanding one.

As Albert Samain was a close friend of their father's, it is not surprising that both Nadia and Lili Boulanger set his verses. *Versailles*, a setting of Samain composed from 17 to 21 April 1906, was premiered by Jane Bathori on 30 October that year at the Grand Palais des Champs-Elysées, accompanied by the composer. Her manuscript reveals that, again like Fauré, Boulanger was willing to edit poems. She omitted the third verse, a description of the gardens of Versailles ('Voici tes ifs en cône et tes tritons joufflus / Tes jardins composés ou Louis ne vient plus / Et ta pompe arborant les plumes et les casques' / 'Here are your cone-shaped yews and your chubby-cheeked Tritons / Your formal gardens where Louis no longer treads / And the parade-ground pomp of your feathers and helmets), surely because she believed these words are totally unsuited to musical setting. She differentiates each verse she set by using contrasting textures, and again her use of enharmonic changes of key is perhaps the most interesting feature of the song.

---

[3] 'La première présente une idée musicale d'une allure simple, et d'une expression juste et très sincère. Un accompagnement d'un tremolo à l'aigu, confié aux violons, jouant avec sourdines, ne manque ni de distinction, ni d'une poésie un peu figurative. Le second ouvrage reste également dans une note rêveuse. Aucune recherche d'effet n'en déflore le charme. Il s'achève comme il a commencé, triste, grave et solennel. Ce sont là deux jolies impressions d'une âme d'artiste.'

Her three settings of Heine are rather more interesting, not least because she sets both the original German texts and a French translation (by Michel Delines), scrupulously altering the rhythms and stress patterns for each text. The first of these is *Larme solitaire*, or in the German original, *Was will die einsame Thräne*, whose manuscript is dated 'Gargenville, 1er août 1908'. The opening of the song is quiet and marked 'Grave, résigné', but it gradually builds up to a climax of almost orchestral power. It ends as it began in C minor, with four bars of arpeggios on the tonic chord, a favourite Boulanger closing device. *Ne jure pas!* ('O schwöre nicht!') was written in 1908, as was *Ach die Augen sind es wieder*.

Besides these songs, most of Nadia Boulanger's early compositional activity focused on her attempts to win the Prix de Rome. Her cantatas, and those by her sister, will be examined in more detail later, but here it is appropriate to mention the choral works which both sisters wrote in preparation for the first round of the competition. Nadia Boulanger set two poems by Charles Grandmougin[4] – a favourite of the Conservatoire – in 1905 and 1906. The first of these, *Les sirènes*, a practice composition for the Prix de Rome first round, is of particular interest because Lili Boulanger set the same text. I will therefore discuss both these compositions later.

In 1906, Nadia Boulanger wrote *A l'aube* for mixed chorus and orchestra; like many of her larger-scale works, this piece is somewhat problematic. There is no evidence that it was ever performed, though as the copy in Lyon Conservatoire is not in the composer's hand, it is reasonable to wonder why a copyist was engaged for this work. Moreover, the copyist makes some fundamental errors, missing out words of the poem, or aligning parts incorrectly, frequently placing semibreves in the middle rather than at the beginning of the bar. The purpose of this work is also unclear, as a choral work written for the preliminary round of the Prix de Rome would have a piano rather than orchestral accompaniment. But the most problematic feature of the piece is the fact that some pages are missing; it is therefore impossible to perform without significant input from a sympathetic editor.

Armand Silvestre's text is a traditional celebration of dawn, spring and, by extension, love. Again, the composer tends to use a particular rhythmic pattern for each verse, producing a sectional form. While her setting is essentially in D major, there are several unusual touches which tend to blur the sense of key; even the first chord is an inverted seventh on D rather than a tonic triad. Fauré's influence is apparent early in the piece; on p. 3, the music moves from the tonic to F sharp major, using the third of the D major chord as a pivot. Later on, there is a beautiful sidestep from F

---

[4] Grandmougin's poems were set by Fauré in his *Poème d'un jour*, op. 21. His straightforward, often sentimental verse surely did not appeal to Debussy.

sharp major to a Lydian F, highlighting the word 'Pleure' ('Weep'). The orchestration is also attractive and illustrative of the text, with the harp frequently adding colour, and the chorus are given octave As, with the sopranos above the treble stave, at the climax (p. 15, almost exactly halfway through the work) on the word 'luit' ('shines').

The work is continuous up to p. 28 of the 32-page score, but there are gaps from this point. Besides these missing passages, there are some odd moments on the last couple of pages, where some instruments are added in pencil and it is not at all clear how the text fits with the music composed for the chorus. Perhaps Nadia Boulanger lost interest in the piece at a late stage; whether this is the case or whether some pages are missing, it is a great shame that *A l'aube* is incomplete. Her work features some lovely harmonic touches, and her setting transcends the rather conventional poem.

The same could be said of *A l'hirondelle*, her 1908 Prix de Rome chorus, composed 3–7 May to a text by Sully-Prudhomme which is rather similar in style to Silvestre's work. The poem addresses a swallow, which flies freely over land and sea, and compares its flight to the aspirations of the human soul, concluding that both need 'libre vie, immuable amour' (freedom and constant love). Nadia Boulanger ensures that all five stanzas are given contrasting settings, no doubt in order to demonstrate to the judges that she could handle a wide variety of vocal textures. But surely the judges' attention would immediately have been drawn to the unusual prelude to the work, which eventually settles on the tonic and dominant notes, G and D, after some interesting hints that various other keys may be the principal focus (Ex. 2.6).

Ex. 2.6   Nadia Boulanger, *A l'hirondelle*: prelude

The first verse is set for a homophonic chorus, while the second features imitation and a tenor solo. The third verse begins by continuing this imitative texture, but eventually the chorus come together to highlight a key image in the poem, 'L'indépendance et le foyer' (independence and the hearth) (Ex. 2.7). The elaborate triplets which precede this statement were introduced in the second verse and gradually build up to this point in the work.

Ex. 2.7   Nadia Boulanger, *A l'hirondelle*: 'L'indépendance et le foyer'

The fourth verse is for a solo soprano, and Nadia Boulanger decides to modify the poem by repeating the final two lines of the four-line verse, though there is no parallel repeat in the music. Finally, she recalls several previously heard musical ideas for the last verse. This charming work no doubt ensured that the composer reached the final of the competition, in spite of the controversy surrounding her fugue.

Léonie Rosenstiel, who studied early sketchbooks belonging to Lili Boulanger, asserts that her first compositions date from 1906; these include two songs, one entitled *La lettre de mort* and one, *Les pauvres*, to a text by Emile Verhaeren (a summer guest of the Pugnos), and four bars of a projected violin and piano sonata.[5] The two sisters were both influenced by Debussy, and it appears they had similar literary tastes to the elder composer. Both sisters set poems by Maurice Maeterlinck, and both left operas uncompleted to texts by authors whose works Debussy had also set.

Lili Boulanger's first extant work is a piece for (unspecified) melody instrument and piano. The manuscript is now housed in the Bibliothèque Nationale de France, incorrectly catalogued as a preliminary version of her *Nocturne*; characteristically, Lili Boulanger dated it precisely: 'mercredi le 5 juillet 1910'. Like the later *Nocturne*, however, it is not given a descriptive

---

[5] Léonie Rosenstiel (1978), *The Life and Works of Lili Boulanger* (Cranbury, NJ: Associated University Presses), pp. 51 and 53.

title, but simply entitled *Morceau* ('Piece'). The *Nocturne* was originally conceived for flute and piano, and this instrumental combination also suits the earlier *Morceau*. This piece is in the adventurous key signature of F sharp major, but the composer often contradicts this with tritonal harmonic relationships; rather than move from the tonic to the dominant chord, the first bar opposes a ninth chord on C natural, rather than C sharp, to the tonic (Ex. 2.8).

Ex. 2.8   Lili Boulanger, untitled piece: bars 1–8

Her highly ambiguous harmony – the tonal identity of a chord is often unclear – and frequent use of enharmony show the influence of her sister's composition teacher Gabriel Fauré. Also characteristic of Fauré is the Neapolitan (flattened second) cadence towards the end of the piece. Here, one has the impression that the piece is about to finish, but the composer adds a four-bar coda which restates some of the earlier harmonic ambiguities before coming to rest on chord I in F sharp major. The piece lacks a tempo, dynamic indications and phrasing, perhaps suggesting it was never performed, and the melodic line is rather undistinguished. But the complex tonal relations of this *Morceau* are of more than academic interest, demonstrating as they do the adventurous harmonic experiments of the 17-year-old apprentice composer.

The following year, Lili Boulanger composed a prelude for piano in D flat, whose manuscript is again housed in the Bibliothèque Nationale. This is dated 'dimanche 11 mars 1911', though I doubt very much that it is a complete piece. The work often focuses on pedal notes, either the key note or F (the dominant of the relative minor key, B flat minor), frequently oscillating between these two pedals. Apart from this, the piece is somewhat incoherent, moving from one rhythmic figure to another with no preparation. The last bars of the piece suggest that it is unfinished: after a pedal E flat, repeated in several octaves over a Debussian triplet figure, the pitch suddenly drops to D flat and the piece ends after one crotchet of a bar. This brutal resolution rather suggests that the composer got bored of the piece and decided to bring it to a swift conclusion.

Her *Nocturne* for flute and piano (1911) is of quite different quality. Although the piece is usually heard as a transcription for violin and piano, the manuscript in the Bibliothèque Nationale clearly shows that it was originally conceived for flute. Not only is the piece more idiomatic for the flute than the violin; the echoes of Debussy's *Prélude à l'après-midi d'un faune* are clearer to the listener if the flute is the soloist, as the concluding section of the piece reveals (Ex. 2.9).

Ex. 2.9 Lili Boulanger, *Nocturne*: concluding section

The title *Nocturne* was added by the publisher; Lili Boulanger simply titled the work 'Pièce courte pour flûte et piano'. Jacques Chailley compares the oscillating pedal which underpins much of the piece to Mélisande's song at the beginning of Act III of *Pelléas et Mélisande*, and he perceptively notes that the composer 'avoids the straightforward repetition of the opening section that was then obligatory in works of this type'.[6] The piece was later orchestrated; a score for small orchestra in Nadia Boulanger's hand, dated 1960, also survives in the BN, and one wonders whether this is actually a copy of an earlier orchestration made by the composer, as the work was performed in its orchestral version on 9 June 1924 in the Salle Pleyel. This effective orchestration features subtle alterations in tempo markings and other performance directions compared to the original, though none of these are significant musically.

---

6 Jacques Chailley (1982), 'L'oeuvre de Lili Boulanger', *Revue musicale*, 353–4 [special Nadia and Lili Boulanger number]: 21; '[Lili Boulanger] évite le da capo alors de rigueur dans tout morceau de ce genre.'

Nadia Boulanger's setting of Charles Grandmougin's poem, *Les sirènes*,[7] for two-part soprano and alto chorus and full orchestra, was written in April 1905, when she was still a student. The same text was set by her sister six years later, and presumably both sisters set this poem as practice for the preliminary round of the Prix de Rome. Nadia Boulanger's work demonstrates that, at that stage, she was absorbing the influence of Debussy. Her melodic lines are often modally-tinged, and her frequent use of parallel sevenths, ninths and first-inversion chords show that she is absorbing his musical style; Debussy springs to mind when hearing the first entry of the voices at p. 2 of the manuscript (Ex. 2.10).

Ex. 2.10   Nadia Boulanger, *Les sirènes*: first vocal entry

Like Debussy, she was fond of using pedal points to provide harmonic stability in an otherwise tonally ambiguous context, and the orchestral introduction to *Les sirènes* features a dominant pedal.

This harmonic device was also a favourite of Lili Boulanger's, and the piano introduction to her setting of the same poem is similarly based around pedal points. The vocalises in Ex. 2.11 and elsewhere in the piece echo the third movement of Debussy's *Nocturnes* for orchestra, 'Sirènes', a movement inspired by the same Greek legend as Grandmougin's poem. The composer is experimenting in this work with what were then unusual vocal effects, and perhaps, in this way, paying homage to the composer who most interested her at the time.

Lili Boulanger's setting is for the more unusual combination of a solo mezzo-soprano and chorus of soprano, alto and tenor voices and piano. She started to orchestrate the work in 1912, and the manuscript reveals that she showed the work in progress to Georges Caussade between 22 February and 26 March 1912, but the orchestration remains unfinished. Like her sister's setting, hers is evidently influenced by Debussy, and it is also likely that Lili absorbed ideas from Nadia's composition as the two pieces have much in common. Overall, Lili's setting of *Les sirènes* is more satisfying than Nadia's, being more compact and demonstrating a surer sense of form. Both settings reach a climax at the end of the poem, but while Nadia's fades

---

[7] This work is not related to her later Prix de Rome cantata, *La sirène*, composed to a text by MM. Adenis and Desveaux.

Ex. 2.11   Lili Boulanger, *Les sirènes*, vocalises, bars 23–5

away rather unconvincingly after the climax and ends abruptly, Lili creates an ABA structure by repeating the first verse of the poem, with minor alterations in the piano accompaniment, and ends with soaring vocalises which, as in Nadia's version, appropriately evoke the sirens who tempted Ulysses. Her elder sister does not always follow the poem exactly, as she repeats the opening line of the poem after the second verse; the opening musical material is also recalled at this point in slightly varied form. There are other similarities in the sisters' responses to Grandmougin's poem, the most obvious being their change of texture at the beginning of the second verse of the poem. Here, both sisters introduce a decorative accompaniment, providing a faster-moving accompaniment compared to the first verse, and both also change the vocal texture, using a solo soprano voice rather than the chorus; Lili keeps this soloist for the third of the four verses.

Harmonically speaking, there is a lovely sidestepping modulation from E major to D major on p. 17 of Nadia's version, at the words 'l'eau miroite en larmes d'argent' ('the water sparkles like silvery tears'; a typical example of Grandmougin's sentimental imagery). In the same place, there is an attractive change of harmony in Lili's version. At the end of this verse, both sisters insert a pause before its closing words, 'comme les ondes', and both introduce undulating, appropriately wave-like figuration after these words (Exx. 2.12a and b).

It is likely that Nadia's setting was never seen by Gabriel Fauré, then her composition teacher, as the manuscript appears to be a rough draft; it is

Ex. 2.12a Nadia Boulanger, *Les sirènes*: MS p. 18, at 'comme les ondes'

Ex. 2.12b Lili Boulanger, *Les sirènes*: bars 41–7, at 'comme les ondes'

written in pencil, and key signatures are omitted at the beginnings of pages (unless the music has changed key). Interestingly, a fragment of a reduction of *Les sirènes* for chorus and piano in the Bibliothèque Nationale, dated April 1905, suggests that the piece was originally conceived in its full orchestral version. In this manuscript, the vocal lines are complete, but the piano part peters out after ten pages. This possibly implies that Nadia lost interest in the project, or had more pressing work to complete, but could also be a sign of the lack of self-confidence that characterized her composing career, as we shall see. Her setting of *Les sirènes* remains unpublished, unlike Lili's version.

It is interesting to note how many features Lili's setting has in common with her other early choral works. Three pieces were published by Durand in 2000, in editions by Alexandra Laederich based on manuscript sources in the Bibliothèque Nationale de France: *Sous-bois* (1911) and *La source* (1912, written for the first round of the Prix de Rome), both for full chorus (SATB) and piano, and *Pendant la tempête* (1911) for male chorus (tenor, baritone and bass) and piano. It is likely that these pieces were written as Conservatoire assignments, and, as many of Lili's choral works were published in her lifetime or shortly after her death, it is natural to speculate why these pieces remained in manuscript until very recently. Possibly, Nadia Boulanger refused to sanction publication on the grounds that the pieces were of lesser musical worth compared to other early works by her sister. It is true that (like *Les sirènes*) they are not masterpieces; they are principally of interest because they demonstrate that Lili, by her late teenage years, had a recognizable musical style. The opening of *Sous-bois*, based on pedal points, is strikingly similar to that of *Les sirènes*, and there is a beguiling sidestepping modulation at bar 21. This type of modulation also surfaces in *La source* (at bar 10), which suggests that this is a stylistic trait of the composer. But the choral writing of *Sous-bois* is perhaps rather too imitative in style, and the vocal parts are a little over-ambitious for the average amateur choir at which it was surely aimed: few professional, let alone amateur, tenors would welcome a top B in a choral part (as at bar 53), and the alto line regularly soars above the stave as high as A flat.

A typically French characteristic of Lili Boulanger's style is her fondness for incorporating modal elements within a basically tonal musical language. *Sous-bois* features a whole-tone passage at bars 24–5 (Ex. 2.13), and in the central section of *Pendant la tempête*, she employs C sharp minor with a flattened leading note (bars 48–61).

This extended modal passage enhances the religious imagery of the poem, as at this point, the singers invoke 'Sainte Notre-Dame'. These modal touches, together with frequent enharmonic modulations, reveal Fauré's influence, and Fauré composed many small-scale choral works of this type, whether for concert performance or as part of incidental music for

Ex. 2.13   Lili Boulanger, *Sous-bois*: bars 24–5

theatrical productions. In my view, Fauré, not Debussy, is the strongest influence on Lili Boulanger's style.

I have already mentioned that Lili Boulanger's love of Debussy's music is evident in *Les sirènes*. Not only do the pedal points at the beginning of the work recall his style; she also alludes to what is perhaps the best-known phrase in Debussy's entire output, the opening of the *Prélude à l'après-midi d'un faune*. Léonie Rosenstiel pointed out that she quotes a variant of this motif in her *Nocturne* (1911) (see Ex. 2.9) and the song *Le retour* (1912),[8] but it is also cited in other works. Besides its appearance in *Les sirènes*, it also surfaces in *Renouveau* (1911), another choral work written as a Prix de Rome exercise, and in her winning cantata *Faust et Hélène*. Rosenstiel mentions 'the Boulanger circle's enjoyment of puns and semi-humorous quotations';[9] it is therefore likely that the descending motif was, for Lili Boulanger, a symbol of Debussy.

Her other early choral works are better known. During a summer stay in Gargenville in 1911, she composed *Renouveau*, to a text by Armand Silvestre, who seems to have been a favourite author in Conservatoire circles as his poems were often used for competition purposes. This charming work, about the coming of spring, is in a similar form to her setting of *Les sirènes*, as she repeats the first verse in order to create an ABA' structure. In the A sections, she provides harmonic interest within a light texture by directing the accompanying voices to hum or vocalise to 'Ah' under the melody line. She also reveals a typically French fondness for pedal points, particularly the dominant pedal, in these sections. The slightly slower central section

---

[8] Rosenstiel (1978), pp. 139–40 and 154–5.
[9] Ibid., p. 154.

features whole-tone touches and a series of soloists detached from the chorus. Perhaps the range of her alto solo at fig. 9 is rather over-ambitious for an average amateur choir soloist (Ex. 2.14), though its gradually ascending shape is typical of her solo vocal style.

Ex. 2.14   Lili Boulanger, *Renouveau*: alto solo at fig. 9

Later in this same solo, we again hear an echo of Debussy's *Prélude à l'après-midi d'un faune*. The chorus is dedicated to her Conservatoire composition teacher and neighbour – more precisely 'a mon cher Maître et Ami Paul Vidal en respectueuse gratitude et sincère affection'.

The two choral works she wrote in Gargenville in 1912 are rather different from the others in her catalogue. *Hymne au soleil*, to a text by Casimir Delavigne (used for the Prix de Rome in 1888), again features an ABA' form as she uses the opening words and music to form her conclusion, but the steady procession of crotchets and heavy chordal texture of the A sections is unlike anything else in her choral works (Ex. 2.15) and is surely intended to evoke the great power of the sun.

Christopher Palmer, writing in the *Musical Times*, believes that this powerful opening 'exhibits for the first time a streak of sturdy masculinity, inexplicably at variance with the composer's character and temperament'[10] –

---

[10] Christopher Palmer (1968), 'Lili Boulanger 1893–1918', *Musical Times*, 109: 227.

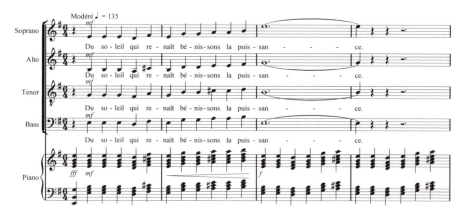

Ex. 2.15   Lili Boulanger, *Hymne au soleil*: bars 5–8

a commonplace critical view on Boulanger's works which inexplicably seeks to draw a parallel between the gender of the composer and the power and volume of her music. The B section features more word painting, at the words 'Sept coursiers' (Seven riders), where she employs a canonic texture to evoke the large number of horses pulling the sun's chariot. An alto solo later in the B section is in a modal C sharp minor; the soloist first appears on her own, and then accompanied by the chorus singing material from the A section.

Pour les funérailles d'un soldat, composed the same year as an exercise for Georges Caussade, is a more striking and original work. The text is derived from Alfred de Musset's poem *La coupe et les lèvres* (though the composer reorders some lines of the poem), and male voices predominate in this military-style work. The piece is essentially in B flat minor, though the seventh is often flattened, a modal inflection within an essentially tonal context. The work opens with a dotted march rhythm played by a drum (Ex. 2.16), and the brass and wind predominate in the orchestrated version.

Ex. 2.17 exemplifies the modal flavour of much of the piece; here, after the words 'Qu'on dise devant nous la prière des morts' (Let the prayer of the dead be said before us) Boulanger introduces fragments of the medieval plainsong 'Dies irae'. This work is dedicated 'a mon cher Maître et ami Georges Caussade en profonde reconnaissance et sincère attachement'.

Boulanger's employment of contrasting vocal textures gives the setting a clear dramatic structure. The chorus basses open the work, followed by the tenors. The full chorus (including the female voices) enters for the first time with the words 'L'âme appartient à Dieu / L'armée aura le corps' (His soul belongs to God / The army will have the body). This statement by the whole community, as it were, is followed by a passage for male chorus only; they sing of carrying the soldier's body to the place of burial. A more

Ex. 2.16   Lili Boulanger, *Pour les funérailles d'un soldat*: opening

Ex. 2.17   Lili Boulanger, *Pour les funérailles d'un soldat*: bars 22–9, featuring *Dies irae*

agitated passage for instruments alone leads up to a section for a solo baritone whose gradual ascending shape is typical of Lili Boulanger's style. This solo statement evokes a friend giving a funeral address. The work ends with a return to the opening musical and poetic material (given this time to the full chorus) and with a vocalise 'Ah!' which effectively moves the piece towards a quiet and reflective conclusion.

Jacques Chailley appropriately remarks that 'the work belongs to that great tradition of funeral cantatas that composers such as Gossec, Lesueur or Berlioz wrote for open-air national ceremonies'.[11] *Pour les funérailles d'un soldat* was received warmly by critics of its first performances. Camille Mauclair was fulsome in his praise during a pre-concert lecture he gave in the Salle Pleyel on 9 June 1924, saying he considered the work to be 'one of the grandest inspirations to have been written since the Funeral March of [Beethoven's] *Eroica* Symphony'.[12] He also attributed prophetic qualities to Boulanger, as she composed the military-themed work before the outbreak of the First World War.

The lovely *Soir sur la plaine* was written in 1913 for the preliminary round of the Prix de Rome; the sunset theme of the poem was very much a favourite of the people who set Conservatoire examinations. Dedicated to the memory of Raoul Pugno, this is a setting of a poem by Albert Samain, who was a close friend of Ernest Boulanger. It is a through-composed work which often features solo voices and subdivisions of the chorus. The opening soprano solo (bars 1–14; Ex. 2.18), which is accompanied by piano tremolandi, strongly resembles the alto solo from *Renouveau* quoted above as Ex. 2.14.

The lush piano part often requires three staves to accommodate the Debussian multi-layered textures which generally include oscillating octave pedal points. Although the work is through-composed, Boulanger creates contrast by using different vocal textures, though there is no real dramatic justification for this as there was in *Pour les funérailles d'un soldat*. The outer two sections feature solo voices as well as the full chorus, but the central section is written for soprano and alto only, each divided into two parts. These magical vocalises are followed by a return to the full chorus for the expansive climax of the work, a grand gesture which paints the words 'la plaine immense'. After this, a gradual diminuendo, featuring more vocalises, effectively leads us to the conclusion of the work, after the words 'Et voici que le coeur du jour s'est arrêté' (And so the heart of the day has stopped).

In 1911, the year she composed *Les sirènes*, Lili Boulanger set Maeterlinck's poem *Attente* (Waiting) for voice and piano, following this in

---

11 Jacques Chailley (1982), p. 24; 'l'oeuvre s'inscrit d'emblée dans la lignée des grandes cantates funéraires que Gossec, Lesueur or Berlioz écrivaient pour les cérémonies nationales de plein air.'

12 Camille Mauclair (1924), 'Lili Boulanger', *Revue musicale*, 10: 152; 'une des plus grandioses inspirations qui aient jamais été révélées depuis la marche funèbre de la *Symphonie Héroïque*'.

Ex. 2.18   Lili Boulanger, *Soir sur la plaine*: bars 1–14

1912 with a setting of his *Reflets*. Both poems are taken from the collection *Serres chaudes*, first published in 1893, and both are enigmatic and charged with symbolism. The narrator of the poems is a mysterious figure who seems almost not to exist on the physical plane, an early version of Mélisande; the striking first lines of *Attente* are 'Mon âme a joint ses mains étranges / A l'horizon de mes regards' (My soul has joined its strange hands / On the level of my gazes). Religious imagery and dreams are constantly evoked, though as befits a subject matter which cannot be explained according to ordinary human logic, these ideas are never rooted in a concrete reality. It is left to Lili Boulanger's music to express the 'meaning' of Maeterlinck's verse. In *Attente*, an oscillating accompanimental figure in the piano, which changes but never resolves, suggests the frustration of waiting. Most impressively, she creates a climax about two-thirds of the way through the song, at the words 'Et dont les lys n'éclosent pas' (Whose lilies do not bloom), where the vocal line reaches its highest note in the song, G sharp; it immediately falls, as does the dynamic level, for the next line, 'Elle apaise au fond de mes songes' (She grows calm in the depth of my dreams) (Ex. 2.19). The song is a remarkable achievement

Ex. 2.19   Lili Boulanger, *Attente*: **bars 15–19**

for a 17-year-old composer, and *Reflets* is of a similar high standard and carries a similar emotional charge.

Perhaps her most touching song is *Le retour*, composed in 1912 to a text by Georges Delaquys – though interestingly, the manuscript shows a second text, a sentimental religious verse entitled *Le nef légère*, under the vocal line. Delaquys was another influential friend of the Boulanger family; a minor poet and sometime journalist, he interviewed Debussy for the journal *Excelsior* in January 1911. Delaquys collaborated with both sisters (he also refashioned the libretto of Nadia Boulanger's Prix de Rome cantata *Roussalka* in 1910) and, significantly, was married to Raoul Pugno's daughter Renée.

Léonie Rosenstiel notes the Debussy echoes in *Le retour*, particularly the near-quotation of the opening of *Prélude à l'après-midi d'un faune* which appears in many of Lili Boulanger's works. Rosenstiel also mentions that as the dedicatee of the song, Hector Dufranne, was a celebrated interpreter of Golaud, 'the fact that Lili chose to allude to … *Prélude à l'après-midi d'un faune* in the introduction to *Le retour* was probably meant quite consciously as a veiled compliment to the singer'. Perhaps it was also a subtle reference to the poet's acquaintance with Debussy.

However, Boulanger's musical style is, again, far closer to Fauré's in this work, and it is perhaps not surprising that the rocking accompaniment of *La retour* echoes Fauré's early Barcarolles, as the song evokes the conclusion of a long sea journey. However, Debussy echoes are apparent in a recurring motif (Ex. 2.20) which initially appears in bars 3–7, marked in Debussian fashion 'comme à travers la brume' (as if heard through fog).

Another recurring ornament, a turn, appears first in bars 19 and 21. Boulanger is a sensitive interpreter of Delaquys's text, which is a straightforward but touching account of Ulysses' feelings as he heads for home. Once again the song is in ABA' form, the outer sections being essentially in F sharp major and the central section in the parallel minor or its relative, A major. Boulanger often uses pedal notes, either a tonic or dominant pedal being almost omnipresent. The climax of the central section

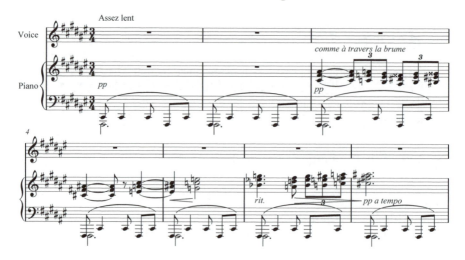

Ex. 2.20   Lili Boulanger, *Le retour*: bars 1–7

Ex. 2.21   Lili Boulanger, *Le retour*: bars 72–81

(from bar 72) highlights in turn Ulysses' anger, his love for his son and his joy in returning home, victorious (Ex. 2.21).

Lili Boulanger is fond of tremolando accompaniments at climaxes which often feel as if she is trying to burst beyond the possibilities of the piano; perhaps she would have orchestrated this song had she had time. In the shortened reprise of the A section, the image of Ulysses floating away on his boat is evident: the vocal line is marked 'en s'éloignant' (moving away), and the piano accompaniment features the markings 'dans le lointain' (in the distance) and, finally, 'en s'effaçant' (disappearing), effectively painting an aural picture of a disappearing ship.

The Prix de Rome

The Prix de Rome was the ultimate goal of the Paris Conservatoire's most talented students of composition. The precise format of the competition varied over the years, but in Nadia and Lili Boulanger's time, there was a preliminary round, in which the candidates composed a chorus to a given text and a vocal fugue. The fugue was in four parts, written on a subject dictated by a member of the music section of the Institut, and four different clefs (soprano, alto, tenor and bass) had to be used. Up to six students were selected for the final round; these happy few had to write a cantata in three weeks, on a prescribed text. This final round took place in Compiègne, where the finalists composed in seclusion, each in his or her own studio without a piano, meeting their fellow competitors only for meals and recreation periods. Each competitor had to sign his or her work – in other words, no submission to the jury was anonymous.

It is clear that the jury, who comprised a number of prominent composers together with members of all sections of the Institut (musicians and those working in other art forms), were looking for a set response to each element of the competition. We know, for instance, that Berlioz's creative early attempts at competition cantatas (including *La mort de Cléopâtre*, written for the 1829 Prix de Rome) were rejected on the grounds that they were too adventurous or, in the view of the jury, unplayable. And Berlioz, who won the competition at his fifth attempt with a conventional, jury-pleasing cantata, *Sardanapale*, wrote an account of the Prix de Rome in his *Mémoires* which has never been bettered:

> In order to show that they possessed the feeling for melody and dramatic expression, the practical knowledge of orchestration and the other skills needed to make a reasonable attempt at a work of this kind [the cantata], the candidates were asked to write a vocal fugue. Each fugue had to be signed.
>
> On the following day the music section of the Institute met, considered the fugues, and made their choice – not always a strictly impartial one, seeing that a certain number of the papers, duly signed, were the work of their own pupils.
>
> The votes having been counted and the competitors nominated, the latter were summoned back soon afterwards to receive the text they were to set to music. The Permanent Secretary of the Academy dictated the classical poem, which usually began: 'E'en now doth Nature greet returning day' or 'E'en now with lustre soft th'horizon glows' ...
>
> When all the scores had been delivered, the grave and reverend signors of the jury met once again, this time with the addition of two members from the other sections of the Institute: a sculptor and a painter, for example, or a sculptor and an engraver, or an architect and a painter, or even two engravers, two painters, two architects or two sculptors; the important thing was that they should not be musicians. ... The scenas – written, as I have indicated, for

orchestra – were performed one after the other, *reduced for piano*, by a solitary accompanist.[13]

The cantata texts were of uniformly low standard, and the same authors' names appear time and again; in the first decades of the twentieth century, Eugène Adenis and Gustave Desveaux-Vérité are responsible for a number of these works. There are always three characters (either two female and one male, or two male and one female), meaning that love triangles were a popular theme. Generally, the cantatas were in two scenes, though some are in three or, exceptionally, four scenes; the length of the composition tends to be around 15–20 minutes. The authors usually provide descriptions of the setting of the action, descriptions which should lead composers to particular musical responses; for example, the sea is a favourite setting, which should prompt a composer to write suitably water-evoking music. Exotic settings were also commonplace. The characters tend to enter one by one, and there is always at least one duet and, usually in the final scene, a trio during which each character expresses his or her thoughts about the situation in which they find themselves. A large number of cantatas end tragically. The aim of this exercise was to enable the competitors to demonstrate facility in writing for the voice (whether solo or in combination) and orchestra, and to show that they are capable of a wide range of emotional expression. Traditionally, the winner of the Prix de Rome would embark on a successful career as an operatic composer.

Ernest Boulanger (a near-contemporary of Berlioz's) was the first family member to participate in the Prix de Rome, winning in 1835. At this time, women were not admitted to the Paris Conservatoire for composition classes, and therefore it was impossible for them to enter the competition. The bar on female entry was only lifted in 1903, a controversial decision made by a left-wing minister, Joseph Chaumié, and the Directeur des Beaux-Arts, Henri Roujon. Fearful that the conservative Académie des Beaux-Arts would not accede to the government's wish to open the competition to women, Chaumié, with Roujon's agreement, deliberately failed to consult the Académie before announcing his decision.[14] In 1903, two women wanted to enter the first round of the music Prix de Rome: Juliette Toutain and Hélène Fleury. However, Toutain failed to appear for the competition and 'publicly accused Théodore Dubois, the director of the Conservatoire, of having forced her to withdraw because he neglected to ensure her good reputation by accommodating her demands'.[15] Toutain's

---

[13] David Cairns (ed. and trans.) (1969), *The Memoirs of Hector Berlioz* (London: Gollancz), pp. 110–11.

[14] See Annegret Fauser (1997), '"La guerre en dentelles": Women and the Prix de Rome in French Cultural Politics' in *JAMS*, 51/1: 92.

[15] Ibid., 95.

father wanted a chambermaid (rather than a male servant) to clean her room, for a chaperone to be present at all times, and for the women to be served meals and enjoy recreation periods apart from the male candidates. In Annegret Fauser's words, 'Dubois refused in principle to give any special treatment to women, but agreed to grant the requests if the other competitors would accept a change of practice.'[16] This passing of the buck came too late to assuage Toutain's father's worries, and his daughter never participated in the competition, although she had actively campaigned for the right to enter. While the authorities acceded to Toutain's father's demands, both Boulanger sisters were accused, for different reasons, of seeking special treatment during the competition, as we will see.

Hélène Fleury had enrolled in Charles-Marie Widor's composition class in 1899, but, her academic career having been interrupted by illness, she left the Conservatoire in 1902, not having won any first prizes. She attempted the Prix de Rome in both 1903 and 1904; although her academic record at the Conservatoire was unimpressive, by 1903, at the age of 26, Fleury was a published composer, and several of her works had been performed in Paris. She chose not to take Toutain's side in the disputes surrounding Toutain's candidacy, no doubt because she would have jeopardized her own chances of success if she had aligned herself with Toutain's family. Indeed, she said in an interview with *Le petit journal*: 'The extreme precautions, which insist that you have lunch and dine separately, walk separately like a little faun, are not at all sensible. I must say that the competitors at Compiègne are well-brought-up people!' Fleury added that she initially took her meals alone, served by a maid, but on the fourth day of the competition the male contestants invited her to dine with them and she accepted their offer.[17]

While she was not successful in 1903, Fleury won the Deuxième Second Grand Prix in 1904, the first woman to win a prize in the competition. The following year, two women, Marthe Grumbach and Marguerite Audan, participated in the first round with Fleury, but (like their fellow candidate Maurice Ravel) none of them reached the final.

In the year of Fleury's success, the journalist Arthur Pougin mentioned the name of Nadia Boulanger in an article about the competition, writing: 'Who knows if she will not triumph in the Grand Prix de Rome as did once her father?'[18] Both Nadia and Lili Boulanger approached the competition in a professional manner, both writing practice cantatas to texts which had

---

[16] Ibid., 96.

[17] *Le petit journal* (10 May 1903), cited in Fauser (1997): 107; 'Les précautions exagérées qui consistent à vous faire déjeuner ou dîner à part, promener à part, comme un petit fauve, n'ont rien de raisonnable. Les logistes de Compiègne sont des gens de bonne société, qu'on se le dise!'

[18] *Le ménestrel*, 70 (1904): 251; 'Qui sait si maintenant elle ne triomphera pas, comme autrefois son père, du grand prix de Rome.'

previously been used for the competition; the formulaic outline of the
cantata texts enabled competitors to hone their skills in practice cantatas of
this type. Nadia Boulanger entered the competition in four consecutive
years from 1906. At her first attempt, she failed to reach the final, but she
did for each of the three following years.

In 1907, Nadia Boulanger reached the final after composing a fugue to
a subject dictated by Théodore Dubois and a short choral work, *Soleils de
septembre*. For the final, the compulsory cantata text was *Selma*, by G.
Spitzmuller. It features the regulation three characters, but is unusual in that
it has four scenes; two or three were far more common. Perhaps Berlioz
would have thought that the most unusual thing about the text is its
opening, as the traditional dawn/sunset scene is, for once, absent. The text
is a typical example of French exoticism; the characters are Selma (a mezzo-
soprano in Nadia Boulanger's setting), Nassim (bass) and Kaïs (a tenor, who
makes his first appearance in scene iii), their names suggesting a North
African or Arabian setting, even if the religious ritual performed by two of
the characters does not.

It is not surprising that such an early work is heavily indebted to other
composers, and Boulanger demonstrates Debussy's influence in many key
passages of the cantata. The short prelude has whole-tone touches, though
a tremolo E acts as a quasi-tonal centre (Ex. 2.22).

Ex. 2.22 Nadia Boulanger, *Selma*: bars 1–6

When Selma enters (p. 2 of the manuscript) she is praying, and the music
moves to a more conventional E major. Her father, Nassim, enters soon
afterwards, and tells us that he has dedicated his daughter to the temple.
Their rather uninspired duo (pp. 5–7) is solidly in C major. The most
interesting passage in the cantata follows this: an instrumental interlude
illustrating a religious ceremony in which Nassim lights a sacred fire and
Selma perfumes the air. It begins with a rather Fauréan sidestep from C
major to E flat major, and continues in a manner that is more than
reminiscent of Debussy's *La damoiselle élue* (Ex. 2.23). The scene concludes
with Selma and Nassim praying, and Nassim warning his daughter of dire
consequences if she disobeys his order to dedicate herself to the gods.

Ex. 2.23   Nadia Boulanger, *Selma*: scene i, interlude

Not surprisingly, therefore, in scene ii we learn of Selma's secret love for Kaïs. She admits her love, again to undistinguished music, and begs the gods to have pity on her. Kaïs enters at the start of scene iii, initially in B major and to a harp-like arpeggio accompaniment. Though there is a brief, daring sidestep to B flat major here, their material is sentimental and unmemorable. They swear to leave together, and sing a duo in which their words alternate; unusually, they never sing together. The compulsory trio appears at the start of scene iv. A tremolo which oscillates between D and G sharp both echoes the introduction, and hints (the tritone interval being dissonant) that there is trouble ahead. Kaïs sings that he fears nothing, and Nassim realizes that he cannot defend his daughter from her lover – but suddenly, she realizes that she is afraid. Her father has a bitter triumph, as he strikes her and she falls to the floor, presumably dead.

Maurice Le Boucher won the competition in 1907, and Jules Mazellier won the 'Premier Second Grand Prix'. Boulanger did not win a prize, perhaps not surprisingly as this was her first time in the final; it was usual for candidates to win one or more of the minor prizes before winning the top prize. While it is therefore possibly not apposite to speculate why her cantata did not win, it is true that her inexperience is evident in several ways. The final page of the manuscript is extremely untidy, giving the impression it was written in a hurry, and time management was clearly one of the elements being tested. It is not clear whether the manuscripts represent a finished product, or whether the work is unfinished, and it is also possible that her unorthodox approach to the duo counted against her, as she did not demonstrate contrapuntal flair in this section. Moreover, the piano reduction I have studied (which is now housed in Lyon Conservatoire) is not always practical; the composer often suggests that a '3ème main' could play some lines, and once she even asks for a '4ème main'. How she handled this in the play-through of the cantatas before the members of the Institut is unknown.

However, Widor, her composition teacher, wrote to her on 30 June, telling her that her performers let her down by not observing her dynamic markings during the Institut play-through of the cantata. He also suggested that there were areas on which she could work: 'Pugno will let you know what we said about your cantata: your technique is superior to that of the other contestants, but unfortunately the effect of your work was greatly diminished in the large hall of the Institut. ... Therefore, we will work on the external, decorative side of things next year; as far as the basics are concerned, you have nothing more to learn. Believe that I am devoted to you and interested in your success, in what is due to you.'[19]

On 9 May 1908, *Le ménestrel* announced that the ten competitors in the first round of the Prix de Rome had, on 2 May, completed the fugue section of the competition, to a subject which had been dictated by Camille Saint-Saëns; also, Théodore Dubois had dictated the poem to be set for chorus, Sully-Prudhomme's *A l'hirondelle*. This bald announcement gives no hint of the turmoil in that year's preliminary round created by Nadia Boulanger's fugue. In the following week's number (16 May), there was still no indication that any problem had arisen; the journal simply lists the six competitors who reached the final round. In order, these were: Gailhard, Mazellier, Delmas, Flament, Nadia Boulanger and Tournier, all of whom studied with Charles Lenepveu, except Boulanger, a Widor student.

However, on 23 May, *Le ménestrel* finally announced that 'There was an incident, connected with Mlle Nadia Boulanger, during the judging of the preliminary round of the Prix de Rome. Although she wrote an instrumental fugue rather than a vocal fugue, she was still admitted to the final round. However, this did not clear everything up, and the incident was brought before the Académie des Beaux-Arts. In its last meeting, the Académie passed judgement and ratified the jury's decision.'[20] As a result of this deliberation, the 'entrée en loge', which had been fixed for 15 May, was put back four days. The result would now not be announced until 4 July.

Boulanger simply said that she believed that the subject was more suited to instrumental treatment, rather than the vocal fugue candidates were supposed to write, so she wrote an instrumental fugue; Ex. 2.24, the fugue subject, shows that she had a point.

---

[19] Letter housed in the Bibliothèque Nationale de France; 'Pugno vous dira comment nous avons parlé de votre cantate: votre technique est supérieure à celle de tous les concurrents; malheureusement l'effet s'est trouvé très diminué dans la grande salle de l'Institut; ... Enfin, nous travaillerons le côté extérieur, décoratif des choses l'an prochain: quand au fond, vous n'avez rien à apprendre. Croyez-moi bien dévoué et intéressé à votre succès, à celui qui vous est dû.'

[20] *Le ménestrel* (23 May 1908): 167; 'Un incident s'était produit au jugement du concours préparatoire pour le prix de Rome, relativement à Mlle Nadia Boulanger, qui, quoique ayant écrit une fugue instrumentale au lieu d'une fugue vocale, fut néanmoins admise au concours définitif. Cependant tout n'était pas fini, et l'affaire fut portée devant l'Académie des Beaux-Arts elle-même. Celle-ci, dans sa dernière séance, a statué sur l'incident et ratifié le jugement du jury.'

Ex. 2.24 Fugue subject for 1908 Prix de Rome competition

One member of the jury – probably Saint-Saëns – wanted to bar Boulanger from the competition on this ground, but the jury came to the following conclusion after hearing all the competing works:

> The jury had again to ask whether Mlle Boulanger should be expelled from the competition for substituting an instrumental fugue for the expected vocal fugue. While regretting that this candidate did not conform strictly to the letter of the regulations, the jury considered that exclusion would, perhaps, be an disproportionate measure when faced with an artist who had just (both through this work, which was satisfactory, and through her chorus with orchestra) given ample proof of her compositional abilities. By admitting her to the final round, the jury used its privilege of judgement, for which it assumes full responsibility.[21]

So, after heated debate, which was reported in the press, she was allowed to proceed to the final round of the competition, but it is certain that her controversial behaviour did not endear her to influential people in the Institut.

The cantata text that year was *La sirène*, a traditional love triangle story in three scenes by Eugène Adenis and Gustave Desveaux-Vérité. The setting is the Breton coast, and the couple at the centre of the tale, Jann (a fisherman) and Anne-Marie (a conventionally pious young woman, his fiancée) are driven apart by a mermaid (la Sirène), who lures Jann to her watery home.[22]

This sea setting naturally gave Boulanger the opportunity to write much arpeggio-based 'water' music. The work opens with a tempest (rather than a sunrise or sunset), portrayed by Boulanger with chromatic rising and falling scales accompanied by tremolandi. A bell-like melody in a modal E minor emerges from this, the whole following the authors' directions: 'A tempest at sea. Outside, one can hear the whistling wind and the roaring

---

[21] Jury report cited in Fauser (1997): 117 (my own translation); 'Il y a eu à examiner à nouveau si, pour avoir substitué une fugue instrumentale à une fugue vocale, Mlle Boulanger ne devait pas être mis hors concours. Tout en regrettant que cette concurrent ne se fût pas conformée strictement à la lettre du règlement, le Jury a estimé que l'exclusion serait peut-être d'une rigueur excessive à l'égard d'une artiste qui venait de faire, tant par ce travail, d'ailleurs satisfaisant, que par son choeur avec orchestre, une preuve largement suffisante de ses aptitudes à la composition. En l'admettant du Concours final le Jury a usé d'un pouvoir d'appréciation dont il assume la responsabilité.'

[22] This plot is more than reminiscent of *L'ensorceleuse*, the 1931 cantata text (by Paul Arosa) set by Olivier Messiaen and his fellow finalists. Messiaen failed to win a prize in this competition.

waves. Bells toll the death-knell.'[23] (This unsubtle harbinger of doom is typical of Prix de Rome cantata texts.) In the first scene, Anne-Marie prays to the Virgin Mary, then complains that Sirens lure away the lovers of mortal women. Right on cue, we hear the 'voix de la sirène' in the distance (p. 8) accompanied by the harp. As in *Selma*, the character first enters humming (bouche fermée).

Anne-Marie meets Jann in the second scene; they sing of their love and Anne-Marie mentions her fear of the Sirens. In a passage which underlines her conventional religious faith, she sings 'ashamed, in a muffled voice, lowering her head': 'And I no longer had faith in the Virgin Mary!'[24] Moved by this admission, Jann swears he will bid farewell to the sea, and the couple look forward to a happy future in the countryside. But, in the third scene, the Siren arrives to tempt Jann, and the compulsory trio ensues. Jann, despite his promise, finds it impossible to be lured away from the sea, and is tempted by the Siren's beauty. He runs after the Siren; they disappear together, and Anne-Marie cries out and drops to the ground, lifeless.

The eventual victor of the competition was André Gailhard (the son of the director of the Opéra) who otherwise made little impact on the musical world, and Boulanger was placed second. Several critics thought Boulanger should have won, some believing that her gender was a factor, others that her status as a Widor pupil disadvantaged her, because all the other finalists were students of Lenepveu.

Boulanger's good relations with the journal *Le monde musical* worked in her favour after the result was announced.[25] The journal usually published an extract of the winning cantata as the musical supplement of its July number, but in 1908, exceptionally, they preferred to publish part of Boulanger's cantata, giving as their reason that the winner did not respond to their request for an extract. Whether this was true or not, Boulanger won some useful publicity thanks to her friends. The journalists from *Le monde musical* recognized the influence of Fauré on her musical style, and predicted that she would win the first prize the following year. But they were not wholly uncritical of her music, and one phrase seems remarkably prescient: 'Although Mlle Boulanger's music has clarity, she would benefit from simplifying her style, only retaining from all her musical knowledge, all her first prizes in harmony, accompaniment, organ and fugue that she won at the Conservatoire, the craftsmanship and suppleness in writing that she has already demonstrated.'[26]

---

23 'Tempête sur mer. – On entend au dehors le sifflement du vent et le rugissement des vagues. – Des cloches sonnent le glas.'

24 'honteuse et d'une voix sourde, en baissant la tête'; 'Et je n'avais plus foi dans la Vierge Marie!'

25 A very favourable review of a concert held in the Boulanger's flat on 30 March 1908 was published in the journal. The (unnamed) journalist described it as 'une magnifique soirée d'art'.

26 *Le monde musicale* (15 July 1908): 202; 'Bien que Mlle Boulanger reste toujours claire, elle gagnera à

The second-placed composer in the Prix de Rome competition was expected to win the following year, and it was impossible to be awarded the same prize twice. Therefore, when Nadia Boulanger entered in 1909, it came as a surprise to many that her cantata, *Roussalka*, won no prize. Some critics assumed this reflected the unwillingness of the jury to award a woman the first prize, though others believed that Saint-Saëns and his supporters would never have allowed her to win after the 'affaire fugue' of 1908.

The text of *Roussalka* was written by the Adenis/Beissier team responsible for several other Prix de Rome cantata texts. It opens with a sunset ('Voici le soir tout voilé de mystère'), and the principal male character, Yégor, falls for a mysterious and ethereal spirit-woman, Roussalka. In Boulanger's version, her first entry (p. 8 of the manuscript) is wordless (Ex. 2.25), as was the first entry of la Sirène in the cantata she wrote the previous year.

Ex. 2.25 Nadia Boulanger, *Roussalka*: first entry of Roussalka, p. 8 of MS

se simplifier et me garder de tout sa science musicale, de tous les premiers prix d'harmonie, d'accompagnement, d'orgue et de fugue, qu'elle obtint au Conservatoire, que le métier et la souplesse d'écriture dont elle fait déjà preuve.'

In the first two scenes, these characters resolve to flee together, but in the third and final scene, a wise man tries to reveal to Yégor the error of his ways. This stock character, 'le Pope' (rather than 'le Pape', the correct French spelling, perhaps to avoid possible blasphemy charges), begs Yégor to remember his Catholic upbringing and return to the Church. Le Pope describes Roussalka as a dangerous seductress: 'elle prend pour séduire une voix qui caresse, mais cette voix ment' ('her seducing voice is a caressing voice, but a lying voice'), and in the compulsory trio, he tells Yégor to follow duty ('le devoir') rather than 'le bonheur' offered by Roussalka. On p. 32 of the manuscript, Yégor sings that he hates religious duty, and he begs Roussalka, accompanied by the inevitable ethereal arpeggios, to take him away. Naturally, this blasphemy does not go unpunished: le Pope announces that the sun is rising, which is a cue for Roussalka to vanish from Yégor's arms.

While this is clearly a satisfying conclusion for the tale, Boulanger's manuscript is unfinished; it peters out on p. 34, as Roussalka 'disappears like melting snow', and I wonder whether she finished the work within the required three-week competition period. There is a frantic note on the final page of the score which was evidently written in haste: 'Monsieur, Please do not worry about the blanks – it doesn't matter. I absolutely must have a second copy for tomorrow, Thursday morning, and the last for tomorrow evening. A thousand thanks and my very best wishes.'[27] What this 'second copy' may be is a mystery to me. While there are no references in newspaper reports to the fact that Boulanger failed to complete her cantata (which would surely have been evident during the play-through of all competing cantatas at the Institut), the incomplete state of her work may explain why she failed to win first prize.

Never one to take a conventional path, Boulanger annoyed other people when a performance of her setting of *Roussalka* in the Concerts Colonne series was announced for 13 May 1909, as cantatas which did not win were inevitably consigned to oblivion. The composer who won the competition, Jules Mazellier, and his publisher threatened legal action for breach of copyright of the text, and the performance could only go ahead once the Boulangers' old friend, Georges Delaquys, made some changes to the text and retitled the work *Dnégouchka*.[28] According to Boulanger's orchestral manuscript, Delaquys's alterations were confined to the final scene; in particular, he renamed the wise male figure 'le Sage', and some pages of the score rename Roussalka 'la Fée' and Yégor, 'le Poète' (occasionally he is

---

[27] 'Monsieur, Ne vous inquiétez pas de ce qui reste en blanc – cela ne fait rien. J'ai absolument besoin d'un second exemplaire pour demain jeudi midi et le dernier pour demain soir. Mille fois merci et meilleurs compliments.'

[28] Perhaps deliberately echoing the title of Rimsky-Korsakov's 1881 opera *Snégourouchka* (The Snow Maiden) which had recently been heard for the first time in Paris.

named 'Yvan'). This version was made, obviously in haste, by a copyist, and features many corrections in Boulanger's hand. The copyist was clearly inexperienced; one of many elementary errors in the score is his placing of the cor anglais part under the bassoons rather than the oboes.

Moreover, there is evidence that Boulanger wanted to make more significant revisions to the score. When Le Sage enters (on p. 52), she adds some new material on the reverse of the page, and writes a note to the copyist: 'Sir, as I am planning a change here, I beg you to leave a blank space allowing room for 7 bars minimum, 10 maximum – for the voices as well as the full orchestra.'[29] Again, the manuscript in the Bibliothèque Nationale is incomplete (it breaks off at the same point at Boulanger's setting of the original Prix de Rome text). As there is no evidence either way as to whether the new cantata was performed in full or in part, I do not know whether it was ever completed, or whether Boulanger cut some passages out of the manuscript as she was unwilling for the complete version to be scrutinized by researchers. The ambiguity surrounding the status of this manuscript is typical of the surviving works of Nadia Boulanger.

Reviews of the performance of *Dnégouchka* on 13 May 1909, conducted by Gabriel Pierné as part of the Concerts Colonne series, were neutral. Writing in *Le ménestrel* (in a review which strangely does not refer to the piece's origins as a Prix de Rome cantata) the critic J. Jemain wrote: 'As for Mlle Nadia Boulanger's cantata, *Dnégouchka*, which is certainly an interesting piece, if rather heavy, I admit I need to hear it again if I am to appreciate all its good qualities.'[30] Unfortunately for Boulanger, he would not have a second chance to hear the work, and Delaquys's collaboration with Lili Boulanger was rather more successful. Moreover, 1909 is the year in which (perhaps not coincidentally) Lili Boulanger started to emerge as a composer.

Lili Boulanger's 'Cantate no. 1', to use her designation, was *Maïa*, a setting of the 1905 cantata text by Fernand Beissier. Typically, the manuscript is dated precisely: 'Prélude avril–mai 1911, St-Raphaël, la suite en 1911 à Paris ou à Gargenville.' The tale is set in Africa, and the three characters are Maïa, a young girl from Galam ('jeune fille du pays de Galam'), Jean, 'le spahi' (an Algerian cavalryman in the French army), who loves her, and a priest-cum-sorcerer, Samba-Hamet. The young lovers are assigned high vocal ranges, as is usual in these cantatas, and also conforming to type, Samba-Hamet is a baritone.

---

[29] 'Prévoyant un changement ici, je vous prie, Monsieur, de laisser un blanc pouvant contenir 7 mes[ures] au minimum ou 10 au plus – pour le chant comme pour l'orchestre complet.'

[30] *Le ménestrel* (19 March 1910): 92; 'Pour la cantate de Mlle Nadia Boulanger, *Dnégouchka*, oeuvre intéressant assurément mais touffue, j'avoue avoir besoin de l'entendre une seconde fois pour en saisir tous les mérites.'

The cantata opens on a lakeside scene at sunset. Entrants for the Prix de Rome clearly had plenty of opportunities to practise writing music suitable for such a scene, and Lili Boulanger responds with a prelude based around pedal points which is already typical of her style. Maïa enters on pp. 5–6 of the manuscript, humming above a pedal note (Ex. 2.26).

Ex. 2.26   Lili Boulanger, *Maïa*: first entry of Maïa, pp. 5–6 of MS

Jean assures Maïa that he loves her in this first scene, but also warns her that he must leave her, revealing the plot as an archetypal colonial love story in which the Frenchman falls in love with a local girl but cannot stay with her forever. The second scene does not move the action forward significantly; at its end, Jean reiterates that he must leave. But the first entry of Samba-Hamet at the start of scene iii provides the necessary catalyst for the story to develop. He enters brandishing a baton, ready to punish Maïa for loving a foreigner. Jean tries to protect his lover, insisting that he should be chastised instead, and Maïa swears to abandon her people for the love of Jean. However, in an echo of Bizet's *Carmen*, a bugle sounds; Jean says that he has 'forgotten' that he must return to his regiment (Ex. 2.27).

After the compulsory trio in which the three characters articulate their contrasting feelings, Maïa poisons herself. Jean is initially stupefied, but not enough to stop him running back to his regiment. The last word goes to Samba-Hamet, who, kneeling by Maïa, says: 'La patrie et les dieux sont vengés maintenant' ('The country and the gods are now avenged').

This nonsense provided a useful introduction to the Prix de Rome cantata style for Lili Boulanger. Her setting also shows that she is already a self-critical composer, as some sections are rewritten and a few pages are missing. It is also possible that the first page of the score is missing, because

Ex. 2.27 Lili Boulanger, *Maïa*: scene iii, bugle call

no tempo marking appears at the top of the first surviving page of manuscript. Also, some dynamic indications have been pencilled in, though these are not present throughout the score, suggesting the work was not written for performance. The first version was written in purple ink, with changes made in black; many of these changes improve the prosody. The most unusual harmonies appear at the start of Jean and Maïa's first duet, in scene ii (p. 13; Ex. 2.28).

Ex. 2.28 Lili Boulanger, *Maïa*: scene ii, beginning of duet

The work is unfinished; the final two and a half bars of Maïa's text are written in pencil, and these words and the final eight lines of text are unset. While this could simply indicate that Lili Boulanger lost interest in the project, on p. 31 of the score there is a note in another hand that the solo piano section she has written is 'trop long'. Overall, the setting anticipates some features of her winning cantata of 1913, *Faust et Hélène*; she likes the male and female voices to be close together (see Ex. 2.31 below), and Maïa, at her death, descends to a low G, just like Hélène as she leaves the scene.

The name character of her next setting of a cantata text, *Frédégonde*, inspired Lili Boulanger to a similar style of vocal writing. Only the first scene of this cantata survives; whether she finished the work or abandoned it is unclear. Boulanger writes at the head of the manuscript that this first scene was 'faite du 17 Sept au Samedi 23 – montrée à Pugno le 24 – montrée à Caussade le Samedi 14 [Oct] 1911'; but, although she must have received feedback from both Pugno and Caussade, no comments from either man appear on the manuscript.

The text, by Charles Morel, again features a love triangle, but this time, the different social status of the characters is the determining issue. Frédégonde (a mezzo-soprano in Boulanger's setting) loves Chilpéric (baritone), and in the first scene of the cantata they meet in his palace. While Chilpéric also loves Frédégonde and begs her not to leave him, he must marry a king's daughter, Galeswinthe. (Galeswinthe does not appear in this scene, but Boulanger sketches a leitmotif associated with this character on the reverse side of p. 17 of her score.) Only the medieval setting and the characters' names distinguish this text from *Maïa*.

Lili Boulanger's score is more finished than her setting of *Maïa*, in the sense that tempi, expression markings and dynamics are indicated in ink, rather than pencil. A concern for musical unity is evident here, too, as the triplet figure which dominates the introduction (Ex. 2.29a) is recalled several times in the accompaniment, and is also the focus of Galeswinthe's motif (Ex. 2.29b).

This 31–bar introduction, in B flat minor, resembles a piano variation, again perhaps showing that the composer was not thinking in orchestral terms. And as in *Maïa*, we can see the compositional process in action up

Ex. 2.29a   Lili Boulanger, *Frédégonde*: recurring triplet figure

Ex. 2.29b   Lili Boulanger, *Frédégonde*: Galeswinthe's motif, pp. 16–17 of MS

to a point, as Boulanger rewrites part of the climactic duet to make the vocal lines more spacious. The most interesting passage in the work appears towards the end (pp. 16–17). Frédégonde asks her lover to give her back her heart, and the strikingly chromatic accompaniment hints at her inner turmoil (Ex. 2.30).

Ex. 2.30   Lili Boulanger, *Frédégonde*: pp. 16–17 of MS

Lili Boulanger entered the Prix de Rome in 1912 and 1913. According to *Le ménestrel*, 1912 was not a vintage year for the competition: their journalist noted that fourteen candidates were admitted to the fugue section of the competition, but that 'The results of the exercise were so weak that the examiners did not believe that they could admit the maximum number of six contestants to the final round; only four proceeded to the competition'.[31] Lili Boulanger withdrew from the final for health reasons, and no first prize was awarded that year, leaving two first prizes available for the 1913 competition.

In 1913, her chorus *Soir sur la plaine*, an appealing work to an Orientalist text which is very much of its time, and fugue admitted her to the final round of the competition. After these qualifying rounds, she was placed second amongst the five finalists, but her cantata won the first prize by an overwhelming 31 out of 36 votes, and hers was considered the finest cantata written for some years.

Any weaknesses in this work, *Faust et Hélène*, can be ascribed to the conventions of the competition and, especially, to the text. Eugène Adenis was again the author, and he based the plot on Goethe's *Faust*. The three characters featured are Faust, Mephistopheles, and a character bearing more than a passing resemblance to Helen of Troy. Although Hélène's nationality is not made explicit, references to the destructive power of her beauty, and the arrival of Greek soldiers in the second part of the cantata, strongly evoke the legend of the Trojan woman whose beauty had the power to launch a thousand ships. The tale is presented as an allegory concerning the

31 *Le ménestrel* (18 May 1912): 158; 'L'épreuve a paru si faible que les examinateurs n'ont pas cru devoir atteindre le maximum des admissibles, qui est de six, et qu'ils n'ont reçu que quatre élèves au concours définitif.'

eternal feminine in Goethe, but is more like an episode in a soap opera in Adenis's version.

Méphistophélès (a baritone) is the first character to enter, describing the beauty of the sunrise so typical of Prix de Rome cantata texts. He is soon followed by Faust (a tenor), who is dreaming of the beautiful Hélène; Méphistophélès mocks his master by alluding to the better-known love of his life ('Marguerite seems no more than a distant memory ...'). When Faust insists that he wants to follow his new love, the poet, in the most amateur manner possible, anticipates the tragic conclusion of the tale when Méphistophélès announces, 'Je crois que ce ne soit le dernier de vos voeux' (I fear this may be your last wish).

Hélène (a mezzo-soprano) is initially reluctant to respond to Faust's advances, being all too aware of the tragic consequences she has brought on many past lovers. But she succumbs, and the compulsory Prix de Rome duet ensues. The second part of the cantata opens with a powerful passage depicting the advancing Greek army, but whatever interest the poet created in the characters quickly vanishes. Here, Hélène is merely an irritating nag who is constantly asking Faust if he still loves her. Faust unsuccessfully tries to chase away the demons pursuing him and, as Méphistophélès predicted, the story ends tragically, with Hélène spirited away and Faust broken-hearted.

Any composer who could create convincing characters and real drama and emotion from this sorry text surely deserves a prize. Her marvellous evocation of sunrise may owe more than a little to Wagner (and Debussy, the opening of whose *Prélude à l'après-midi d'un faune* she again alludes to) in its shimmering textures, but hers is one of the last in a long line of distinguished French Wagnerian compositions, and she moved away from this style in later works. Her vocal writing is both more personal and more innovative than this opening passage. In this cantata and in the psalm setting *Du fond de l'abîme*, Boulanger combines the tenor and contralto voices, exploiting the large crossover in register between the highest male voice and lowest female voice. At the end of the *Faust et Hélène* love duet, the two voices imitate each other at pitch, symbolizing the union of the two lovers, and at its climax, there is an extraordinary passage in which the male voice provides the top line (Ex. 2.31). The score was published by Durand – the only Lili Boulanger work to be published in her lifetime – and not dedicated, as was traditional, to her Conservatoire composition professor, but 'à ma soeur Nadia Boulanger'.

Le ménestrel wrote about the result of the Prix de Rome on 12 July 1913, exactly a week after the competition results were announced. Lili Boulanger's cantata was the third out of six to be played, and in their (anonymous) journalist's words: 'Here are the results of this particularly brilliant concert: Premier Grand Prix: Lili Boulanger; Deuxième Premier

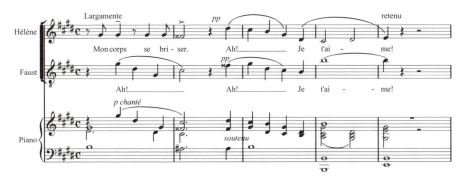

Ex. 2.31 Lili Boulanger, *Faust et Hélène*: scene i, climax of duet

Grand Prix: Claude Delvincourt; Premier Second Grand Prix: Marc Delmas. Mlle Lili Boulanger, the victor of the day, was awarded the first prize by 31 out of the 36 voters.'[32] Significantly, the journal added that 'Monsieur Saint-Saëns' was not in Paris for the competition judgement; the music section judges were Paladilhe, Dubois, Fauré, Widor and Charpentier. Raymond Bouyer wrote in the same journal about the prizegiving ceremony, drawing attention to the still-controversial victory of a female contestant: 'Passing smiles do not contradict the plaudits which greet the victory and the name of Mlle Lili Boulanger, whose first name seems to displease some purists: though she is the winner of the Prix de Rome, she is no less of a woman.'[33]

The cantata, which was given several complete or partial public performances during Lili Boulanger's lifetime, was unusually successful. No doubt it was this success that prompted Boulanger and Adenis to consider a sequel, as a diary entry of 17 February 1915 reveals. Boulanger and Renée de Marquein had gone to a meeting to ask a M. Albers to sing in a performance of the cantata; Lili Boulanger noted that 'Mme Dougnon, Mlle Goug.[?], Mme Strauss and M. Adenis are coming – business discussion about the chorus sequel to Faust by Adenis and me.'[34] She did briefly pursue this project; a crossed-out diary entry of 19 February states 'reçois les vers d'Adenis', and on the following two days, she intriguingly writes 'travaille l'après-midi avec N[adia] et seule au choeur à Faust'. Could this be the

[32] *Le ménestrel* (12 July 1913): 223; 'Voici le résultat de cette séance, particulièrement brillante: Premier Grand Prix: Lili Boulanger; Deuxième Premier Grand Prix: Claude Delvincourt; Premier Second Grand Prix: Marc Delmas. C'est par 31 voix sur 36 votants que Mlle Lili Boulanger, la triomphatrice de cette journée, s'est vu décerner le premier prix.'

[33] Ibid., 227; 'Les sourires intermittents ne contredisent pas les acclamations qui saluent la victoire et le nom de Mlle Lili Boulanger, dont le prénom paraît déplaire à quelques puristes: pour être grand Prix de Rome, on n'en est pas moins femme.'

[34] 'Mme Dougnon, Mlle Goug., Mme Strauss, Mr Adenis viennent – parlons affaires p[ou]r choeur suite Faust Adenis et moi.'

chorus that Caussade heard during a visit on 18 March, according to another diary entry? Unfortunately there is no more information about this project after this date, and the chorus appears not to have survived.

The sisters' mixed fortunes in the Prix de Rome had a critical impact on their future careers as composers. While Nadia Boulanger paved the way for her younger sister's success, by winning one of the minor prizes and by drawing the public's attention to the family's achievements, she also made enemies in the establishment through her unconventional behaviour. Amongst many ironies in Nadia Boulanger's career, perhaps the most striking is the fact that she became notorious as a student who bent the rules, whether in the *affaire fugue* or her previously unheard-of recycling of a losing cantata for later public performance, but would surely not have tolerated such behaviour from one of her own students. The perfection she demanded from others sits uncomfortably, too, alongside her hastily completed cantatas and the scrappy manuscript of *Dnégouchka*. It would be fair to say that 'Do as I say, not do as I do' could have been an appropriate motto for Nadia Boulanger as a composition teacher.

Lili Boulanger, on the other hand, could have used her success in the Prix de Rome as a launch pad for a successful composing career. It is clear that she used the competition as was originally intended; in other words, it provided her with experience and confidence in handling large-scale musical forms and forces. She planned to move on from the small format and clichéd dramatic situations of the Prix de Rome cantata to the composition of a full-length opera: *La princesse Maleine*, a setting of Maurice Maeterlinck's play. But fate would not permit her to realize this aim.

CHAPTER 3

The Music of Nadia Boulanger

The story of Nadia Boulanger's composing career after her student days is essentially a story of failure. Her final known works were composed in 1922, and in the rest of her long life, she arranged some of her sister's works, but there is no evidence she wrote any original compositions. Indeed, she generally discouraged comment about her creative works; many of her colleagues and pupils have spoken of her refusal to discuss her music after she abandoned composing. Although her music continued to be performed after her retirement from creative work, she never actively encouraged performances and often said that she had no talent as a composer. Fauré, her former teacher, was just one composer who questioned why she abandoned creative work, but Nadia Boulanger replied: 'If there is anything of which I am very sure, it is that my music is useless.'[1] In this chapter, I will focus on the public reception of those works that were performed while she was trying to establish herself as a composer. Most importantly, I would like to explore the reasons behind the ultimate failure and premature termination of her compositional career.

Nadia Boulanger focused on a narrow range of genres as a composer, and her choice of these genres was perhaps prompted as much by pragmatism as by her own ambition. Her preparation for the Prix de Rome competition ensured a concentration on works for chorus and piano and practice cantatas in the first decade of the twentieth century. The catalogue of her works (see Appendix A) shows that most are songs for voice and piano, though many of these songs were orchestrated. This focus on an essentially domestic genre is not surprising from a woman composer in the early years of the twentieth century. However, the fact that she orchestrated a number of her songs shows that she wanted to develop her skills in this medium and perhaps reach out to a larger audience; the pressures of earning a living as a teacher surely prevented her from writing many new works for the orchestral concerts in which she participated. She wrote only a few pieces for orchestra, the most significant of which are a *Rapsodie variée* for piano and orchestra (*c.* 1912) written for Raoul Pugno, the premiere of which was conducted by Boulanger herself; and a problematic opera, *La ville morte*, composed jointly with Pugno. Her other pieces comprise a few organ

---

[1] Cited in Don G. Campbell (1984), *Master Teacher: Nadia Boulanger* (Washington: Pastoral Press), p. 31.

65

works, some piano pieces and three short works for cello and piano. Most of these chamber works were commissioned for specific occasions.

Anyone wishing to study Nadia Boulanger's music must contend with several formidable problems. Firstly, some of her works have simply not survived: I have found references to a number of songs in publishers' catalogues or newspaper reports, but have not been able to trace manuscripts or even, in some cases, printed copies (even the Bibliothèque Nationale de France does not possess copies of all her published works). Boulanger's highly self-critical attitude towards her music undoubtedly led her to destroy some of her works. Several of her surviving manuscripts exist in a fragmentary state; indeed, almost all her large-scale works in manuscript are incomplete. The manuscript of her *Rapsodie variée* bears so many signs of extensive revision that it is unperformable in its present state.

Another problematic factor is her collaboration with Raoul Pugno. Two of Boulanger's most substantial achievements as a composer – the song cycle *Les heures claires* (1909) and the opera *La ville morte* (1910–13) – were written with her mentor. Although, as we will see, both composers' hands are evident on the manuscripts of both these works, it is not possible to evaluate the true extent of each composer's contribution to the music in the absence of definitive statements from both composers. While one may not necessarily consider that this is a problem for anyone interested in the works in question – arcane questions of authorship do not make a difference to the listener – it does mean that crucial questions related to Boulanger's personal musical style are hard to answer. It is true, however, that joint compositions of this type were not rare in French music of the late nineteenth or early twentieth century, and I am sure Nadia Boulanger was happy to associate her name with Pugno's not only because of their close friendship, but because this would draw public attention to her creative work.

However, this strategy backfired for her in both the short and long term. Contemporaries assumed that the older man Pugno was therefore the dominant partner in this collaboration, and tended to minimize Boulanger's contribution to their joint works. Unfortunately, even Pugno himself sometimes downgraded Boulanger's contribution; in an interview with the Boston-based magazine *The Musician* about *La ville morte*, he does not mention that she is the joint composer at all.[2] Gossip about the true nature of their relationship was also rife, and this was disastrous for a young woman living in a society where women were severely punished for not behaving correctly, or for not appearing to behave correctly. Nadia Boulanger and Raoul Pugno obviously spent time alone together because they worked together, behaviour which placed the young woman at risk of

---

[2] Cited in Léonie Rosenstiel (1998), *Nadia Boulanger* (London and New York: Norton), pp. 99–100.

moral censure. As Nadia Boulanger was so closely associated with Pugno, his death in 1914 had a devastating impact on her composing career. She wrote no large-scale works after his death, probably because it would have been far more difficult for her to secure performances without his influential support. Finally, it is fair to say that modern critics, who prize the individual creative genius, do not look favourably on her collaboration with Pugno, and it is also true that contemporary researchers interested in women's participation in music have tended to maximize Boulanger's contribution to their joint works.

Boulanger's choice of poets and poems is an important factor in any discussion of her contribution to the *mélodie* genre. She occasionally set contemporary verse, by Maurice Maeterlinck (*Les heures ternes, Cantique de soeur Béatrice*) and his fellow Belgian Emile Verhaeren (*Les heures claires*), but most of her songs set verses by distinguished nineteenth-century poets, most notably Paul Verlaine and Heinrich Heine (in French translation). Some later songs set texts by her friends Georges Delaquys, Camille Mauclair and Renée de Marquein, and one *mélodie* features her own, regrettable, verse (*Soir d'hiver*).

In 1909, she composed a song cycle jointly with Raoul Pugno, their first collaborative work. The cycle, *Les heures claires*, sets eight poems by the Belgian Emile Verhaeren, whose work clearly interested both Boulanger sisters, as one of Lili Boulanger's first works is a setting of his poem *Les pauvres*. Questions about the nature of the collaboration between Boulanger and Pugno are fascinating, but perhaps ultimately unanswerable. However, the manuscript in the Bibliothèque Nationale shows material in both composers' hands for most of the songs, as Table 1 reveals.

The dates reveal that the work must have been composed during vacation periods from teaching, and Boulanger writes at the end of the manuscript that the whole cycle was composed at 'St-Jean – Gargenville, 13 avril–13 août 1909'. The difference between the two composers' handwriting is clear, not least because Boulanger writes sharp key signatures in an unusual manner, with the F sharp towards the bottom rather than the top of the treble clef stave. However, there is no hiatus from one composer to the other; indeed, in 'C'était en juin', the triplet accompaniment figuration continues smoothly throughout. Although this manuscript is almost certainly a neat copy of the songs rather than work in progress, it is not a final version as there are no tempo markings present.

The songs form a loose cycle in that they are composed to poems by one author and are linked in mood, though there are no specific musical connections from one song to another and the poems do not form a sequential narrative. If anything, the songs are rather too similar; most are in a moderate tempo (only the fifth and seventh songs are at all lively); most are based on one accompaniment figure (often an oscillating or arpeggiated

Table 1. Manuscript (BN Ms 16273) of *Les heures claires*

Title and number of song	Date and place of composition	Hand(s)
1. Le ciel en nuit s'est déplié	13 avril 1909, St-Jean	Neat copy in Pugno's hand
2. Avec mes sens, avec mon coeur	16 avril 1909, St-Jean	In Boulanger's hand, but words from 'Je ne cesse de longuement me souvenir' are in Pugno's hand
3. Vous m'avez dit	18 avril 1909, St-Jean	In Pugno's hand, but date is in Boulanger's hand
8. S'il arrive jamais [follows no. 3 in this manuscript]	22 avril 1909, St-Jean	Neat copy in Pugno's hand
4. Que tes yeux clairs	20 juillet 1909, Gargenville	Neat copy in Pugno's hand, date in Boulanger's hand
5. C'était en juin	3 août 1909, Gargenville	In both hands: Pugno until words 'les oiseaux/Volaient dans l'or et dans la', Boulanger from 'joie …'
6. Chaque heure où je songe à ta bonté	7 août 1909, Gargenville	Boulanger's hand on first page, until words 'Et de si loin', then Pugno's hand
7. Roses de juin	13 août 1909, Gargenville	Pugno writes first line; Boulanger follows until Pugno takes over at 'et de velouté douce'; Boulanger concludes song from 'Roses de volupté'. Dates in Boulanger's hand

line); and the subject matter is steady happiness in a relationship rather than the extremes of passion.

The first song, 'Le ciel en nuit s'est déplié', features enormous 7/4 bars and a wide variety of accompaniment figures in the first eight bars of the piano part (Ex. 3.1): a complex contrapuntal texture followed by various arpeggiated accompaniments.

Ex. 3.1 Nadia Boulanger and Raoul Pugno, *Les heures claires*, 1 ('Le ciel en nuit s'est déplié'): bars 1–8

The accompaniment of 'Avec mes sens' is more coherent, and the directions to the singer are strikingly vivid: 'avec ferveur' and 'plus intense encore' are just two of the explicit indications for the singer to follow. The third and sixth songs, 'Vous m'avez dit' and 'Ta bonté', are more Fauréan in their use of simple, processional chordal accompaniments. Ex. 3.2, the opening of 'Ta bonté', anticipates Boulanger's Maeterlinck setting *Cantique (de soeur Béatrice)* (see Ex. 3.5a below), and both are highly reminiscent of Fauré's *Lydia*. The direction 'avec une religiosité émue' situates the song very clearly in the late Romantic period.

In addition to these songs, the manuscript book features other material which can almost all be attributed to Boulanger. After the song cycle, there are three pages of an unfinished song in Boulanger's hand entitled *Jean de Bois s'en va t'en guerre*. The song is in a modal G minor (with a flattened

Ex. 3.2   Nadia Boulanger and Raoul Pugno, *Les heures claires*, 5 ('Ta bonté'): bars 1–5

seventh), but only the first page features an accompaniment as well as a melody line. There are also sketches for *Dnégouchka*, the revised version of *Roussalka*, her Prix de Rome cantata of 1909; the character's names 'Yégor' and 'La fée' are indicated, and interestingly the composer uses figured bass symbols as harmonic shorthand. Finally, there is a sketch for the first song of *Les heures claires* in Pugno's hand.

The conductor Odaline de la Martinez wrote in a programme note about a selection of Nadia Boulanger's songs that 'The songs written with Raoul Pugno are unusually appealing. They manage to blend Pugno's old-fashioned Romantic chromaticism with Boulanger's ear for sharp dissonances and the tendency to give her harmonies a more colouristic role.'[3] While this appears a reasonable assumption – Boulanger was the younger composer in the partnership and we know that she was interested in Debussy – there is no evidence proving that there is such a stylistic difference between the two composers in their joint works, nor that Boulanger is responsible for the more harmonically daring passages in their joint works.

Nadia Boulanger's Maeterlinck setting, *Heures ternes*, is one of her finest works. Its manuscripts are undated, but we know that it was given its first public performance in April 1910, and published by Heugel as the eleventh of a collection of twelve songs in 1914. The rough copy of the song reveals that someone had a high opinion of it: a note, not in Nadia Boulanger's hand, reads 'Prière de copier celle-ci de suite pour 6h ce soir / le chant très bien fait – et très soigné' (Please copy this one immediately for tonight at 6 p.m. / the vocal line [is] very well made – and very carefully constructed). The other surviving manuscript copy is unusually neat for Nadia Boulanger, and is therefore presumably the copy made for this private première. Like the two Maeterlinck poems chosen by Lili Boulanger, *Heures ternes* focuses on feelings of desolation, darkness and a sense of futility; the sense that the

---

[3] Programme note for CD 'Fleurs jetées' by Rebecca de Pont Davies (mezzo-contralto) and Clare Toomer (piano), Lorelt LNT 106 (1996).

Ex. 3.3   Nadia Boulanger, *Heures ternes*: bars 1–8

narrator is waiting for something to relieve these feelings is omnipresent. Nadia Boulanger's setting admirably conveys this mood: the piano introduction, combining pedal points with dissonances, encapsulates the restlessness which goes nowhere and unresolved tensions of the poem (Ex. 3.3).

For the final verse, she again superimposes a pedal note on chromatic harmony, a favourite device of both Nadia and Lili Boulanger. The influences of both Debussy and Fauré are again perceptible: the climax of the song, at bars 31–3 (Ex. 3.4), features parallel chords, whole-tone harmonies and unresolved seconds, reminiscent of Debussy, and the obsessional sequences of the previous phrase echo Fauré's contemporary style.

Heures ternes is one of Nadia Boulanger's most impressive achievements as a composer, perhaps because it is a rare example of her setting a first-rate poem. In comparison, her setting of Maeterlinck's *Cantique (de soeur Béatrice)*, published in 1909 (which later became the sixth in the series of

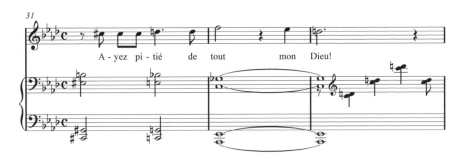

Ex. 3.4   Nadia Boulanger, *Heures ternes*: bars 31–3

twelve songs published by Hamelle), is far more conventional, no doubt partly because she chose a poem which expresses pious sentiments in a straightforward manner. Most of Nadia Boulanger's songs, whether written on her own or in collaboration with Raoul Pugno, also reveal a taste for uncomplicated poetry, and like Fauré in his early years, it seems she was not too concerned about the literary merit of the texts she chose.

The poem originally appeared at the beginning of the second act of Maeterlinck's play *Soeur Béatrice* (1901), and was later published in his collection *Chansons complètes*. Its narrator is a nun who sings of the necessity to raise oneself above the disappointments of love. The opening bars of her setting sound like a homage to the opening bars of Fauré's *Lydia* (c. 1870)[4] (Exx. 3.5a and b); this slow procession of chords is virtually identical to Fauré's song, though without the modally inflected vocal line.[5] But Boulanger decided not to emulate the paradoxical quality of Fauré's music; the ascetic chordal accompaniment of *Lydia* contrasts with the erotic imagery in Leconte de Lisle's poem, whereas Boulanger matches the mood of poem and music in traditional fashion.

Ex. 3.5a   Nadia Boulanger, *Cantique (de soeur Béatrice)*: bars 1–5

Ex. 3.5b   Gabriel Fauré, *Lydia*: bars 1–6

---

[4] It seems this song was a popular model for French composers: Vladimir Jankélévitch suggests that the opening bars of Henri Duparc's *Phidylé* are closely related to *Lydia*, though Duparc's piano accompaniment quickly becomes more texturally complex than Fauré's. Ernest Chausson's *Hébé* also bears a strong resemblance to *Lydia*. (See Vladimir Jankélévitch (1988), *Fauré et l'inexprimable* (Paris: Agora), p. 55.)

[5] Fauré employs the Lydian mode – no doubt, as Robert Orledge suggests in his 1983 book *Gabriel Fauré* (London: Eulenberg, pp. 50–1) he intended this musical pun.

Some years later, she transcribed the song as a *Lux aeterna* for voice, harp, violin and cello for a Mass commemorating her sister's death, a transcription which serves to emphasize the conventionally pious sentiments of the *Cantique*.

This song was premiered by the tenor Rodolphe Plamondon at a concert organized by the Grands Concerts Symphonia in Paris on 13 Feburary 1910, together with *Prière*, another religious song which exemplifies a type of poem which was considered suitable for young ladies in the late nineteenth and early twentieth centuries. Sentimental religious songs grace the catalogues of so many women composers of the nineteenth century, including Augusta Holmès (*La belle Madeleine*, *c.* 1880) and Cécile Chaminade. Boulanger composed *Prière* on 22 January 1909, according to the manuscript. It begins in A minor, but not unexpectedly ends in the tonic major, with an added sixth, evoking the sentimental religious style favoured by César Franck and his followers. Again, she changes the texture of the accompaniment for each of the three verses of the poem. Overall, the setting, and in particular Boulanger's marking 'd'une grande bonté' as a direction to the singer, is very much of its time.

Rapsodie variée / Fantaisie variée

It is a great pity that Boulanger's *Rapsodie variée* for piano and orchestra now only exists in a fragmentary state, as it is one of her few large-scale works. Even its title is uncertain: contemporary reviews call this piece *Rapsodie variée* (a practice which, to avoid complication, I will follow here), the orchestral manuscript now housed in Lyon Conservatoire is titled *Fantaisie*, and the Bibliothèque Nationale manuscript, a reduction for two pianos, is entitled *Fantaisie variée*. Pugno was the first soloist and the probable inspiration behind the work, not least because he had composed a *Concertstück* for piano and orchestra which he premiered in Paris in 1900. This connection is all the more plausible because Boulanger conducted the Pugno work (with the composer again at the piano) for her debut on the podium on 17 April 1912 in La-Roche-sur-Yon.[6]

The work is essentially a theme and variations for piano and orchestra which plays continuously, though it is divided into several sections which are differentiated in tempo and mood. Overall, the work (as far as it can be studied) is highly Romantic in character, written for a conventional large orchestra including cor anglais and contrabassoon, and its harmonic language is tonal though highly chromatic. The theme (Ex. 3.6) is initially presented by the orchestra and then repeated by the soloist before being developed.

---

6 Rosenstiel (1998), p. 97.

Ex. 3.6   Nadia Boulanger, *Rapsodie variée*: theme, bars 1–8

Both surviving manuscripts feature pages which have been pinned or pasted together, and while it is possible to examine material on those pages which are pinned together, the passages which have been pasted over remain a mystery. Moreover, these are not simply compressions of the original, as the pages either side of the cuts do not segue neatly. The BN manuscript can is summarized in Table 2.

Boulanger was evidently unhappy with the structure of the work, although the Lyon manuscript is in a copyist's hand and is dated '1914' – two years after the work's premiere. This manuscript features several crossed-out orchestral parts as well as a number of cuts (as in the BN manuscript). Although the Lyon orchestral manuscript features a Heugel stamp, which suggests that it was a pre-publication copy, it was never actually published.

The two lengthy cuts she made are significant in that the first (32–7 in the BN manuscript) is a highly Romantic passage, marked 'avec une grande émotion' and the second (42-7), as far as I can see, features conventional virtuoso display material. Neither of these sections is effective musically as they do not lead anywhere in particular and do not feature distinctive material. It is also possible that Boulanger later recoiled from the heart-on-sleeve emotional display of the music at pp. 32–7. Interestingly, she seems to begin the work confidently, but the last pages of both manuscripts feature crossed-out material and few dynamics, suggesting that she was less certain about the work by this stage. This loss of confidence – or, perhaps, loss of interest – is apparent in other manuscripts by this composer and is the strongest evidence explaining the reasons for her eventual abandonment of composition.

Most intriguingly of all, Boulanger's theme strongly resembles the theme of a work written by her sister in the same period. Lili Boulanger's *Thème et variations* for solo piano is in the same key, C minor; the themes of both works are slow and stately, both being marked 'Lent, grave'; and these themes share a time signature and similar melodic outlines (Ex. 3.7 shows the theme of Lili Boulanger's work, which is presented by the right hand only).

The two works share a common ancestor in Fauré's Theme and Variations in C sharp minor for solo piano, a connection which will be

Table 2.   Sectional divisions in Nadia Boulanger's *Rapsodie variée* (BN Ms 19509)

Page numbers	Tempo/expression marking
1–10	Lent – Grave: statements of the theme by the orchestra and then piano.
11–13	Plus doux: highly chromatic, often featuring parallel chords.
14–16	Un peu plus lent: appogiatura figures, rising to a climax.
17	Moins lent (crotchet = 84): conventional arpeggio material based around a D flat or C sharp pedal. Bassoon solo.
18–19	Allegro: brilliant scalar passages.
20–26	Più vivo: essentially in B minor with a dominant pedal. The orchestra effectively reinforces the piano's material.
27	Moderato: no key signature, though D minor is implied. Ascent and accelerando leads to next section.
28–31	Initially A tempo (crotchet = 96), though this is a recitative-like section with frequent tempo changes in which the theme is fragmented.
[32–7, 38–90]	Pinned together and crossed out. Marked 'Avec une grande émotion'. 38–top of page 39 are pasted over. The theme is accompanied with duplets or triplets, in Brahmsian or Fauréan fashion.
Bottom of p. 39–p. 43	Sans lenteur, avec une certaine nonchalance: back in C minor, resembles the opening of the work.
[43–5, 46–7]	43–5: pasted together. 46–7, a conventional virtuoso passage, are pinned together.
48–53, 54–6	Attempts to follow on from end of p. 43, but this does not form a convincing join. 'Joyeux' and 'éclatant' climaxes, clearly in C minor. 54–6: essentially filler material (diatonic or chromatic scales and a glissando).
57–8	Accelerando, building up to a restatement of the theme.
59–62 (end)	Scherzando: chromatic harmony. Lacks dynamic markings.

Ex. 3.7 Lili Boulanger, *Thème et variations*: theme

explored at greater length in Chapter 4. While neither work was published
in the composers' lifetimes, the differences between Lili Boulanger's
polished end product and Nadia Boulanger's fragmentary, problematic work
for piano and orchestra encapsulate the contrasting fortunes of the sisters'
composing careers.

Pugno was the soloist for the first performance of the *Rapsodie variée*, in
Berlin on 17 January 1913, with the composer conducting the Blüthner
Orchestra. The concert was devoted to music by female composers, and
contemporary critics viewed the event, and Boulanger on the podium, as a
curiosity.[7] The *Rapsodie variée* was first heard in Paris only a month later (on
9 February) and received mixed reviews. Amédée Boutarel, a critic with *Le
ménestrel* (a journal which always reviewed Pugno's performing and
composing activities enthusiastically), wrote: 'The work is divided into two
sections: a slow introduction and a rondo that might be called "theme and
variations" in the broadest sense. The composer employed cyclic form; a
single principal motif dominates the two sections and is subjected to
development that sometimes radically changes its character, sometimes not.
From the melodic point of view, the ideas are beautiful, pleasant, and not
bereft on occasion of a seductive vitality. The orchestration seems excellent;
a tendency to use the brass instruments, rather insistently, for gentle
pianissimo effects, is clear. Overall, this is a worthy composition that
sounds well and comes over well.'[8]

Boutarel seems to be trying to persuade his readers (and perhaps himself)
of the value of Boulanger's work, but an anonymous reviewer in *Le courrier
musical* was blunter in his lack of enthusiasm. This reviewer wrote that
'Monsieur Raoul Pugno interpreted it with all his heart, with his customary
authority. I'd like to be able to speak well of it, if only out of respect for
the admirable artist who presented it … But I owe it to the truth to admit

---

7 Ibid., p. 102.

8 *Le ménestrel* (15 February 1913): 53: 'L'ouvrage se divise en deux parties, une introduction d'un
movement lent et un rondo que l'on pouvait appeler "thème et variations" dans le sens le plus large.
La forme cyclique est celle adoptée par le compositeur: un motif principal unique domine dans les deux
morceaux et s'y développe avec des modifications de structure plus ou moins accusées. Au point de vue
mélodique, les idées sont jolies, agréables et non dépourvues parfois de vivacité entraînante.
L'orchestration paraît excellente; elle laisse apercevoir une tendance heureuse à employer les cuivres, non
sans une certaine insistance, pour des effets moelleux dans le pianissimo. En somme, il s'agit ici d'une
composition de valeur qui sonne et qui chante.'

that I don't like that sort of music.' Léonie Rosenstiel, quoting this reviewer, said that he 'disliked its lack of unity of emotion or colour, its triple-metre sections that resemble Sevillanas – those of Montmartre, not of Seville – its Mazurka which suffered from "Viennese insipidity" and the rest of the work, which failed to live up to the promise of the opening bars; it fell rather quickly into the most banal repetitions'. The reviewer summed up his or her feelings by describing the piece as 'a juvenile work'.[9]

Organ and chamber works

In 1911, Boulanger wrote a set of three organ works for an *Anthologie des Maîtres Contemporains de l'Orgue*, a two-volume anthology edited by the Abbé Joseph Joubert. Her contributions appear in the second volume, which was published in 1912. This volume features potted biographies of all contributing composers, and Boulanger's naturally draws attention to her Conservatoire prizes; it also mentions that she is currently writing 'several works', including *La ville morte* with Pugno.

Boulanger's three works are a *Prélude* (dedicated to the editor of the anthology), *Petit canon* and *Improvisation*. For all three pieces, she seems to have prized harmonic interest over melodic or rhythmic invention. The *Prélude* is rhythmically repetitive and very four-square, and almost always features a melody in one hand and accompaniment in thirds in the other. It begins in F minor, ending in the tonic major, but its central section is in the surprising key of C sharp minor. After this highly chromatic central section, the original theme reappears louder and differently spaced. In the *Petit canon*, the canonic imitation occurs at the distance of a quaver and an octave lower and, as in the *Prélude*, the piece concludes with a reprise of the opening ideas. The *Improvisation* begins in E flat minor, and is largely based on ostinato patterns, either alternating B flat–C flat or G flat–A flat. While on the surface this may seem like a Debussian device, the harmonic language (which is highly chromatic but still essentially rooted in tonality) and scoring for the organ militate against this impression. The work wanders through a number of keys and, like the *Prélude*, ends in the tonic major, the *tierce de Picardie* being a deliberately archaizing device.

As Boulanger was herself a fine organist, it is perhaps surprising that her only other organ work is a short *Pièce pour orgue sur des airs populaires flamands*, composed in 1915 and published by Ricordi in 1919. The work was premiered by the composer on 22 March 1915 at a concert arranged by the Union des Femmes Professeurs et Compositeurs de Musique at their headquarters, 27 rue Blanche, in the 9th arrondissement in Paris (not far

---

[9] Rosenstiel (1998), p. 105.

from her home in rue Ballu). This connection reveals that Boulanger did occasionally ally herself with women's organizations, though in later years she refused to identify herself with the feminist cause.

Nadia Boulanger's chamber works tend to be grouped in threes, though there is rarely any strong musical connection between different pieces in the group; presumably she thought that a group of short pieces would be easier to market than single works. Her *Trois pièces pour piano* are typical in that they are problematic works which seem to have been composed in a hurry. Only the manuscript of the first piece is dated ('5 juin 1914'), and it is reasonable to assume that the others were composed about the same time.

All three pieces are two pages long. For the first, Boulanger hesitated over her choice of tempo, changing her mind from 'Assez lent' to 'Sans lenteur'. This piece is essentially in D minor with a constant D pedal (Ex. 3.8 illustrates the opening), though the music is highly chromatic and the final 'chord' is octave Ds with an added C.

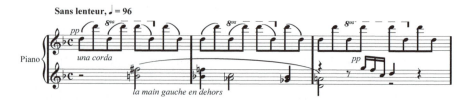

Ex. 3.8   Nadia Boulanger, *Trois pièces pour piano*, 1: bars 1–3

She moves the music from the high to low register from bar 13 to 18, at which point there is a counterbalancing ascent until bar 20, the end of the piece. Despite this gesture, the overall impression is of a piece which does not go anywhere. The second piece is harmonically very similar to the first, as it is also in D minor with an omnipresent D pedal. However, rhythm is, for once, the principal focus of this piece, and reiterated rapid triplets give it something of the cod-Spanish feel which the review quoted above also noted in her *Rapsodie variée*. The manuscript is very scruffy and lacking a tempo indication, and it is possible that the work is unfinished as the end is unconvincing.

The third piece in the group is neater and more like a finished product, though again there is no tempo indication, and misplaced sharp accidentals give the impression that the piece was written at great speed. This time, the key is B minor, and an ostinato rhythm (quaver–crotchet–quaver) is the main unifying factor in the piece. Again, Boulanger frequently uses a tonic pedal and, as in the second piece, she occasionally injects rhythmic interest by using triplets. The three pieces are not strong works, an opinion perhaps shared by their composer, who did not publish them.

Nadia Boulanger's later works rarely resemble those of her sister, but a fascinating exception to this is the third of her *Trois pièces* for cello and piano, published by Heugel in 1915. This short work, in C sharp minor, is roughly contemporary with Lili Boulanger's *D'un soir triste* and *D'un matin de printemps*. The former work exists in a sketchy version for cello and piano, almost certainly in Nadia Boulanger's hand. Whether there is any definite connection between the two sisters' decisions to write for cello and piano is impossible to establish. What is clear, however, is that Nadia Boulanger's third piece for this combination has a good deal in common with her younger sister's *D'un matin de printemps*. Despite its minor key, Nadia's piece is an uncharacteristically lively work. Its principal theme – an almost nursery-rhyme-like tune and punchy accompaniment – is more reminiscent of Poulenc than anything else in her own catalogue of works (Ex. 3.9).

Ex. 3.9   **Nadia Boulanger, *Trois pièces pour violoncelle*, 3: bars 15–20**

After a central section in 5/8, the opening ideas recur in varied form; this section is followed by a more exact reprise of the opening material. The concluding bars of Nadia's cello piece and Lili Boulanger's *D'un matin de printemps* are strikingly similar (Exx. 3.10a and b).

La ville morte

One of Nadia Boulanger's most intriguing works is *La ville morte*, an opera she wrote in collaboration with Raoul Pugno. Like many women composers of her generation, Nadia Boulanger was subjected to many offensive sexist comments in the press, not least in the magazine *Femina*, which greeted the news of the composition of *La ville morte* in 1910 with the announcement: 'This is the first time that a collaboration has been established between a "female composer" and a composer.'[10] Many half-truths regarding the

---

[10] Cited in Rosenstiel (1998), p. 91.

Ex. 3.10a   Nadia Boulanger, *Trois pièces pour violoncelle*, 3: concluding bars

Ex. 3.10b   Lili Boulanger, *D'un matin de printemps*: concluding bars

Boulanger/Pugno collaboration are in print, not least, I suspect, because it seems no writer has studied the manuscripts of the work.

Camille Mauclair noted that Pugno brought to the opéra-comique genre 'more grace, a surer technique and more taste' than one normally encountered.[11] Pugno was already experienced in the art of collaboration, having written the ballets *Viviane* (1886) and *Le chevalier aux fleurs* (1899) with André Messager and Clément Lippacher respectively, and Boulanger and Pugno had, as we have seen, written a song cycle, *Les heures claires*, as a team in 1909. Moreover, *Musica* claimed in January 1913 that they were planning to write a second opera, *La rédemption de Colin Muset*, though no music seems to have been composed for this project.[12]

It appears that Pugno and Boulanger jointly conceived the opera project, and Pugno persuaded his friend Gabriele d'Annunzio to adapt his play *La città morta* (1898) as an opera libretto.[13] *La ville morte* no doubt appealed to the composers because a collaboration with d'Annunzio, a notorious figure in the theatrical world, would have drawn the public's attention to the work,

---

[11] Obituary of Pugno in *Le ménestrel* (17 January 1914): 17; 'plus de grâce, de science et de goût'.

[12] Cited in Rosenstiel (1998), p. 103.

[13] The pianist and playwright met frequently at Pugno's Sunday afternoon salon.

and I believe that the strong resemblance between his libretto and that of Debussy's *Pelléas et Mélisande* must have been a potent source of attraction, though it must be said that d'Annunzio's work suffers from comparison with Maeterlinck's. Of course, d'Annunzio also collaborated with Debussy in *Le martyre de Saint-Sébastien*, a work composed in 1913, shortly after his Boulanger/Pugno project.

D'Annunzio compressed the five acts of his play into four when converting his text into a libretto. Set in Mycenas, the opera features four principal characters: Anne, Hébé (Bianca Maria in the play), Anne's husband, Alexandre, and Léonard, Hébé's brother. The two female characters are close friends, and Alexandre and Léonard are also close; Alexandre says they are 'like brothers'. Briefly, Alexandre is in love with Hébé, and Léonard is jealous of this relationship as he harbours incestuous feelings towards his sister and is obsessed with her purity; Hébé returns Léonard's feelings. Anne, who is blind, spends most of the opera in a state of despair because she realizes her husband no longer loves her. In Act III, Léonard admits to Alexandre that he loves his sister, and resolves to drown her in the Perséia fountain. The short final act of *La ville morte* is centred on Hébé's corpse and, in a further parallel with Act V of *Pelléas et Mélisande* (in which the characters group around Mélisande's deathbed), it features a single scene. Léonard insists that only he understands his sister's soul, echoing Arkel's words as he watches Mélisande die.

The suffocating relationships parallel the self-contained world of the inhabitants of Allemonde, and d'Annunzio's concentration on the four principal characters compounds this oppressive atmosphere: a Nourrice (Anne's former wet-nurse) has a small role, and the inhabitants of *la ville morte* intervene twice in the form of a chorus and children's chorus. There are other close links between d'Annunzio's and Maeterlinck's libretti. All four characters in *La ville morte* yearn to leave, just as Pelléas constantly mentions his desire to travel. Both operas feature a blind character (though Anne regains her sight in the closing bars of *La ville morte*, when she touches Hébé's dead body), and the populations of both Allemonde and the 'dead city' are dying; the inhabitants of 'la ville morte' open Act III with an invocation to Elijah, a prayer for rain to relieve their thirst. In a clear parallel with Act III, scene i of Debussy's opera, the third scene of Act I of Boulanger and Pugno's work features Hébé unknotting her long hair. Finally, a fountain is an important meeting place in both operas.

The musical language of the opera is rooted in tonality, though often highly chromatic and with modal inflections: in other words, in a style typical of French late Romantic music. Given the libretto's connections with *Pelléas et Mélisande*, it is significant that many passages are highly indebted to Debussy, who was a favourite composer of both Nadia and Lili Boulanger and an inspiration to both sisters. The vocal writing echoes the parlando style of much of *Pelléas*, and Nadia Boulanger wrote at the beginning of the Act I sketches: 'La voix suivra intimement le sens des mots, et soulignera chaque intention, tout en conservant une simplicité, une sorte de gravité non dépourvue d'énergie. Le rythme sera bien définie.' (The voice shall be closely bound up with the meaning of the words, and shall at the same time retain a simplicity and gravity which is not devoid of energy. The rhythm shall be well defined.) The harp and celesta are used for pictorial purposes, to evoke freshness, the sun, or the Perséia fountain in which Hébé is drowned at the end of Act III. Parallel chordal progressions abound, a bar is often immediately repeated, and a single rhythmic figure, possibly an ostinato pattern, to unify a scene is another stylistic trait common to Debussy's only completed opera and the Boulanger/Pugno collaboration. Ex. 3.11, taken from the first act of the opera, shows an ostinato figure underlining the sense of suffocation felt by Hébé.

Ex. 3.11   Nadia Boulanger and Raoul Pugno, *La ville morte*: Act I, Hébé, OS p. 120

These Debussy connections initially led me to believe that Nadia Boulanger would have played the principal role in the composition of the opera. I felt it was unlikely that Pugno, a composer working in the conservative genres of the opéra-comique, ballet and character piano piece, would be absorbing the influence of such a revolutionary figure at this late stage in his career. However, if the manuscripts available for study are any guide, it is not possible to distinguish between the composers' styles, and both Pugno and Boulanger are responsible for obviously Debussian passages.

The question of their respective roles in composing *La ville morte* is the most fascinating of all. Most of the work was composed at Gargenville, during summer holidays, and in a letter to d'Annunzio, dated 2 July 1911, Boulanger assures the playwright that the first two acts are virtually complete, and describes its composition in strikingly emotional terms: 'I do not know how we will manage, but I am certain that each note will come from our hearts – and I think that one thing cannot fail to give our score a lasting value: the sincerity and intense feeling that our two hearts will bring to it.'[14] Boulanger's biographer Jérôme Spycket endorses d'Annunzio's belief that she composed the music for the female characters, whilst Pugno dealt with the male roles,[15] but there is no evidence whatsoever for this. If this were indeed true, Pugno would have composed a good deal less than Boulanger, as the female characters have more substantial roles and are more convincingly drawn than the cardboard Alexandre and Léonard. Boulanger was the principal correspondent with the librettist; despite her youth and inexperience, she did not hesitate to badger d'Annunzio for texts and berate him for his slow responses to her letters.

Table 3 lists the manuscripts available for study. Sometimes we can see that both composers have worked on a page of the score: pp. 17–26 of the sketches for Act I provide the clearest evidence of this compositional teamwork. Boulanger has written p. 18, but the next page, featuring striking chromatic harmony, is written by Pugno. He is also responsible for a very Debussian passage on pp. 21–2, based on triplet rhythms, and his sumptuous orchestration reacts to the character's mention of 'le soleil'; Boulanger adds a harp glissando to the texture at this point. On pp. 25–6, there is no stylistic hiatus at all as Pugno's writing is replaced by Boulanger's. There are, however, differences in their working methods: Boulanger invariably includes expression markings and other details when composing, whereas for Pugno, the notes themselves were apparently the priority; he is also far less likely than Boulanger to write words under the vocal lines.

Of course, these differences in handwriting do not necessarily prove who composed what, but the joint nature of the compositional process cannot easily be refuted. It is, however, logical to suppose that the Prelude to the opera is entirely Boulanger's work. The neat manuscript is in her hand, and is dated November 1913 – only two months before Pugno's death during an ill-advised concert tour to Russia he undertook shortly after a serious operation. This Prelude, though longer and texturally more substantial than the Prelude to Act I of *Pelléas et Mélisande*, is similarly repetitive (Ex. 3.12).

Perhaps the discovery of correspondence between the two composers would reveal more about their working methods; only one complete letter from Pugno to Boulanger is available for study, together with what is clearly the final page of a longer letter, and these sources shed no light on their collaborative process. It is possible that their correspondence forms part of the Boulanger archive deposited in the Bibliothèque Nationale de France

---

14 Letter cited in Doda Conrad (1995), *Grandeur et mystère d'une mythe: 44 ans d'amitié avec Nadia Boulanger* (Paris: Buchet/Chastel), p. 34; 'Je ne sais comment nous réussirons, mais je sais bien que chacune des notes sera venue des profondeurs les plus intimes de nous-mêmes – et il me semble qu'une chose donnera, ne peut pas ne pas se donner, une valeur à notre partition: c'est la sincérité et l'émotion intenses que nos deux coeurs lui donnent.'

15 Jérôme Spycket (1987), *Nadia Boulanger* (Lausanne: Payot), p. 34.

Table 3. Manuscripts of Boulanger and Pugno's _La ville morte_

Material	Location	Date	Hand(s)	Comments
Prelude to Act I	Bibliothèque Nationale de France (BN), Paris (MS 19676)	November 1913	Boulanger	19 pp.; does not appear in vocal score or Act I MS
Act I: sketches	BN (MS 19676)	Undated	Boulanger and Pugno	31 pp.
Act I: full orchestral score	Heugel	6 September 1923	Boulanger	214 pp.
Act III: full orchestral score	BN (MS 19675)	Undated	Boulanger and Pugno	126 pp.
Complete vocal score (Acts I–IV)	BN (MS 19674)	Undated	Boulanger and Pugno	_c._ 300 pp. (not numbered)

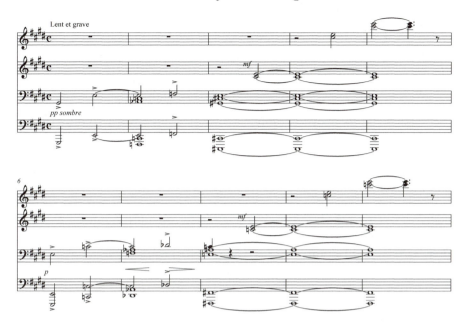

Ex. 3.12   Nadia Boulanger and Raoul Pugno, *La ville morte*: Prelude, bars 1–10

and inaccessible to scholars until 2009, but it is equally possible that Pugno and Boulanger saw each other so frequently in the summer months that it was not necessary for them to correspond.

After Pugno's death on 3 January 1914, many obituary writers, according to Rosenstiel, 'reflected the ardent hope that the Opéra-Comique would produce *La ville morte* as soon as possible', though 'most, like [Camille] Mauclair [in *Le ménestrel*], were far more interested in it as evidence of the departed Pugno's genius than as witness to Nadia's talents as a composer'.[16] The casting of the opera was complete by July 1914, sets and posters were designed (though d'Annunzio, rather than Boulanger, was asked to approve them), and chorus rehearsals were scheduled to start on 17 August. However, the outbreak of the First World War meant all plans were put on hold. The work attracted the attention of Gustave Samazeuilh in 1942, when he wrote an article for *L'information musicale* entitled '"La ville morte" en musique'. Here, he calls on Boulanger to 'complete the unfinished orchestration of *La ville morte*'.[17] I have not found orchestrated versions of Acts II or IV of the opera, though it would have been surprising for the

---

[16] Rosenstiel (1998), pp. 118–19.

[17] 10 July 1942: 1021–2 (the article had previously been published in *Le Temps*, which appeared in the unoccupied zone of France, on 30–31 May 1942).

Opéra-Comique to have proceeded so far in its plans to produce the opera in 1914 if it was only half-orchestrated. On 15 and 16 July 2005, the work was finally heard for the first time at the Chigiana Festival, Italy, though this version was orchestrated by Mauro Bonifacio.

A manuscript copy of Act I of *La ville morte* in Nadia Boulanger's hand, owned by the publisher Heugel, is dated 6 September 1923, after Boulanger had supposedly abandoned composition. Léonie Rosenstiel mentioned that in 1923, 'Albert Carré, the director of the Opéra-Comique, at d'Annunzio's suggestion, had looked up the score for *La ville morte*, which had been lying in the back of a file drawer since the war.'[18] Boulanger eagerly supported this projected performance, perhaps because she was more motivated to publicize this collaborative work rather than music she composed without Pugno. Carré's interest in the score must have provoked her to prepare the September 1923 manuscript, and characteristically, she made several alterations to Act I in the process. Though most of the differences between the vocal score prepared by both composers and this 1923 manuscript are minor, one is quite extraordinary. On pp. 102–4 of the manuscript, the pianist's right hand plays tremolandi on the black notes of the keyboard, superimposed on a white-note cluster played with the left forearm (Ex. 3.13).

Ex. 3.13   Nadia Boulanger and Raoul Pugno, *La ville morte*: Act I OS p. 102, cluster

* NB's note on score: 'Toutes les touches blanches seront enfoncées en posant le coude et l'avant-bras sur le clavier – donner un peu plus de poids dans le grave'
(All the white keys depressed by placing the elbow and forearm on the keyboard – give a little more weight to the lower notes)

As far as I know, this is the first piano cluster in Western European classical music, pre-dating Bartók's First Piano Concerto and *Out of Doors* Suite by three years.[19] Ex. 3.13 is all the more striking as it occurs in a harmonic context which is highly chromatic (though rooted in tonality) with modal inflections – therefore far from revolutionary.

---

18 Rosenstiel (1998), p. 168.

19 Was Nadia Boulanger familiar with the work of American composers, such as Ives and Cowell, who

Boulanger's 1923 revision of this act is symptomatic of her highly self-critical attitude towards her music, though it also suggests that she was not always as reluctant to promote her music as is believed. Unfortunately, and for an unknown reason, Carré did not follow through his plan to produce *La ville morte* in the 1923–4 season of the Opéra-Comique. Some years later, Leonard Bernstein expressed an interest in performing *La ville morte*, and Boulanger sent him a score. Rosenstiel states that Bernstein and Boulanger met early in 1946,[20] though I am, as yet, unaware when Boulanger sent the conductor a copy of the score of the opera. Her hopes of a production of her collaboration with Pugno were again to be dashed; not only did Bernstein never conduct *La ville morte*, he failed to return the score.[21] The correspondence from Boulanger to Bernstein, now housed in the Library of Congress, Washington, does not shed any light on this possibility of a performance of the opera; indeed, there are no references to *La ville morte* in these letters.[22]

La ville morte is without doubt Nadia Boulanger's most significant achievement as a creative artist, and the discovery of other manuscripts of the opera (and of further correspondence between its joint composers) would reveal more about her fascinating collaboration with Pugno. Its sorry history, from Pugno's untimely death to these fruitless attempts to have the opera produced, must have caused Nadia Boulanger much anguish and frustration, and the difficulties she encountered in obtaining a performance of the work must have reinforced her lack of self-belief in herself as a composer.

Nadia Boulanger's last songs

Boulanger's composing career petered out in the early 1920s, and her last known compositions are a set of four songs to texts by Camille Mauclair, dating from 1922, and a setting of a poem by her friend Renée de Marquein (writing under the pseudonym François Bourguignon), *J'ai frappé*. Mauclair's poems are intended to be popular in flavour; he often uses colloquial language and writes about everyday issues. Mauclair was a supporter of the feminist movement, and Boulanger took a passing interest in politics under

---

experimented with clusters from around 1912? Cowell's music was featured on a Paris concert programme in November 1923 (therefore, two months after Boulanger's date on the revised manuscript of Act I of *La ville morte*), and around this time, Ives's experiments were unknown outside his immediate circle of friends. I should like to thank Professor David Nicholls for his suggestions of possible sources for Boulanger's cluster.

[20] Rosenstiel (1998), p. 336.

[21] Letter to the author from Alexandra Laederich, secretary of the Fondation Internationale Nadia et Lili Boulanger, 21 July 1998.

[22] I am indebted to the Fondation Boulanger, Amberson Inc. and Mark Horowitz, Curator of the Bernstein Collection at the Library of Congress, for enabling me to study this correspondence.

his influence, writing a piano piece for a women's organization. Rosenstiel insinuates that Boulanger was attracted to him, but that this attraction was not mutual.

Of the five poems set by Boulanger, two (*Chanson* and *Le couteau*) are subtitled 'populaire', explaining the uncomplicated character and colloquial diction (e.g. 'J'ai un couteau dans l'coeur', imitating normal spoken French diction rather than conventional poetic diction which gives a value to every syllable). *Doute* is rather more akin to Boulanger's early songs in its involved chromatic accompaniment, and *Au bord de la route* features a pedal F throughout; the song, in F minor, has a piano accompaniment marked 'tortueux'. Finally, *L'échange* again features a chromatically saturated musical language, this time with the vaguely Spanish flavour (Ex. 3.14 illustrates the final bars of the song) that is one of the more peculiar characteristics of her music.

Ex. 3.14   Nadia Boulanger, *L'échange*: bars 34–8

The contrast between the sisters' compositional careers is best demonstrated by their musical responses to war: Lili's setting of the *De profundis* (Psalm 130, *Du fond de l'abîme*), for soloists, chorus, orchestra and organ, expresses the suffering and pain of the times, and her *Vieille prière bouddhique* (1916) could, according to Fauser, be interpreted as 'a prayer for peace for humanity'.[23] War is also a central theme of her opera *La princesse Maleine*. Although written in 1912–13, Lili Boulanger's work for male chorus and orchestra, *Pour les funérailles d'un soldat*, was appropriately premiered in the war years. These are all large-scale, public works, whereas Nadia was moved to compose a song to an embarrassingly bad text of her own, *Soir d'hiver*. The narrator of the song is the mother of a baby boy who is waiting for her husband to return from the front; she expresses her love for her husband and son, and concludes that the baby has 'un coeur d'homme' (Ex. 3.15).

---

23 Fauser (1997): 75.

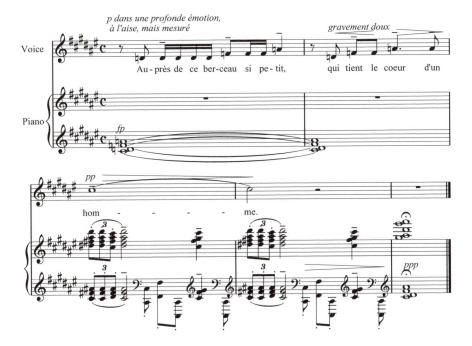

Ex. 3.15   Nadia Boulanger, *Soir d'hiver*: final 5 bars

Clearly, this song focuses on domestic, female concerns; concerns which, poignantly, did not mirror the composer's real-life situation as a single, childless woman. Moreover, the rather overwrought climax of the song exemplifies the essentially late-Romantic musical language she favoured – a language far removed from the Stravinskian neo-classical style she promoted later in life. One has to wonder whether Nadia Boulanger was reluctant to promote her music because her stylistic tastes seemingly changed dramatically under the influence of Stravinsky. The highly Romantic emotional world of her music also contrasts greatly with the dour, serious public image she assiduously cultivated as a teacher.

The most personal work in Boulanger's output is her final song, *J'ai frappé*, a slow, dense work that she surely intended to be her farewell to composition. It is reasonable to presume that the text was written especially for Boulanger, perhaps at her prompting (Ex. 3.16 illustrates the final bars of the song).

The words seem to sum up her feelings of failure connected with her unsuccessful compositional career. In a lecture on modern French music given in the Rice Institute in 1925, Nadia Boulanger briefly mentioned her sister's songs, saying: 'Even when Mademoiselle Boulanger is commenting on the verses of another, it seems as though the words were

Ex. 3.16   Nadia Boulanger, *J'ai frappé*: bars 11–22

her own.'[24] This Romantic view of the relationship between a composer and her texts, expressed only three years after Nadia Boulanger composed *J'ai frappé*, endorses this interpretation of her own final work. Judging by the text – 'I have knocked on closed doors / But only the echo of my heart responded' – Boulanger knew that this would be her last musical composition as, in her view, the continuation of her creative career was futile. While her surviving works do not reveal a strikingly original voice, it would have been fascinating to see her respond as a composer to musical developments of the twentieth century in the rest of her long life. If the story of Nadia Boulanger's compositional life is essentially a story of failure, this is surely because, tragically, she never received the support and encouragement she needed after Pugno's death.

---

24 In *The Rice Institute Pamphlets*, 13/2 (April 1926): 150–1.

CHAPTER 4

The Music of Lili Boulanger
after 1913

Lili Boulanger's victory in the Prix de Rome was a turning point in her composing career. As the first female winner of the music Prix de Rome – and as a member of an eminent musical family – she received a good deal of press attention, much of which focused on her gender and fragile appearance rather than her music. Her prize-winning cantata was published by Durand, and the publisher Ricordi gave her career a great boost when he signed her on an exclusive contract in 1913; this ensured her of a regular monthly income and assigned the rights to future compositions to the Italian publisher.

Despite her always precarious health, Lili Boulanger composed prolifically during her stay in Rome. As a winner of the Prix de Rome, she was obliged to compose works in particular genres during each year of her stay in the Villa Medici, and these works were sent to Paris at the end of the year and the composer's progress was evaluated by the Institut. While the precise rules and regulations for the Prix de Rome changed over the years, composers were always required to write a religious vocal work.[1]

The compositions written or started by Lili Boulanger in Rome should therefore be considered in the context of these regulations. For example, the 1894 regulations (which were modified only slightly in 1897) state that 'In the first year of his or her stay, [the composer should] firstly: compose a substantial work for a chamber formation of his or her choice, preferably a string quartet. Secondly: compose six short songs, with orchestral accompaniment and a separate reduction of this for voice and piano.' Sketchbook evidence reveals that Lili Boulanger toyed with various chamber works during her time in Rome (though she does not appear to have considered the string quartet genre). Her song cycle, *Clairières dans le ciel,* may perhaps have been written in response to the requirement to write a group of songs, but this cycle of thirteen songs goes far beyond the letter of the regulations. Her three Psalms, the most considerable works she composed in Rome, may again have been partially prompted by the requirement for a

---

1 Alexandre Dratwicki (2005), 'Les "Envois de Rome" des compositeurs pensionnaires de la Villa Médicis (1804–1914)' in *Revue de musicologie*, 91/1: 123.

third-year *pensionnaire* to 'Firstly: either compose an oratorio on French, Italian or Latin words; or choose either a solemn Mass, a Te Deum, a large-scale Psalm …'.[2] One of the other possibilities open to a third-year *pensionnaire* was the composition of an opera. Although Lili Boulanger's stay in Rome was curtailed by her illness and by the First World War, meaning she never became a third-year *pensionnaire,* she eagerly seized upon the opportunity to write large-scale vocal works of the types suggested by the Prix de Rome regulations. She noted ideas for future works, not all of which she completed, in a small red exercise book. This 59-page sketchbook is now housed in the Bibliothèque Nationale (MS 19435), and while not all of these sketches can be precisely dated, she was scrupulous about dating manuscripts of completed works.

Her *Thème et variations* for piano was completed in Rome on 12 June 1914 (and is therefore certainly the work she was, according to her diary, copying out on the 13th), though sketches for the work dated as early as 1911 survive.[3] A serious and substantial work, it requires considerable power and, ideally, large hands, and uses the full range of the piano. The work is in C minor, though the theme is highly chromatic (see Ex. 3.7). Initially, this theme is stated unaccompanied; it is followed by a harmonized version and then variations as follows:

1.   Lent (avec grandeur, mais sombre, douloureux) [Slow, grand but sombre and painful]
2.   sur la tête de la thème (très tenaillé, douloureux) [on the head – i.e. the initial motif – of the theme, very tormented, painful]
3.   Thème à la partie supérieure (assez lent, plus simple, plus de grandeur) [Theme in the upper part – quite slow, simpler, grander]
4.   La basse et surtout le chant bien en dehors [The bass and, above all, the melody to the fore]
5.   Très calme [Very calm]
6.   Thème modifié [Altered theme]. Features rippling figurations
7.   Thème totalement modifié, pas très lent, très large [Totally changed theme, not too slow, very broad]. In 4/4 time
7 bis. Plus vite [faster]; the dynamic level drops to *pp* (from *ff*). Following this 'variation 7b', variation 7 is repeated, creating a tripartite variation
8.   Reprendre no. 1 [repeat no. 1]

Variations 1–4 play continuously; this is interestingly reflected in the manuscript, as Boulanger only starts numbering the variations from the

---

2 Ibid., 119.

3 This means that she was composing the work at the same time as her sister was writing her *Fantaisie/Rapsodie variée* for piano and orchestra; see Chapter 3 for further details.

fourth one, as if the first few were a single unit. The composer's descriptions of the first variations in particular are strikingly explicit and dramatic.

The work has much in common with Fauré's Theme and Variations in C sharp minor, op. 73 (1895), which may well have served as a model for Boulanger's piece. The character and keyboard layout of Fauré's theme closely resemble Boulanger's theme (Ex. 4.1: Fauré theme), and neither work ventures from the home key in the variations (only Fauré's eleventh and final variation, in the tonic major, departs from this rule).

Ex. 4.1   Gabriel Fauré, *Thème et variations*: theme, melody line

The elliptical harmonic shifts in Boulanger's theme owe a good deal to Fauré's harmonic style, and her use of the Neapolitan sixth in its penultimate bar is another of Fauré's harmonic traits. Moreover, the predominantly chordal piano textures are also reminiscent of the piano style of Nadia Boulanger's composition teacher. Lili Boulanger's other piano works are also very close to Fauré in style, far closer than to Debussy with whom she is more often compared.

However, vocal works are a larger and more significant proportion of Lili Boulanger's catalogue, and her deep religious faith is reflected in her most important works. While religious belief was expected of people of her background, the composition of religious choral music was not encouraged at the Conservatoire because of its secular, republican ideals. Lili Boulanger completed three Psalm settings and a *Pie Jesu*, and her red sketchbook reveals that she toyed with other settings of religious texts. Much material in this book is clearly preliminary work for her largest choral piece, *Du fond de l'abîme* (the *De profundis*, Psalm 130). Elsewhere in this sketchbook, there are ideas for a setting of the Kyrie (p. 23) and a text (probably Psalm 134) which she presumably considered setting: 'Voici, bénissez l'Eternel; vous, tous les serviteurs de l'Eternel, vous qui assistez toutes les nuits dans la maison de l'Eternel / Elevez vos mains dans la sanctuaire, et bénissez l'Eternel. L'Eternel te bénisse, de Sion – lui qui a fait les cieux et la terre.'

Psalms 24 and 129

Lili Boulanger completed two short psalm settings in Rome: Psalm 129 ('Ils m'ont assez opprimé dès ma jeunesse') and Psalm 24[4] ('La Terre appartient à l'Eternel'). Many writers on Boulanger have been unable to resist the temptation to interpret these psalm settings in the light of the composer's slight physique and supposed personality traits. Rosenstiel simply notes that the composer must surely have identified with the title of Psalm 129 (Many a time from my youth up have they afflicted me), and the chunky chords and strident scoring, dominated by brass instruments, of Psalm 24 have been contrasted with the fragile appearance (and, of course, the female gender) of the composer, as if there were a connection between a composer's size and the scale and intensity of the work he or she is capable of writing.

It is far more interesting and fruitful to explore the musical characteristics of each work, not least because the two settings have a good deal in common. Both are essentially in minor keys, though with modally flattened sevenths (Psalm 24 in E minor, Psalm 129 in D minor), and both combine straightforward melody lines (which are well within the grasp of a competent amateur choir) with harmonically adventurous accompaniment. The opening bars of Psalm 129 feature mirror writing, with the bass voices descending as the upper voices ascend (Ex. 4.2), and the lead up to the first vocal entry well reflects Boulanger's expression mark 'Contained but agitated inside'; the dominant pedal, A, and climbing melodic line contrast strongly with the highly chromatic inner voices (E7 first inversion with flattened seventh/E flat7 first inversion with flattened seventh).

Ex. 4.2   Lili Boulanger, *Psaume CXXIX*: bars 1–5

When the voice enters at bar 31, it is the lowest line of the texture. (Ex. 4.3)

---

[4] Psalm 24 is dedicated to Jules Griset, an industrialist and director of the Chorale Guillot de Saint-Brice.

Ex. 4.3   Lili Boulanger, *Psaume CXXIX*: vocal entry, bars 31–4

Boulanger often distinguishes different sections of a piece by using different accompaniment figures for each. This is the case for this Psalm, as Table 4 illustrates.

Table 4.   Sections of Psalm 129

Bars	Characteristics
1–30	Orchestral introduction
31–43	Vocal entry: uses chords from introduction
44–84	Triplets in accompaniment (text: Des laboureurs ...), orchestra only 55–67
85–94	Return to texture, dynamic (*f*) and instrumentation of opening
95–110	Sudden decrease in dynamic to ***pp***; chord plus rocking accompaniment

Although the vocal score indicates no change in the vocal line at bar 95, in Igor Markevitch's 1960 recording there is a change from unison male chorus to a solo baritone at this point. Also, female voices enter for the first time here, vocalizing on the syllable 'Ah!' and doubling the treble lines of the orchestra. The psalm ends, as often in Boulanger, not with the final word of the text but with the syllable 'Ah!' (Ex. 4.4). In Psalm 129, this gesture underlines the rocking, lullaby-like concluding section, while in Psalm 24 and the *Vieille prière bouddhique*, the 'Ah!' is a final exclamation.

The vocal scoring of Lili Boulanger's setting of Psalm 24 essentially divides the work into four sections, as seen in Table 5. This shows a clear progression towards the full chorus entry at the climax and conclusion of

Ex. 4.4   Lili Boulanger, *Psaume CXXIX*: concluding bars

Table 5.   Sections of Psalm 24

Bars	Vocal texture
1–57	Male chorus
58–72	Tenor solo
73–80	Half the male chorus
81–149	Full chorus (SATB)

the work, a dynamic progression which is similar to that in her *Vieille prière bouddhique*.

While the introductory bars, for brass and timpani (Ex. 4.5), could be viewed as being in a modal E minor, the complete lack of tonic-dominant movement and emphasis on the interval of an open fifth reveal a more original harmonic world, one which is distinctly different from the Germanic Romantic harmonies of earlier works such as *Faust et Hélène*.

Ex. 4.5 Lili Boulanger, *Psaume XXIV*: bars 1–6

Boulanger adds dissonant seconds to her chords (often an added fourth), perhaps echoing Ravel's practice, and her avoidance of I–V harmonies could be inspired by Fauré, who often substituted I–iii for I–V. When the voices enter, the harmony is again ambiguous: it could be interpreted as I–ii, though the second chord is perhaps more likely to be perceived as the top two notes of the dominant seventh.

Bar 39 of Boulanger's Psalm 24 is the beginning of a section marked 'Sans rigueur' which contrasts with the strident opening of the psalm. Here, she uses mirror writing, a texture not unlike the opening of Psalm 129 (Ex. 4.6; compare with Ex. 4.2 above) and the accompaniment is formed of a series of layered ostinati.

Ex. 4.6   Lili Boulanger, *Psaume XXIV*: bars 39–43

These ostinato accompaniments have a mechanistic feel which was very much in vogue when Boulanger composed her Psalm: Satie, Poulenc and many other composers were fond of this type of accompaniment. Indeed, had Lili Boulanger lived, it would have been fascinating to see whether she would have established herself as an equal of near-contemporaries such as Honegger, Milhaud and Poulenc.

Psaume CXXX (Du fond de l'abîme)

Boulanger worked on her setting of Psalm 130 in Rome, as is clear from an examination of her sketchbook. On pp. 54–5, she sketches a fugue on the words 'Si tu prends garde', though this material is not used in the definitive version (at these words, the contralto soloist enters for the first time); and on p. 42 she appears to be considering titles for this work. The title ideas she writes down are: Le glas avec le Dies irae (Deathknell with Dies irae); Carillon baptême (Bell pealing for a baptism); Chant grave (Serious song); Chant d'émotion personnelle (Song of personal feeling); and Chant de paix planant au-dessus tout (Song of all-enveloping peace). The dedication of *Du fond de l'abîme* to her late father explains the more personal ideas for titles, and her first idea is the only one to make specific reference to the Dies irae plainsong which plays such an important role in the work. Perhaps these titles were discarded in favour of the first line of the text, because she felt that they were too personal and therefore inappropriate for a large-scale, public work.

Her setting is for tenor and contralto soloists – a favourite Boulanger combination – mixed chorus and a large orchestra, including organ. Boulanger underlines the dark text by emphasizing the lower instruments in her orchestration, including the sarrusophone[5] and heavy brass.

Like Psalm 129, the *De profundis* is in eight short verses; unlike Psalm 129, Boulanger does not set the text continuously, and this work is a good deal longer than her two other surviving psalm settings. Instead, she frequently repeats the opening verse; she also occasionally adds 'Ah!' vocalises, as in several previous works.

Annegret Fauser, writing in the *New Grove*, suggests that '[Lili Boulanger's] imaginative use of instrumental colours, as at the beginning of her Psalm 129 with its dissonant organ rumble from which the melodic line emerges, was later to influence composers such as Honegger in his *Jeanne d'Arc au bûcher* (1934–5).'[6] Two themes, A and B (Exs. 4.7a and b) act as unifying forces.

Ex. 4.7a   Lili Boulanger, *Psaume CXXX*: theme A

Ex. 4.7b   Lili Boulanger, *Psaume CXXX*: theme B

---

[5] The sarrusophone is used here as a replacement for the contrabassoon. The instrument was patented in 1856 by Pierre Louis Gailhot, who named it after the bandsman Pierre Auguste Sarrus (1813–76); as Sarrus was also an instrument maker, it is possible he had a hand in the design of the instrument bearing his name. Although the instrument exists in seven pitches (from sopranino to contrabass), only the contrabass version was widely used. It found favour with several French composers, most notably Saint-Saëns (in his opera *Les noces de Prométhée*, 1867) and Ravel, who used it in *L'heure espagnole* (1907–9) and *Rapsodie espagnole* (1907–8). It is likely that Boulanger discovered the sarrusophone through her teacher Paul Dukas, who used it in *L'apprenti sorcier* (1897). See Blaikley, Baines and Waterhouse's article 'Sarrusophone' in S. Sadie (ed.) (2001), *The New Grove Dictionary of Music and Musicians*, vol. 22, pp. 296–8 for further information.

[6] See article by Annegret Fauser at www.grovemusic.com.

A appears for the first time at the start of the work, initially played by a solo cello and tuba and in a modal G minor. While Boulanger does not quote the 'Dies irae' plainsong (as she did in her earlier *Pour les funérailles d'un soldat*), there are echoes of this melody in this theme. The second principal theme, B, is often associated with the brass and is more chromatic; it first appears when the trumpets enter at bar 26 of the score, heralding an increase in tempo and dynamics. These sudden shifts in mood are typical of Boulanger's setting.

The overall structure of the psalm could be illustrated as shown in Table 6 overleaf. It is clear from Table 6 that the contralto is given far more material than the tenor, who simply follows the contralto's lead when he first enters in section 8. The interlocking relationship between the two solo voices could be compared to *Faust et Hélène*, and Boulanger was fond of combining the lowest female and highest male voices. While the extraordinary climax in her Prix de Rome-winning cantata featured the female voice as the lower of the two lines (see Ex. 2.30 in Chapter 2), in *Du fond de l'abîme* the two solo voices end section 8 on a unison. While the two principal themes and text repetitions help to unify the setting, the form is sectional and individual sections are often unified by one or more ostinato figures. The first entry of the contralto soloist is typical of this, as it is based on several ostinati in a manner reminiscent of Boulanger's other psalm settings (Ex. 4.9).

Ex. 4.8 Lili Boulanger, *Psaume CXXX*: chorus, section 3

Table 6. Structure of *Du fond de l'abîme*

Section Characteristics

1.	Introduction: focuses on lower pitched instruments in the orchestra. Theme A opens the work; Theme B introduced at increase in tempo.
2.	Chorus enters with verses 1 and 2 of the psalm (Du fond de l'abîme je t'invoque, Iahvé / Adonaï, écoute ma prière, que tes oreilles soient attentives aux accents de ma prière; Out of the depths have I cried unto thee, O Lord / Lord, hear my voice: let thine ears be attentive to the voice of my supplications), followed by 'Ah!' vocalise.
3.	Sudden increase in tempo accompanied by rising, French overture-like scale patterns. Chorus sing verses 1 and 2 again at the original slow tempo, constantly returning to a pivot note (Ex. 4.8).
4.	Chorus sing verse 3 (Si tu prends garde aux péchés qui donc pourra tenir Iahvé, If thou, Lord, shouldest mark iniquities, O Lord, who shall stand?) in recitative style. Solo cello to fore in accompaniment. Ostinato in orchestra leads to new, loud statement of verse 1.
5.	Chorus 'Ah!' leads to contralto entry singing verse 3, supported by solo cello and ostinati in orchestra (Ex. 4.9). Vocal line rises towards climax on verse 3.
6.	Agitated; trumpet has Theme B again. Chorus emphatically repeat verse 3, then diminuendo to …
7.	Contralto solo (verses 4, 5 and 6: Mais la clémence est en toi afin qu'on te revere / Mon âme espère en Iahvé, j'espère, je compte sur sa parole / Plus que les guetteurs de la nuit n'aspirent au matin mon âme espère en Adonaï; But there is forgiveness with thee, that thou mayest be feared / I wait for the Lord, my soul doth wait, and in his word do I hope / My soul waitest for the Lord more than they that watch for the morning: I say, more than they that watch for the morning) accompanied by harp ostinato, and separate flute ostinato. Chorus altos join soloist, followed by rest of chorus.
8.	Contralto and tenor soloists in canon (verse 7: Car en Iahvé est la miséricorde et l'abondance de la délivrance, Israël espère en Iahvé; Let Israel hope in the Lord: for with the Lord there is mercy, and with him is plenteous redemption) with flute and harp ostinato; soloists end on unison.
9.	Verse 8: soloists and reduced chorus (C'est lui qui délivrera Israël de toutes ses iniquités; And he shall redeem Israel from all his iniquities). Material derived from contralto melody line from section 7. Repeats word 'Israël'
10.	Verses 1 and 2 repeated with 'heartbeat' accompaniment. Faster, excited passage follows, repeating verse 8.
11.	Coda: orchestra in lowest regions. Chorus repeat 'je crie vers toi' (from verse 1), 'Israël' and finally 'Du fond de l'abîme' with 'Ah!'

Ex. 4.9   Lili Boulanger, *Psaume CXXX*: contralto solo enters

In section 10, Boulanger returns to the opening two verses of the psalm, and introduces a 'heartbeat' accompaniment which is reminiscent of the 'Libera me' section of Fauré's Requiem. Nadia Boulanger often conducted both works, and in conversation with the British conductor Simon Johnson, she highlighted the section quoted above and emphasized the importance of maintaining the steady heartbeat rhythm.[7]

Some sketches for *Du fond de l'abîme* survive in a sketchbook now housed in the Bibliothèque Nationale (MS 19435). While it is not absolutely certain that these sketches all represent ideas for this work, or if some were intended for works never completed by Lili Boulanger, they give us some insights into her creative process. The most interesting of these sketches (Ex. 4.10) suggests that the work was originally going to be a Requiem. Although only one word of the Requiem text is present (Dona [eis requiem] or [nobis pacem]), the dedication of *Du fond de l'abîme* to the composer's late father makes the possibility that it was conceived as a Requiem plausible. Instead, the sketch fits the words 'Car en Iahvé est la miséricorde'

---

[7] Information communicated to the author by Peter O'Hagan.

Ex. 4.10   Lili Boulanger, sketch for *Psaume CXXX*

from the seventh verse of *Du fond de l'abîme*, as Boulanger sketches rhythmic notation above the stave which fits these words. A few pages later (p. 23), sketches for a Kyrie further reinforce the notion that this work was originally intended to be a Requiem.

Boulanger's use of ostinato figures is also apparent in these sketches, particularly on p. 52 of the sketchbook, where the contralto solo setting of verses 5 and 6 of the psalm is sketched. The vocal line is underscored by a repeated harp pattern which is marked 'A' when it appears for the first time; the letter alone is subsequently used to denote repetitions of this bar.

Vieille prière bouddhique

Started in Rome in 1914 and completed in 1917 in Arcachon, *Vieille prière bouddhique* is a work for chorus and orchestra composed to an old Buddhist text. Its subtitle – Prière quotidienne pour tout l'univers (Daily prayer for the universe) – draws attention to the religious function of this text, which was communicated to Boulanger by her friend Suzanne Karpelès in 1914. Karpelès is also responsible for the translation into French.[8] Léonie Rosenstiel says that the original is in Pâli and is 'a sort of Buddhist meditation on Universal love', adding 'Lili Boulanger's choice of this text is one further expression of her interest in considerations of peace and happiness, and is not simply an attraction to oriental exotica for its own

---

8 Léonie Rosenstiel (1978), *The Life and Works of Lili Boulanger* (Cranbury, NJ: Associated University Presses), p. 197.

sake'.[9] Certainly, Lili Boulanger was greatly affected by the suffering caused by the First World War, and while the attraction to peace and love is itself universal, her choice of this text can surely be rooted in the very specific circumstances in which the work was composed.

The text articulates the desire for universal love and fellowship, and these eternal desires are expressed in music which appropriately returns constantly to the same idea. The *Vieille prière bouddhique* can be divided into sections based on the vocal texture and dynamics employed (Table 7).

Table 7.   Sections in *Vieille prière bouddhique*

Bars	Vocal texture
1–36	Full chorus (soft dynamic); Verse 1 bars 1–20, verse 2 bars 20–37
37–49	Flute solo with orchestral accompaniment
49–70	Tenor solo
70–80	Full chorus; humming accompaniment
80–99	Full chorus (loud dynamic)
99–108	Coda: 'Ah!'

Ostensibly in C minor, the work lacks the third of the chord much of the time and the D is often flattened, producing a modal rather than tonal melodic and harmonic language. Harmony, however, is often limited to sustained fifth-based chords or (more rarely) parallel chordal progressions; this is essentially a melody-based work. In the opening bars (Ex. 4.11), the voices in octaves introduce the descending figure that permeates the piece.

Ex. 4.11   Lili Boulanger, *Vieille prière bouddhique*: opening bars, melody line

This whole-tone fragment covers the ambit of a tritone; like Debussy, Boulanger uses the whole-tone mode to blur traditional tonal relationships, and the final bar features both the C/G perfect fifth and a D flat – a tritone away from G and therefore a pitch which undermines our sense of tonality at the end of the piece. As in many of Boulanger's choral works, the chorus is sometimes directed to hum, providing timbral variety. This hummed material tends to focus on the C/G perfect fifth, an interval which had a private significance for the composer. In the first pages of her diary for 1912, she scribbles down fragments of a private language, some of which is based on musical notes. It is surely not a coincidence that the motif signifying 'Lili' is 'do sol do sol' (C–G–C–G), as this motif is prominent in the *Vieille prière bouddhique*.

The first and last sections are almost identical in their vocal material, though Boulanger uses canonic imitation to provide variation. The central, contrasting section is typical of her choral works in that a solo voice provides contrast with the surrounding choral sections, though the contrast is of texture rather than material as much of the tenor's material repeats the opening music. However, the tenor constantly returns to F sharp, rather than the C central note of the opening material, again highlighting the importance of the tritone. Perhaps the most obviously 'exotic' element of this work is the flute solo, which elaborates the choral material (Ex. 4.12) and evokes a generic musical East Asia in its timbre and its sinuous arabesque shapes.

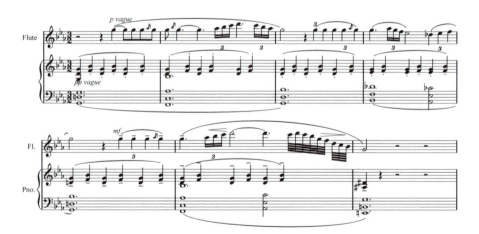

Ex. 4.12   Lili Boulanger, *Vieille prière bouddhique*: flute solo

Clairières dans le ciel

This song cycle for voice and piano (often performed by a soprano, though the texts suggest a tenor is the most appropriate voice) was composed in 1914 to poems by Francis Jammes (1868–1938). Boulanger selected 13 poems from a collection, *Tristesses* (1905), which Jammes wrote following his return to the Catholic faith. She took some time to settle on which poems she wanted to include and the order in which they should appear.

Many sketches for *Clairières dans le ciel* can be found in a black and red sketchbook which is now housed in the Bibliothèque Nationale de France (MS 19438). The fifth page of this sketchbook features initial ideas for the sequence of poems in the cycle (I have noted the eventual ordering in brackets after each song title):

1. Elle était descendue … (1)
2. Elle est gravement gaie (2)
3. Parfois, je suis triste (3)
4. Au pied de mon lit (5)
5. Si tout ceci n'est qu'un pauvre rêve (6)
6. Nous nous aimerons tant (7)
7. Vous m'avez regardé avec toute votre âme (8)
8. Par ce que j'ai souffert (11)
9. Venez, ma bien-aimée (not included)
10. Demain fera un an (13)

A second list underneath this one indicates some other ideas:

3 bis   Un poète disait (4)
5 bis   Je ne desire point? (not included)
5 ter   O mon coeur (not included; 5 bis and 5 ter are crossed out)
6 bis   Je garde une médaille d'elle (12)
6 bis   (sic) J'ai quelqu'un dans le coeur (not included)
7 bis   Les lilas qui avaient fleuri (9)

The tenth poem of the cycle, 'Deux ancolies', is not mentioned in either of these lists and was therefore perhaps a late addition.

Neat copies of several songs appear from p. 71 of the sketchbook. Four of them appear as a group, dated 'Déc[embre] 1913 1er Janvier 1914 Paris. Copiée le samedi 31 Oct. 1914 à Nice [while Boulanger was staying with her friend Miki Piré]'. By this stage in the composition of the cycle, she had decided on the ordering of the first seven songs.

Significantly, she notes under the copy of 'Elle était descendue': 'toutes ces mélodies devraient être chantées avec le sentiment d'évoquer un passé resté plein de fraîcheur' (all these songs should be sung with the feeling of evoking a past that is still fresh in the mind). The thirteen poems trace the development of the first love relationship of two young people, from first meeting through to disillusionment, and the final poem looks back on the affair a year after the first meeting of the two lovers. The narrator is clearly an inexperienced young man, as a line in 'Les lilas qui avaient fleuri' reveals: 'et j'avais espéré je ne sais quoi de vous' (and I do not know what I hoped for from you). While he dreams of a more intimate relationship with the woman he loves in 'Nous nous aimerons tant', the future tense of the verb is significant; it appears that their relationship is unconsummated, and perhaps one that exists more in the mind than in reality. Similarly, while the narrator looks back in sadness on the end of the relationship, there is no mention of a break-up in the poems, again suggesting that the woman is idealized and the affair happened more in his imagination than in reality.

Lili Boulanger, who was aged 20 when she started composing the cycle, was the ideal composer of songs to these poems. A young woman herself, her feelings for various male friends (notably Jean Bouwens) were heartfelt and genuine, even though they did not lead to a full-blown relationship; her ill-health put paid to any hopes she may have had of a serious affair. Léonie Rosenstiel has suggested that she identified with the object of the narrator's love; the 5 foot 9 inch tall Lili had 'la grâce déguingandé d'une fille trop grande', as the first song in the cycle puts it. And the fourth song, 'Au pied de mon lit', initially focuses on a religious icon which the narrator had received from his mother; Lili Boulanger had a similar Russian medal, a gift from her best friend Miki Piré.

Fauré is again the strongest influence on Boulanger's musical style. Like Fauré, she tends to use one accompaniment figure in each song, though the texture changes if there is a sudden mood shift. The young and raw emotions are evident in the explicit shifts in mood in both poem and music in the third song, 'Parfois je suis triste'. And similarly in 'Les lilas qui avaient fleuri', Boulanger again highlights the drama of the narrator's feelings; initially he sings of the beauty of spring flowers, but at the line 'Mon coeur devrait mourir au milieu de ces choses', the music makes it clear he is distressed because he is thinking of his lover (Ex. 4.13).

The final song, 'Demain fera un an', is by far the longest in the cycle. Here, the narrator looks back on the affair, though his feelings are still raw and he feels lost without his love. Appropriately, Boulanger quotes material from earlier songs, linking the evocation of memories in the poem with the recall of music heard earlier. In the final page of the song, the repetition of the first line of the first poem is heralded by the repetition of the introductory bar, though this recall tails away when the narrator sings that there is 'plus rien qui me soutienne' (Ex. 4.14).

Boulanger's technical prowess in this song recalls the eighth and final number of Ravel's *Valses nobles et sentimentales* (1911), composed shortly before *Clairières dans le ciel*; Ravel's final waltz similarly quotes from the seven previous waltzes, and it would be interesting to know whether Boulanger knew the Ravel work.

Orchestrations of some of the songs also survive; though I do not know

Ex. 4.13   Lili Boulanger, *Clairières dans le ciel*, 9 ('Les lilas qui avaient fleuri'): bars 13–18

Ex. 4.14   Lili Boulanger, *Clairières dans le ciel*, 13 ('Demain fera un an'): recall of opening bars

of any public performances of these versions, the blue conductor's markings in some of the manuscripts suggest that they were indeed performed. The dating and authorship of these orchestrations is problematic. The Bibliothèque Nationale catalogue states that they are in Nadia Boulanger's hand, and I wonder whether Nadia Boulanger is also responsible for this work. Lili Boulanger scrupulously dated her manuscripts, and some stylistic features of the orchestrations are more characteristic of her sister's work.

The first of these orchestrations is of 'Elle était descendue …'; although the direction 'enchaînez' is noted at the end of the song, an orchestrated version of the second song, 'Elle est gravement gaie', appears not to have survived. The orchestra is a standard one: double woodwind (but three flutes), four horns, two harps, celeste (which plays an important role), triangle, solo voice and strings. The orchestrator (Nadia or Lili Boulanger) adds additional material to the song and extends the introduction by one bar.

Four other orchestrations are grouped together and numbered '1–4' in red on the manuscript. The group comprises songs 7, 10, 6 and 5; it is possible that someone considered they work well as a mini-cycle, though I would disagree as they neither form a coherent narrative nor a coherent musical unit. Moreover, the first and last songs in this group, 'Nous nous aimerons tant' and 'Au pied de mon lit', are emotionally introverted and largely slow in tempo and would not make very effective opening and closing numbers. The orchestration features double woodwind (plus a cor anglais), four horns, sarrusophone, one trumpet, harp, celeste, timpani, cymbal, voice and strings. Yet another volume features orchestrated versions of the final three songs of the cycle. Only the simple chordal twelfth song, 'Je garde une médaille d'elle', does not feature additional material.

Clairières dans le ciel was not published until after Lili Boulanger's death; Ricordi wrote to the composer on 19 December 1916 that 'as two-thirds of our employees are mobilized, it has been impossible for us until now to make a proof copy of *Clairières dans le ciel*'.[10] In that same year, 1916, Boulanger wrote an isolated song, *Dans l'immense tristesse*, completing it on 24 August. She had been introduced to the works of the author of the poem, Bertha Galeron de Colonne, by Marthe Bouwens.[11] The poet was, allegedly, blind, deaf and unable to speak. Boulanger's five-minute-long

---

[10] Cited in Jérôme Spycket (2004), *A la recherche de Lili Boulanger* (Paris: Fayard), p. 316; 'Les deux tiers de nos employés étant mobilisés, il nous a été jusqu'ici impossible de tirer une épreuve des *Clairières dans le ciel*.'

[11] This was perhaps Galeron de Calonne's volume of poems *Dans la nuit*, published in Paris in 1890. The poet, born Bertha Galeron, married the playwright Ernest Calonne and collaborated with him in a play *Chez la Champmeslé*, which was published in 1886.

setting of the poem is dedicated 'à ma chère Claire Croiza', the celebrated contralto. As the ambit of the melodic line ranges from B flat below middle C to D flat just over an octave above this note, it is ideally scored for this voice.

Originally titled *Dans la sombre tristesse*, this is an extraordinarily dark setting which has few parallels in the solo vocal literature as a study of despair. While it is generally not helpful to interpret Lili Boulanger's works in the light of her personal circumstances, perhaps *Dans l'immense tristesse* could justifiably be connected to her biography. Around the time of its composition, her goddaughter Madeleine Delaquys, the daughter of Georges Delaquys and Raoul Pugno's daughter Renée, was very ill; she died on 5 September 1916 at the age of 5, less than two weeks after the song was completed. And the critic René Dumesnil, writing in 1938, believed that '*Dans l'immense tristesse* reflects the preoccupations which weigh on us all at the moment'.[12] While Dumesnil's observation was written the year before the outbreak of the Second World War, Boulanger's setting was composed in the middle of the First World War, justifying the belief that the war years could have inspired it.

The setting of the song is a cemetery; a young woman comes across a stranger who asks what business she has in the cemetery, and eventually we learn that the woman is searching for the grave of her child. At the end of the poem, the narrator reports that the mother sings her child a lullaby. In B flat minor, though often with a flattened second, the music again recalls Fauré in its modally tinged language and the steady procession of chords of much of the piano accompaniment. The music becomes more chromatic in places to reflect the mother's profound anguish. Boulanger often uses pedal notes, usually a dominant pedal, to evoke the sound of bells; indeed, the first appearance of this idea is marked 'comme une cloche' (like a bell). While bells are not explicitly mentioned in the poem, Boulanger is here providing an imaginative response to the text by enhancing the churchyard imagery in musical terms; the bells also provide a welcome registral contrast in an accompaniment that, reflecting the dark mood of the poem, is predominantly in the bass or medium register. This repeated B flat in the context of a sombre scene instantly evokes Ravel's 'Le gibet', the second piece in his *Gaspard de la nuit* (1907) which Boulanger, a friend of the composer, surely knew.

At bars 35–7, the central and crucial point of the song, the pedal is transformed from octaves to minor seconds (Ex. 4.15).

Before this point, we were not aware why the woman is in the cemetery, but after this line of the text (Alas! The heart breaks) we learn that she is seeking her child's tomb. These unresolved minor seconds, together with

---

12 René Dumesnil (1938), *Portraits de musiciens français* (Paris: Plon), p. 20.

Ex. 4.15   Lili Boulanger, *Dans l'immense tristesse*: bars 35–7

the parallel triads Boulanger occasionally uses, show her mixing elements of Debussy's style with a primarily Fauréan musical language.

La princesse Maleine

The musical and literary connections between Debussy and the Boulanger sisters come to the fore in their unfinished operas. Annegret Fauser, writing in the *New Grove*, claims that Lili Boulanger started composing an opera, *La princesse Maleine*, in 1911,[13] and Léonie Rosenstiel stated that 'By early March of 1912, Lili Boulanger had begun to work on setting Maurice Maeterlinck's *La princesse Maleine* as an opera. In fact, her first sketch is dated March 9.'[14] However, documentary evidence for either of these timescales is lacking, and Rosenstiel admitted that 'Lili Boulanger's sketches for *La princesse Maleine* were not made available [to me] for detailed analysis'.[15]

Maeterlinck's vogue with French composers spread well beyond Debussy, and indeed he is now better known via his opera libretti than as a playwright or poet. Born in 1862, he was encouraged by fellow Belgian poet Emile Verhaeren (some of whose poems were set by Nadia Boulanger and Raoul Pugno in their song cycle *Les heures claires*), Stéphane Mallarmé and the influential Parisian critic Octave Mirbeau, all of whom admired his first play, *La princesse Maleine*. This play was first performed in Paris in February 1890, only a year after it was written, and it almost immediately attracted the attention of composers. Fauser claims that in 1891, Debussy himself was interested in setting the play, but Maeterlinck refused because, at the time, he would only consider giving permission to Vincent d'Indy.[16] Also, Erik Satie would have liked to make a musical setting of the play, and it is

[13] Annegret Fauser (2001), 'Boulanger, Lili', in *The New Grove Dictionary of Music and Musicians,* 2nd ed., vol. 4, p. 96.

[14] Rosenstiel (1978), pp. 145–6.

[15] Ibid., p. 284.

[16] Ibid., pp. 72–3.

possible that a *Danse* for small orchestra he composed in 1890 was originally intended as music for a project based on *La princesse Maleine*.[17] Satie's enthusiasm for medieval settings is shown in his puppet opera, *Geneviève de Brabant* (1899–1900), whose blonde, passive heroine has a good deal in common with Maleine. Pierre de Bréville composed an overture to *La princesse Maleine* in 1891, and in 1907, Paul Dukas's opera *Ariane et Barbe-Bleue*, based on a Maeterlinck libretto, was premiered in Paris. Moreover, Lili Boulanger had set two of his poems, *Attente* and *Reflets*, for voice and piano, and her elder sister's songs *Heures ternes* and *Cantique (de soeur Béatrice)* are also based on Maeterlinck texts.

Lili Boulanger was therefore seriously interested in Maeterlinck's work, and any opera with a libretto by him would certainly have attracted a good deal of critical attention. But why was she particularly attracted to *La princesse Maleine*, a play its author, with the benefit of hindsight, considered problematic? Many critics have drawn parallels between the frail, sickly composer and the character of Maleine. Nadia Boulanger herself claimed in an interview with Léonie Rosenstiel that her sister felt 'a strong emotional identification with the heroine of Maurice Maeterlinck's play, *La princesse Maleine*', and Rosenstiel, for one, believed that this was so because 'she felt that she, too, had a tragic destiny'.[18] Maeterlinck further fuelled this speculation when he presented the composer with an autographed photograph of himself, inscribed 'to my dear little collaborator Lili Boulanger who, by order of the gods of music and Fate, is to give to the Princesse Maleine the soul for which she has been waiting'.[19] While the first part of this inscription was no doubt intended to be affectionate rather than patronizing, his words also suggest that he supported the generally held notion that Lili Boulanger identified with the heroine of his play.

Whether or not this was the case, the play had other attractions for Boulanger. All available evidence points to the opera being composed during the First World War, and we have already seen that she was actively involved in war work and genuinely concerned about those who were suffering as a result of the hostilities. Fauser, for one, believes that 'the outbreak of World War I is reflected in her choice of *La princesse Maleine* (a fairy tale with war as its central theme)'.[20] But perhaps the key to her interest in the play was the connection between Maeterlinck and Debussy and, as we shall see, there are many significant links between *La princesse Maleine* and *Pelléas et Mélisande*, as well as many traces of Debussy's influence in Boulanger's musical language. Debussy's *Pelléas et Mélisande*, premiered in

---

[17] Private information from Robert Orledge.

[18] Rosenstiel (1978), pp. 42 and 43.

[19] Cited ibid., p. 122: 'à ma chère petite collaboratrice Lili Boulanger qui doit donner à la Princesse Maleine, de par la volonté des dieux de la musique et du Destin, l'âme attendu'.

[20] Fauser (2001), p. 96.

1902, was soon recognized as a supremely important contribution to French opera, and indeed, contemporary composers including Henri Dutilleux and Pierre Boulez have testified to its importance and hinted that its ideal fusion of music and the French language is perhaps unsurpassable. While the importance of *Pelléas* in French musical history is not questioned, Debussy's choice of a text by Maeterlinck situates the opera very much in its own time. Fauser has justly emphasized the importance of the *femme fragile* in French-language literature of the late nineteenth and early twentieth centuries,[21] and Mélisande is the quintessence of this fragile blonde character type, a favourite of Maeterlinck's.

Late in 1914, Lili Boulanger's publisher Tito Ricordi contacted Maeterlinck regarding a possible operatic setting of the play by her, and on 4 January 1915, Ricordi wrote to the composer:

> Monsieur Maeterlinck would be delighted to entrust you with 'La Princesse Maleine' and would not be opposed to us restructuring the play, making cuts, etc. etc. Therefore, it's for you to decide if you still want to set this poem to music. If that is the case – I hope it is – it would be very easy to arrange Maeterlinck's drama as a libretto – and if you will allow it, I will undertake this task myself.[22]

Maeterlinck wrote to Boulanger on 16 February 1916, giving permission 'avec le plus grand plaisir' to set his play, and stating that the collaboration shall happen according to an agreement between them and Ricordi.[23] And it was indeed Ricordi who cut the long play and fashioned the libretto for Boulanger,[24] who was thinking about the music by May 1916.[25] The composer, publisher and playwright eventually met to discuss the text in Nice on 22 or 23 June that year, an earlier meeting having been cancelled due to Maeterlinck's concerns about his sick mother. Maeterlinck wrote to Boulanger on 24 June that he found Ricordi's adaptation of the play 'very skilful and successful'.[26] But on 16 August 1916, Lili Boulanger was clearly anxious about some aspects of the collaboration, and wrote to her sister, asking for her advice about contacting both Maeterlinck and Ricordi. The letter is worth quoting in full:

---

[21] Annegret Fauser (1997), 'Lili Boulanger's *La princesse Maleine*: A Composer and her Heroine as Literary Icons', *Journal of the Royal Musical Association*, 122: 68–108.

[22] Letter in the BN, cited ibid., 75: 'Monsieur Maeterlinck est tout disposé à vous confier "La Princesse Maleine" et il ne s'oppose pas à ce qu'on y fasse des remaniements, des coupures, etc. etc. C'est donc à vous de décider si vous voulez encore mettre en musique ce poème. Si c'est oui – ce que j'espère – il sera très facile d'arranger le drame de Maeterlinck en livret lyrique – et si vous me le permettez je ferai moi-même cette besogne.'

[23] Cited in Spycket (2004), p. 286.

[24] See Fauser (1997): 82–3, for full details regarding the cuts Ricordi made to Maeterlinck's play.

[25] Ibid., 76–7.

[26] Letter in the Boulanger collection, BN: 'L'adaptation me paraît très habile et très heureuse.'

16/8/16 from Gargenville to Paris

My little Nadia,

This letter for Ricordi seems fine to me. The other one too. But, I don't know why, I can't bring myself to send them without you having seen them. The one for Maeterlinck has strange writing – the ink wouldn't mark the paper – and I started it too low down the page – I would have redone it, but I couldn't find more paper like that.

On the other hand, read it carefully, and let me know if you think that Ricordi, having it for one reason or another in his hands, wouldn't be a little annoyed by it, because after all, the publishing house is him, isn't it – nothing can be done without his say-so – but on the other hand ... what do you think???

Do whatever you think best.

If you don't think the handwriting of the letter for Maeterlinck is <u>good enough</u>, but <u>the content is</u>, don't send it – I'll redo it tomorrow when you come back, and [you should] send him a telegram more or less like this: Would be very grateful to you if you would return the signed contract to Ricordi. Letter follows – thank you, compliments, sincerely yours ... or something along those lines.

Another thing – bring me, if you can, a little bottle of cucumber milk from Roberts. My deepest love for you and my best kiss,

In haste, Bébé[27]

The very close relationship between the sisters, in particular Lili Boulanger's continuing professional dependence on Nadia, is evident.

Aged 15 at the start of the play, Maleine is a pale, sickly character, the daughter of King Marcellus and Queen Godelive, rulers of part of Holland. She falls in love with Hjalmar, the son of the king of another part of Holland, who is also called Hjalmar. The young Hjalmar, however, is intended for Uglyane, the daughter of Queen Anne of Jutland. Quite the most evil character in the play, Queen Anne has left her first husband for King Hjalmar, but also tries to seduce his son. When Maleine refuses to renounce young Hjalmar, Anne imprisons her and her nurse (la Nourrice). They break out of prison and return home, only to find that their home

---

[27] Letter in the Fonds Nadia Boulanger in the Bibliothèque Nationale, Paris: '16/8/16 de Gargenville à Paris. Ma petite Nadia, Cette lettre pour Ricordi me semble bien. L'autre aussi. Et puis, je ne sais pourquoi, je n'arrive pas à pouvoir les envoyer sans que tu les aies vues. Celle de Maët.[erlinck] a un drôle de touché – l'encre ne marquait pas – puis, j'ai commencé trop bas – je l'aurais bien refaite, mais n'ai pu trouver du même papier.

D'un autre côté, lis-la bien et regarde si tu ne crois pas que Ricordi l'ayant p[ou]r une raison ou une autre entre les mains n'en serait pas un peu péché, car, après tout, la maison, c'est pourtant lui – rien ne peut être fait sans son ordre – d'un autre côté ... alors???

Fais ce que tu crois bien.

Si tu ne trouves pas le letter p[ou]r Maët.[erlinck] <u>assez bien</u> comme écriture, mais <u>bien comme rédaction</u>, ne l'envoie pas – je la referai demain à ton retour et envoie-lui un télégramme à peu près ainsi: Vous serais très obligée attendre p[ou]r renvoyer maison Ricordi traité signé. Lettre suit – merci complime[nts] sincère souvenir ... ou un équivalent.

Autre chose – rapporte-moi, si tu le peux, petit flacon de lait de concombres de chez Roberts.

Ma grande tendresse autour de toi pour toi mon meilleur baiser

En hate, Bébé'

has been destroyed during the war between the two parts of Holland. They then flee to Ysselmonde, where Hjalmar lives, and Maleine gets work as Uglyane's chambermaid. (The action of Act I takes place in Harlingon, Maleine's home, though the remaining four acts of the play are set in Ysselmonde.)

At the start of Act II, Maleine and her nurse are lost in the forest as they flee their home. The setting moves later in this act to a wood in the park with a fountain. Hjalmar believes he is to meet Uglyane by the fountain, as Maleine has sent him a note in Uglyane's name asking him to meet her there. He glimpses Maleine in half-light, and she reveals her true identity. Having previously believed Maleine was dead, Hjalmar falls in love with her.

Act III does not move the story on very much, but what action there is serves to highlight the personality traits of various characters. Hjalmar talks to his father the King, who is ill, almost blind, and constantly talks about his desire to leave. The King is so shocked to see Maleine (whom he believes to be dead) that he faints. Anne asks the King to choose between Maleine and her, and asks her doctor for some poison, as she wants to kill Maleine. When Hjalmar and Maleine return from a walk, Maleine's nurse enters accompanied by seven dwarves.

Act IV features the climax of the drama. Anne's principal aim is to ensure that Maleine is alone, away from her nurse, and in the third scene, we see Maleine in her bedroom, alone apart from her dog, Pluton. In the following scene, Anne and the King predict that there will be a storm that night – an obvious harbinger of doom – and in what was surely not intended to be a moment of comic relief, the seven dwarves enter, chanting litanies in Latin. Then Anne and the King enter Maleine's bedroom; the King refuses to kill her, and Maleine cries out, correctly believing that Anne is going to perform the evil deed. Anne strangles Maleine. The nurse enters the room, followed by Hjalmar and Anne's young son Allan. In the final, fifth act, all the principal characters eventually acknowledge Maleine's death and seven nuns enter her bedroom. Hjalmar stabs Anne and himself, and the final words are given to his friend Angus: 'Encore une nuit pareille et nous serons tout blancs!' At the very end, only the seven dwarves, singing a Miserere and carrying the corpses onto beds, remain.

As *La princesse Maleine* was Maeterlinck's first play, some of its more absurd moments could be ascribed to inexperience; the fact that he recycles several ideas from this play in later works, not least *Pelléas et Mélisande*, also suggests that he believed certain ideas were worth salvaging in new contexts. *Pelléas* is overall a more practical play than *La princesse Maleine*, partly because it has a smaller number of principal characters and partly because the stage action is simply less gruesome. And as the text of *Pelléas et Mélisande* is a good deal sparer, one could argue that there is more room for musical amplification in this play compared to *La princesse Maleine*.

There are many significant connections between *Pelléas et Mélisande* and the two opera libretti set by the Boulanger sisters. Most obviously, *La princesse Maleine* is based on a Maeterlinck play which, like *Pelléas*, has a *femme fragile* at its centre. Other striking similarities in these two plays are listed below:

- Many of the characters have cod-medieval names
- There is a love triangle in both plays (Pelléas/Mélisande/Golaud and Maleine/Hjalmar/Uglyane)
- Both plays feature complex stepfamily relationships
- There is a young boy character in both plays: Golaud's son Yniold (by his first marriage) in *Pelléas et Mélisande*, and Anne's son Allan (from her first marriage) in *La princesse Maleine*. Neither boy has a substantial role, but there are clear similarities between Allan constantly calling his mother 'petite mère' and Yniold's oft-repeated 'petit père'
- The names of the towns in which most of the action takes place – Allemonde and Ysselmonde – are very similar. Also, the inhabitants of the towns are ill and the place is clearly doomed (also paralleled in Nadia Boulanger's opera *La ville morte*)
- A forest plays a significant role
- There is an elderly, blind male character in both plays: King Hjalmar (*La princesse Maleine*) and Arkel (*Pelléas et Mélisande*), though neither is necessarily the wise sage one might expect this type of character to be. In *La ville morte*, Anne is a blind character, though she is a young woman
- In Act I, scene ii of *La princesse Maleine*, the nurse, Maleine and her mother sing while spinning ('filant leur quenouille'). There is a similar scene in *Pelléas*, which is memorably illustrated by Fauré in his incidental music for the play but omitted by Debussy
- On many occasions, characters in both *La princesse Maleine* and *Pelléas et Mélisande* speak of their desire to leave the suffocating world in which they live; Pelléas and King Hjalmar in particular constantly talk about leaving, though neither moves towards action
- Maleine and Hjalmar arrange to meet by a fountain in the middle of a wood in Act II, scene vi; it is dark and Hjalmar is initially unaware that the girl he is meeting is Maleine. This is like a combination of Act II, scene ii of *Pelléas*, where Pelléas and Mélisande meet by a fountain, and many occasions in this play when Mélisande says she prefers to see Pelléas in shadow, rather than in the light.

Although very little music survives, two different copies of the libretto exist. It seems that at least four music sketchbooks containing music for the opera have not survived, as the single, small, bound manuscript book dating from the last year of Boulanger's life (which is now housed in the Bibliothèque Nationale) makes reference to various numbered red notebooks. In this small sketchbook, Boulanger has written many notes to herself saying that she must finish the opera, most poignantly a note on p. 30 of the sketchbook written in December 1917: 'I must finish everything before 1 January. I MUST!!! Can I?'[28] Her very last sketch for the opera is dated 13 February 1918 – possibly the last time she put pen to manuscript paper.

Judging by the content of this sketchbook, I find it very difficult to believe that the opera could have been nearly finished by the time she died, as Fauser and other writers claim. Charles Koechlin makes reference to *La princesse Maleine* in his in-depth analysis of Debussy's *Pelléas et Mélisande*,[29] but the only significant extant extract of the opera is a scene featuring Hjalmar, the central male character, and his friend Angus, entitled 'scene ii' and copied between 27 and 29 October 1917, presumably for a private performance.[30] This is based on the original Act I, scene iii of the play and is scored for voices and piano, presumably a short score to be orchestrated at a later date. A 10-bar prelude precedes the entry of the voices (Ex. 4.16); its slow parallel chordal movement is highly reminiscent of the prelude to *Pelléas et Mélisande*.

Ex. 4.16   Lili Boulanger, *La princesse Maleine*: prelude, bars 1–10

---

[28] 'Il faut tout finir avant le 1er Janv[ier]. Il faut!!! [underlined three times] Le pourrai-je?'

[29] Cited in Spycket (2004), p. 355.

[30] Information from the manuscript (BN Ms 19469).

Likewise, Hjalmar's touching description of Maleine could easily be taken for Pelléas's musings on Mélisande. Debussy's influence is evident in the multi-layered instrumental writing, where the bass underpins the texture and a pedal inner part (here, the dyad f/g) provides continuity and an anchor in a constantly shifting harmonic texture (Ex. 4.17).

Ex. 4.17   Lili Boulanger, *La princesse Maleine*: Hjalmar's aria

The sketchbook also features ideas for leitmotif-type material (providing another connection with Debussy's opera; themes for Maleine, Fate (Fatalité) and Queen Anne are all labelled). Most poignantly, some material of a more personal nature that has no connection to the opera is in this sketchbook. On the very first page, Boulanger has written a monody for voice in which she gives way to self-pity, a very rare example of her giving vent to her anguish and pain in musical form. The monody is supposed to be 'en si♭ mineur', though the key signature does not reflect this, and the rhythmic notation, which does not always fit in the time signature, also indicates that the sketch was not at all intended for performance or public appraisal. Boulanger's text speaks of the pain she feels in her legs, back and other parts of her body, pains which are relentless and for which she sees no end in sight (Ex. 4.18). ('I have pains in the back. I have pains, little pains. I have pains in the back, the whole back, little pains. I have pains … in the back, in the whole back. I can't go out because it's raining. Now I'm hot, I'm not cold any more, but I'm too hot. I'm pretty ill, poor little thing. Why am I always in pain? It's not fair, poor little thing, so little. Being too hot, being too cold, that's my lot. It's not fun.')

Ex. 4.18 Lili Boulanger: from sketchbook

A short extract of Act IV, scene iii can be found in her sketchbook; here, it is hard to resist drawing a parallel between Maleine's situation and that of Lili Boulanger. In this scene, Maleine is alone in her bedroom with her dog, Pluton (Boulanger adored dogs and there was always a dog in her home), and talks about her illness. She says 'je crois que mon coeur va mourir.'

Chamber works

Several of Lili Boulanger's works were written in different versions for different instrumental formations, a practice no doubt encouraged by her publisher to ensure the widest possible market for her works. *Cortège* is a case in point: she signed a contract with Ricordi on 29 January 1918 for both solo piano and piano and violin versions of this piece:[31] Exx. 4.19a and b illustrate the opening bars of both versions.

Ex. 4.19a   Lili Boulanger, *Cortège*: opening of piano version

Ex. 4.19b   Lili Boulanger, *Cortège*: opening of violin and piano version

This unpretentious chamber work, which evokes a carnival procession rather than the funeral that an English interpretation of the title might suggest, is one of her most frequently performed works, together with the earlier *Nocturne* for violin (or flute) and piano; in *Le ménestrel* on 30 November 1923, the critic Maurice Léna reported that *Cortège* had been

31 Rosenstiel (1978), p. 285.

performed recently by the violinist Albert Spalding in an afternoon recital at Carnegie Hall. Its appealing freshness and dotted rhythms are reminiscent of the later work *D'un matin de printemps*. While Boulanger has benefited from frequent performances of her chamber music for violin and piano, the popularity of these works has perhaps given a false impression of the range and quality of her musical output, as these pieces in the more traditionally 'feminine' salon genre are more easily accessible than her large-scale works for choral and orchestral forces.

The short piano pieces *D'un jardin clair* and *D'un vieux jardin* were composed in 1914, either at the Villa Medici or shortly before her arrival in Rome. A rough sketch of the opening bars of *D'un jardin clair* appears in her red notebook (BN Ms 19438) after sketches for *Clairières dans le ciel* (Ex. 4.20).

Ex. 4.20   Lili Boulanger, *D'un jardin clair*: opening bars

It is very likely that Boulanger did not choose the titles of the published versions, both because she tended to avoid descriptive titles and because there is no surviving evidence that she had these titles in mind. As with her *Thème et variations*, Fauré is the most considerable influence on these works.

According to Léonie Rosenstiel, 'Both *D'un soir triste* and *D'un matin de printemps* were conceived by the composer in three different versions simultaneously'; she also claims that 'These were the last pieces that Lili Boulanger wrote with her own hand.'[32] *D'un matin de printemps*, like her earlier *Nocturne*, exists in versions for either flute or violin with piano accompaniment, and there are a few insignificant differences between the flute and violin versions of the melody line. All these differences result from a concern to make the solo parts idiomatic for the instrument (double stopping for the violin, for instance). There is also an orchestral version of this work in which the solo line is absorbed by various solo groups of the orchestra.

This lively, playful work anticipates Poulenc's music in places, not least in bars 10–13 (Ex. 4.21), where a two-bar melody is then immediately

---

[32] Ibid., p. 199 (after conversations between Nadia Boulanger and Léonie Rosenstiel in 1973 and 1975).

repeated a semitone higher – a Poulenc fingerprint that appears in almost every work he composed.

Ex. 4.21   Lili Boulanger, *D'un matin de printemps*: bars 10–13

The acidulous unresolved dissonances of the piano accompaniment also suggest that Boulanger would have been very much at home in Les Six (Ex. 4.22). While these chords could be connected with Debussy's style in that their harmonic function is secondary to the pure enjoyment of the sonority, the lively rhythmic impetus of this passage is more reminiscent of Poulenc.

Ex. 4.22   Lili Boulanger, *D'un matin de printemps*: opening bars

The case of *D'un soir triste* is more complex; as the surviving manuscript material in the BN is incomplete, it is difficult to be certain of the composer's intentions for this piece. Rosenstiel writes that 'Lili was able to finish *D'un soir triste* in a version for string trio as well as for cello and piano before her strength deserted her. The orchestration of this work she managed to complete, but the nuances were filled in by Nadia, following the indications in Lili's trio score.'[33] However, the version for three instruments is for the traditional piano trio formation of violin, cello and piano rather than for string trio. The cello and piano version is incomplete, notably in the piano accompaniment, and the transcription is sometimes rather impractical. For example, bars 49–54 of the piano trio version (Ex. 4.23a) are transcribed with the cello line identical in both versions, but the

---

[33] Ibid., p. 130.

piano part of the cello and piano duo version is uncomfortably thickened with the addition of the original violin line (Ex. 4.23b).

Ex. 4.23a   Lili Boulanger, *D'un soir triste*: piano trio version, bars 49–54

Ex. 4.23b   Lili Boulanger, *D'un soir triste*: parallel passage for cello and piano

There is also an orchestral version which is complete, though this appears to be in Nadia rather than Lili Boulanger's hand. *D'un soir triste* is a rather sober and sombre work whose principal theme is, however, related to the principal theme of *D'un matin de printemps* in its melodic shape and use of dotted rhythm (Ex. 4.24).

This theme appears in several related guises, with the note values often

Clarinet in A

Ex. 4.24   Lili Boulanger, *D'un soir triste*: principal theme of orchestral version

being halved or doubled compared to the original version. The orchestrations of both works are for large orchestras featuring the sarrusophone (though it does not have a significant role in either work), and *D'un soir triste* has a prominent harp part. Double basses with a fifth string are essential as the low C is sometimes used as a pedal note. A hire score owned by BMG (formerly Durand) is made by a copyist and features several crossings-out, but it is impossible to tell whether these were sanctioned by Nadia (or indeed Lili) Boulanger or whether they were made by a conductor. Whatever the case, it is true that the piece would benefit from lighter scoring in some places, for instance at fig. 6 where a harp melody is virtually inaudible.

Unusually for Boulanger's music, *D'un soir triste* does not have a key signature but is essentially in the Phrygian mode. Like many of her works, much of the piece is a slow procession of chords and pedal notes are often featured. At fig. 12, the pedal played by the timpani is a dyad (minor second) rather than a single pitch. Occasionally, the primary melodic line is preceded by an upwards swooping gesture reminiscent of the French overture style. Fig. 13 features a typical Boulanger ostinato pattern played by the celesta, harp and violas, with one unusual feature: the middle C pedal note is given to the flute. Perhaps the most interesting section of the piece is around fig. 16, preceding the restatement of the principal theme; here, muted brass predominate and the music has a military feel somewhat reminiscent of *Pour les funérailles d'un soldat* in its rhythm, dark scoring and use of brass and percussion. One could speculate whether these echoes were deliberate on the part of the composer, given that *D'un soir triste* was composed in the middle of the First World War.

Pie Jesu

Lili Boulanger's final completed work is a setting of the *Pie Jesu* text from the Requiem Mass. While this may seem fitting, Léonie Rosenstiel mentions that 'The first of Lili Boulanger's sketches for the *Pie Jesu* are to be found in a composition book she used between 1909 and 1913. These jottings contain the "Amen" and four measures of the bass, which forms an ostinato during the opening measures of the work. It is possible that this was envisioned by the composer as part of a complete Requiem Mass, because a sketch for a Kyrie appears in another of her composition workbooks – one that she used later, between 1913 and 1916. In any event, Lili was never to complete this Mass in its entirety.'[34] According to the published score, the *Pie Jesu* was started in Rome and completed in Mézy, in the house in which Lili Boulanger died, in 1918. Too weak to write, Lili dictated most of the work to her sister. Nadia recalled, 'when she could no longer write, she dictated note by note, line by line … the work which she had conceived within her'.[35]

The work exists in two versions: for voice, harp, string quartet and organ; and for voice and organ. Equally, two transpositions of the work are published, one for a high voice, one for medium voice. The composer (and publisher) do not specify whether a male or female voice should be employed, though in practice, all current recorded versions feature a female voice.

Boulanger's preference for layered textures is apparent in the *Pie Jesu*, a preference which is ideally suited to the scoring for organ. The mood of this piece shifts from anguished intensity to calm acceptance of fate. This transition is not dictated by the short, repetitive text, but is the composer's musical interpretation of the text. Expression markings, musical texture and harmonic shifts combine to create the overall effect, as demonstrated below.

The expression markings over the vocal line undergo a significant shift over the course of the piece. In bar 3 of this 56-bar work, the singer is asked to be 'très expressif' (Ex. 4.25), a marking reinforced in bar 11 with the indication 'plus intense'.

Ex. 4.25 Lili Boulanger, *Pie Jesu*: bars 1–4

---

[34] Ibid., 200. Rosenstiel does not mention that this sketchbook also features ideas for *Du fond de l'abîme*; these ideas are mentioned on pp. 101–2 of the present book.

[35] Nadia Boulanger, interview with Léonie Rosenstiel, cited ibid., 282: 'quand elle ne pût plus écrire, elle dictait note par note, ligne par ligne … l'oeuvre qui s'était conçue intérieurement'.

At the approximate mid-point of the work (bar 27), the direction 'plaintif' signals a decrease in intensity (Ex. 4.26), and at bar 43, the direction is 'très calme et clair'. While the marking 'expressif' makes another appearance at bar 48, the mood of the concluding bars is summarized by the final expression marking, at bars 51–2: 'sans couleur, très calme'.

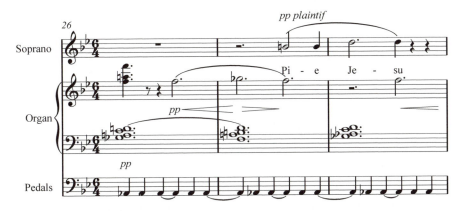

Ex. 4.26   Lili Boulanger, *Pie Jesu*: bars 26–8

The harmonic language of the *Pie Jesu* makes this shift in mood all the more explicit, as shown in Table 8.

Table 8.   Harmonic movement in *Pie Jesu*

Bars	Harmony
1–25	Highly chromatic
26–43	Pedal bass (A flat and D natural)
44–56	Exclusively white notes

While the work begins in a modal G minor (with a flattened leading note), constant chromaticism blurs any sense of a tonal centre. The shift to a pedal bass at bar 26 gives the music greater stability, though Boulanger avoids a traditional perfect fifth relationship between the two notes forming the pedal, instead using the unstable tritone. At bar 44, the two flats of the initial key signature are cancelled, and from this point, accidentals are completely avoided. This final section centres on the note G, providing a sense of closure and completion of the circle. However, the final chord condenses the archetypal classical cadence into one chord, being a superposition of chords V and I in the key of C major (the common note in these chords being G; Ex. 4.27).

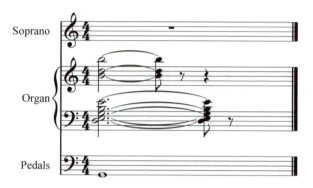

Ex. 4.27 Lili Boulanger, *Pie Jesu*: final chord

Lili Boulanger's career was summed up not long after her death by Camille Mauclair, the friend and collaborator of her elder sister. Although, in the mode of his times, he patronizingly refers to her as a 'child', he also pinpoints the essential mystery of Lili Boulanger's music: 'This child can have known nothing of harsh reality and passions. However, through her evocative imagination, she gave them a strong and potent expression.'[36] Rooted in the French tradition, particularly Fauré and Debussy, her music is nevertheless a distinctive contribution to early twentieth-century music; though she died at the age of 24, an individual voice is already apparent in her works. Had she lived, Lili Boulanger would doubtless have been recognized internationally as a significant voice in French music and one of the first truly great women composers.

---

[36] Camille Mauclair (1924), 'Lili Boulanger', *Revue musicale*, 10: 150; 'Cette enfant ... n'a presque rien pu connaître des réalités et des passions. Elle les a pourtant douées d'une expression forte et merveilleuse par la vertu d'une imagination évocatrice.'

CHAPTER 5

Nadia Boulanger as Teacher

Although Nadia Boulanger's reputation as one of the greatest music teachers of the twentieth century is secure, surprisingly little is known about her approach to teaching and the content of her classes. Nadia Boulanger herself is most to blame for this, as she rarely revealed anything of importance about her life or work to interviewers and turned down offers to publish her teaching materials. She was always keen to emphasize that the musical work, rather than the performer or a commentator on the music, should be the centre of attention.[1] The aura of mystery that she created only enhanced her reputation, giving her students the impression that they belonged to an elite group.

Although one might presume that a teacher of her eminence would have taught only elite students, Boulanger taught a surprisingly varied student body that included those with little previous knowledge of harmony as well as successful students who were promising young composers. The three principal types of student she taught can, in general, be placed into separate categories by virtue of their financial status and their gender. Some of her students were young female amateurs who viewed music as an essential accomplishment for someone of their background; others were men who aimed for a professional career in music, usually as composers or performers. The third principal group – women who sought a career as music teachers – often considered Nadia Boulanger as a role model. Speaking of one of these students, Boulanger told Bruno Monsaingeon: 'I have a pupil who has made wonderful progress ... in 25 years. 25 years is a long time! But now she can teach piano, in a small American town, to people who want to have a few lessons.'[2] Many of her female students had similar career objectives, though fortunately most graduated from her classes after far fewer years of study.

While she was, of course, obliged to tailor the content of classes to the abilities of her students, there are several common threads running through

---

[1] For instance, in an interview with Irene Slade (recorded in 1960 on an LP preserved in the National Sound Archive).

[2] Bruno Monsaingeon (1980), *Mademoiselle: Entretiens avec Nadia Boulanger* (Paris: Van de Velde), p. 54; 'J'ai une élève qui a fait des progrès fantastiques ... en 25 ans. 25 ans, c'est long! Mais elle peut aujourd'hui professer dans une petite ville américaine, enseigner très honnêtement le piano à des gens qui ont envie de faire un peu de piano.'

her teaching career. In particular, the transmission of a central Western musical culture, based on great composers and the masterpieces they wrote, was fundamental to her outlook. Also, for many of her students, she represented the prestige, civilized qualities and socially desirable aspects of French culture. Boulanger handed down this cultural heritage to students from many different countries and backgrounds.

Boulanger began teaching in autumn 1904, when she was a student at the Paris Conservatoire, in order to support herself and her family. She continued working almost until her death at the age of 92 in 1979, although in her last decade she was blind and extremely frail. She obtained her first official position in a music school – the private Conservatoire Femina-Musica – in autumn 1907, probably thanks to Raoul Pugno. This establishment, in the words of Léonie Rosenstiel, 'catered primarily to well-to-do young Parisiennes', and was bankrolled by the periodicals *Femina* and *Musica*. Rosenstiel also notes that she would have been paid half the salary that a man would have earned for the same job.[3] This post entailed teaching elementary piano and the class known as *accompagnement au piano*. The latter was not simply a 'piano accompaniment' class, but rather one in which students were taught auxiliary disciplines that included score reading, transposition and figured bass realization.

Female pupils from financially comfortable families were, then as now, the most substantial and most lucrative market for a music teacher. Very few of Nadia Boulanger's female students became professional composers. One exception was Marcelle de Manziarly, a pupil and friend from 1912 until the end of her life, although Manziarly, coming from a wealthy family background, never had to earn a living as a composer.

Nadia Boulanger's first pupils were young women from well-to-do families. She did not come into contact with different types of student until she obtained posts in music schools that offered entrance scholarships. One of these institutions was the Ecole Normale de Musique, founded in Paris in autumn 1919 by Alfred Cortot and Auguste Mangeot, the editor of the journal *Le monde musical*, as a more liberal competitor of the Conservatoire. The Ecole Normale lacked the qualifying examinations of that establishment and did not have upper age limits for enrolment. In common with all institutions with that title, one of the principal functions of the Ecole Normale was to train teachers, although it also attracted students who were not aiming for a professional career. In Léonie Rosenstiel's words, 'Deserving poor students could find scholarships there; the Ecole Normale's society pupils subsidised the poor but gifted, their tuition money serving as the school's financial cushion, its insurance against bankruptcy.'[4]

---

3 Léonie Rosenstiel (1998), *Nadia Boulanger: A Life in Music* (New York and London: Norton), p. 64.
4 Ibid., p. 145.

Boulanger taught harmony, counterpoint and organ, and thanks to Mangeot she obtained a post as concert reviewer for *Le monde musical* from 1919.

She was appointed professor of composition at the Ecole Normale in 1935, though her official role was as co-professor with Stravinsky. Rosenstiel quotes an article in *Le monde musical* on their joint appointment: 'This is the first time the celebrated composer will participate in the teaching of Composition and there is no need to say that his advice will be of inestimable value to the young musicians. In giving Mlle Nadia Boulanger his collaboration, the master of *Perséphone* gives our illustrious female musician testimony to the high regard he has for her as an artist.'[5] It is clear that Stravinsky, rather than Boulanger, was the main draw for the students. According to Eric Walter White, the class at the Ecole Normale 'consisted of two classes a week: one devoted to the analysis and criticism of the students' compositions, the other to a study of works by the great masters. Stravinsky came to the second of these classes about once a month; and when he did, it was his own compositions, particularly recent scores like *Perséphone* and the Concerto for Two Solo Pianos, that came up for discussion.'[6] White also quotes Maurice Perrin, a student in this class, who said: 'Nadia Boulanger would sit at the piano and play a reduction. ... She would stop at a certain passage, point out subtle harmonic relations, throw light on some surprising modulation, try to explain why it sounded so well, and then turn towards Stravinsky as if for confirmation, and ask him if he had anything to add. But he nearly always confined himself to saying: "Mais c'est de la musique tonâle!"'[7]

Much to her disappointment, Boulanger was not appointed to a permanent teaching post at the Paris Conservatoire until 1946 (when she was named professor of *accompagnement au piano*). She was employed as a teacher at the institution as early as 1909, after her final attempt at the Prix de Rome; from this date, she acted as assistant to a professor of harmony, Henri Dallier. Very early in her teaching career, she actively sought posts in prestigious institutions; indeed, she was far from reluctant to approach the directors of these institutions and urge them to consider her as a faculty member. In an undated letter in the Archives nationales (almost certainly written in 1919, when three professorships in harmony fell vacant), addressed to the director of the Paris Opéra, Boulanger solicits his support for her application for a post as a harmony teacher at the Conservatoire. After giving a brief résumé of her teaching career, she writes: 'Moreover, all those I have loved have lived, in a manner of speaking, at the Conservatoire, and the ties that bind me to my old school are as ancient as they are deep. My father and grandfather taught there, my grandmother

5 Ibid., p. 259.

6 Eric Walter White (2/1979), *Stravinsky: The Composer and his Works* (London: Faber), p. 110.

7 Ibid.

started her great career there, my mother studied there, and my poor little sister studied there. In memory of her, I devote my entire self to young people.'[8] The letter reveals that she was willing, if necessary, to advance her career through nepotism and by appealing to others' sympathy, and that it was clearly essential for a future Conservatoire teacher to have the backing of influential figures if he or she were to be considered for a post.

Even though three of her students (Marcelle Soulage, Pierre Menu and Renée de Marquein) entered the Prix de Rome competition in 1919, none of them listed Nadia Boulanger as his or her teacher. Perhaps this was not so surprising, since the Prix de Rome was a competition organized by the Conservatoire, whose students would not have wished to associate themselves too closely with a teacher from outside its walls.[9] The following year, Annette Dieudonné entered the Prix de Rome, though she failed to progress beyond the preliminary round. Dieudonné studied with Boulanger for fourteen years from 1910 and became one of her closest confidantes and work colleagues. Nadia Boulanger often sent new pupils to Dieudonné to study solfège with her, and while some appreciated the thoroughness of her training, others remarked that she completely lacked Boulanger's gifts of communication.

It is perhaps surprising that very few of Boulanger's best students were French (Jean Françaix being the best-known exception), although she was often described as the greatest living French music teacher of her time. However, Boulanger gained a particularly strong reputation in the USA. Her first American students came to Paris to study with her in the early 1920s, either at the Ecole Normale or privately at her home in rue Ballu. Boulanger was also one of the founders, in 1921, of the Conservatoire Américain in Fontainebleau, which enhanced her association with students from the United States. She eventually learned to speak English well, if in a charmingly idiosyncratic manner, although in the early 1920s she confessed to knowing only a few words of the language in which her American students were to be taught.[10]

The Conservatoire Américain was a singular institution. It was not, strictly speaking, a conservatory, since classes ran for only three months a year, during the summer (Nadia Boulanger once said: 'Summer is the best time to work').[11] Although catering for American students (and, later, those

---

8 As Boulanger applied for a teaching post in harmony in 1919, and the letter is written on black-edged notepaper (suggesting she was in mourning for her sister, who died the previous year), we can assume that the letter was written then. 'De plus, tous ceux que j'ai aimés ont vécu en quelque sorte au Conservatoire et les liens qui m'attachent à la vieille maison sont aussi anciens que profonds. Mon Père et mon grand-Père y furent professeurs, ma grand-mère y commença sa glorieuse carrière, ma Mère y a été élève et ma pauvre petite soeur y fit ses études.'

9 Rosenstiel (1998), p. 147.

10 Rosenstiel (1998), p. 25.

11 Charles F. Dupêchez (1981), 'Le Conservatoire Américain de Fontainebleau', unknown source: 'Les

of other nationalities), it was based in Fontainebleau, to the south of Paris, and the musical education dispensed by Boulanger and others at this institution was quintessentially French. Moreover, many of Boulanger's colleagues in Fontainebleau were also professors at the Paris Conservatoire. Unsurprisingly, therefore, the pedagogic ideals of that establishment were also the focus of the Fontainebleau institution.

The Conservatoire Américain was founded by the American Walter Damrosch, a conductor and the president of the American Friends of Musicians in France, an organization founded during the First World War. We have already seen that during the First World War, both Nadia and Lili Boulanger had been involved with charities concerned with Franco–American relations, and Nadia Boulanger played in several benefit concerts organized by Damrosch. Together with an American colleague, Damrosch founded a school for bandsmen in France after the war. This college, whose director was Francis Casadesus, was so successful that the idea for a permanent French-based music school for American students was mooted, and this idea resulted in the Conservatoire Américain.

In addition to providing music education of high quality, the purpose of the Conservatoire Américain was to give students a taste of French civilization and culture, and, as a corollary, to perpetuate the notion that this was a necessary adornment for students from the New World. At the opening festivities for the Conservatoire Américain, Damrosch said to the students: 'Learn French and the French people, they have the civilisation of the ages ... Their civilisation must be kept for the benefit of the world and it is a supreme privilege for you to share in its rich rewards.'[12] Aaron Copland, one of the institution's first students, said of Nadia Boulanger: 'Her intellectual interests and wide acquaintanceship among artists in all fields were an important stimulus to her American students: through these interests she whetted and broadened their cultural appetites.'[13] Some of the students received grants from American foundations; for instance, Virgil Thomson's studies in France were financed by a bursary from Harvard.

For Boulanger's amateur students, the social cachet of studying at the Conservatoire Américain was comparable to a year spent at a Swiss finishing school by a well-to-do young British lady. This 'civilizing' function ensured also that the popular nineteenth-century view of music as a desirable social grace was sustained. Léonie Rosenstiel notes that the American students 'soon realized that Fontainebleau was a social as well as

---

vacances, c'est le meilleur moment pour travailler.' This article, and many other sources cited in this chapter, was found in the archive of the Lyon Conservatoire library; many of these sources lack complete references.

12 Cited in Rosenstiel (1998), p. 153.

13 Aaron Copland, 'Nadia Boulanger: An Affectionate Portrait' (typescript at the Conservatoire National Supérieur de Musique, Lyon; later published in *Harper's*, October 1960).

an artistic experience',[14] and it is fair to say that Boulanger's value to her students was not confined to the classroom. She kept a close eye on the social development of her students, inviting them to parties, where she ensured that their behaviour was proper and correct. In Rosenstiel's words, 'In order to be accepted at the highest level of French society one had to act like a well-brought-up European, not like an uninhibited American. Any student of Nadia's who wanted to move in the exalted social circles of the Princesse de Polignac had first to learn how to behave as if he or she belonged there.'[15] (While the American author is right to stress the importance Nadia Boulanger attached to correct social behaviour, she does not mention that Princesse Edmond de Polignac (1865–1943) was herself the heiress to the Singer sewing machine fortune whose marriage was the union of her money with her husband's title. The Princesse always spoke French with an American accent.) From 1921 onwards, a select group of students was invited to spend part of the summer at the Boulangers' country home in Gargenville, which was regarded as a highly prized invitation.

Boulanger's time was devoted to her students. Her mother drilled the value of hard work into her from her student days, and her schedule left her with so little free time that, as Robin Orr wrote in his obituary of Boulanger, 'Other than her lifelong and devoted friend, Mademoiselle Dieudonné, few could be sure if she ever ate a square meal'. Orr, a former student, also mentioned that 'Her energy was prodigious. She could work from 8 a.m. till after midnight day after day. Studying with her at Gargenville … one might be summoned for a lesson at 10 p.m. It might last one hour, two hours – one would never know.'[16] Many other students confirm her extraordinarily full schedule, and the British composer and pianist David Wilde claims that she described sleep as 'five hours of nothing'![17] According to Wilde, she would attend Mass, eat breakfast and deal with her voluminous correspondence before starting to teach at 8 a.m.

Philip Glass, who studied with her from 1963 to 1965, described the pressures of this timetable from a student's point of view: 'When I studied with her, for example, the only way to live up to her standards and to turn out the amount of work she expected every week was to get up between 6 and 7 in the morning and work all day long. And, if I did that every day, I would turn up at my lesson and Boulanger gave me the impression that I had done just about the very minimum.'[18] Glass, for one, found her

---

[14] Rosenstiel (1998), p. 156.

[15] Ibid., p. 215.

[16] Robin Orr (1979), 'A Note on Nadia Boulanger' in *Musical Times*, 999.

[17] David Wilde (2003), talk on 'Working with Nadia Boulanger' during a one-day conference at the Royal Academy of Music, 19 October 2003.

[18] Philip Glass, interview in 1992 with Helen Tworkov and Robert Coe; in Richard Kostelanetz (ed.)

example daunting; he wrote: 'Boulanger set herself up as an incomparable model of discipline and dedication, and she expected you to be just like her. And that was almost impossible, because she seemed beyond what any human being could really hope to be.'[19]

It is probable that her relationship with her pupils was, for her, a replacement for the intimate relationships with a partner or with children that she never had, not least because her interest in her pupils' personal, as well as musical, development often exceeded the bounds of a healthy teacher–pupil relationship. Many accounts suggest that she expected her students to confide in her, and that she did not hesitate to express disapproval of the personal relationships of her students. As a devout Catholic, she disapproved of Roger Sessions's divorce and did not hesitate to tell him (even though he was never officially a student of hers). In Sessions's words, 'The night before I went to court in Reno, Nevada, I had a long letter from her begging me not to. She knew nothing at all about the circumstances. She begged me not to do it, telling me how I'd feel and so forth.'[20] She was also sometimes jealous of those students who, having been close to her, married someone outside her orbit.

Paris has always been a magnet for artists from all over the world, and in the early decades of the twentieth century the city was a fashionable destination for American artists working in every genre. For instance, the writers Henry Miller, Gertrude Stein, Ernest Hemingway, among many others, left their mark on Parisian artistic life and directly or indirectly encouraged other Americans to make the pilgrimage to the city. The height of popularity of Paris amongst American expatriate artists coincided with the zenith of Nadia Boulanger's reputation as a teacher, in the 1930s. In Roger Sessions's words: 'I never thought that she was anything less than a quite remarkable musician, except that she was not exceptional in that respect in Europe. She was the first European who really took seriously American students. If I may say so, somewhat cynically, she made a very good thing out of it.'[21] And as late as 1951 a journalist could write of the teacher: 'En Amérique, son nom est synonyme de tout ce que l'école française a de haut et d'excellent.'[22] From 1949, Nadia Boulanger was the director of the Conservatoire Américain.

Her illustrious American composition pupils included Aaron Copland, George Antheil, Elliott Carter and Roy Harris, and she also taught many American amateur musicians. As Virgil Thomson, one of her first American

---

(1997), *Writings on Glass* (New York: Schirmer), p. 323.

[19] Ibid.

[20] Andrea Olmstead (1987), *Conversations with Roger Sessions* (Boston: Northeastern University Press), p. 222.

[21] Ibid., p. 220.

[22] J. de Montalais, article dated 10 March 1951.

pupils, wrote in 1962: 'Nadia Boulanger … has for more than forty years been, for musical Americans, a one-woman graduate school so powerful and so permeating that legend credits every American town with two things – a five-and-dime and a Boulanger pupil.'[23] For her part, Boulanger believed that the training her American students received from her in Europe was particularly valuable to them because, according to her: 'they [Americans] do very well at school, they are very talented but … in many cases, they do not start from a solid base as their ear is not properly trained … Why is this the case? Because little children must not be tired!'[24] She considered that it was her job to rectify this lack of rigorous study and hard work that she detected in her American pupils.

Boulanger's connections with the USA were further cemented during numerous visits when she taught and led masterclasses. She was even offered a professorship at the Curtis Institute in 1925 (following representations from her student Kathleen Wolff and Walter Damrosch's brother), but after much hesitation, she turned this opportunity down because her mother would not have wanted to live abroad.[25]

She did, however, refuse to teach a small number of potential students, including George Gershwin and Iannis Xenakis. Gershwin was turned down because she felt he had already found his voice; according to David Wilde, she preferred his songs to his concert works (including *Rhapsody in Blue* and a Piano Concerto). Xenakis approached her soon after his arrival in Paris after the Second World War, but in his words, 'she turned me down, saying I wasn't mature enough and that she was too old to start with a boy my age'.[26] As Xenakis was then in his late twenties and Boulanger's teaching career lasted until her death in 1979, this was perhaps an excuse rather than a reason, and she did point him in the direction of Annette Dieudonné, who then taught at the Conservatoire. Xenakis showed her a trio he had written for voice, flute and piano, and said: 'I went to her classes a few times but when she saw that the rules of traditional harmony were like fetters for me, she said I'd better see Messiaen. And that's what I did.'[27] Dieudonné's advice proved fortunate for Xenakis, who found a congenial and understanding teacher in Messiaen.

It is perhaps paradoxical that Nadia Boulanger was a sought-after teacher of composition who was not herself active as a composer for the great majority of her teaching career. A journalist writing for *Samedi-Soir* noted

---

23 Virgil Thomson, article in *New York Times Magazine* (4 February 1962).

24 Monsaingeon (1980), p. 26: 'Ils font des études brillantes, parce qu'ils ont des gens très doués, mais … les bases ne sont pas assurés dans beaucoup de cas, leur oreille n'étant pas développée … Pourquoi? … parce qu'il ne faut pas fatiguer les enfants!'

25 Rosenstiel (1998), p. 202.

26 Bálint András Varga (1996), *Conversations with Iannis Xenakis* (London: Faber), p. 26.

27 Ibid., p. 27.

that she could have become a composer, but she 'insists that she gave up writing because she had nothing new to say'.[28] Not only a perfectionist as a composer, Boulanger showed little interest in musical works besides those she considered to be masterpieces. Her teaching materials abound with references to 'works by the masters', and she firmly believed that the study of music was the study of musical masterpieces. As she once said: 'Just as I accept God, I accept beauty, I accept feeling, I also accept the masterpiece.'[29]

This was not to say that she was uninterested in music outside the Western European classical tradition. Aaron Copland remembers that she was curious about everything, and that she was fascinated by the complexity of the jazz rhythms he was introducing into his music during the mid-1920s. Copland wrote: 'She had the teacher's consuming need to know how all music functions, and it was that kind of inquiring attitude that registered on the minds of her students.'[30] Her liking for Gershwin's songs, as well as her acceptance of Astor Piazzola and Quincy Jones as students, shows her respect for vernacular forms of music.

D. F. Aitken, writing in the *Radio Times* in 1936, believed that Nadia Boulanger's pupils thought that she was the greatest teacher in Europe 'because she has no axe to grind. Years ago she gave up the idea of being herself a composer … since she is not primarily a composer, she has no style of her own to impress on her pupils, no ready-made pattern by which to turn out so many little Boulangers with five years' struggle in front of them before they can recover any semblance of individuality.'[31] Although this is perhaps not an accurate assessment of the process of teaching composition, Aitken was right to emphasize that Boulanger was not a professional threat to her students, since she was not a competitor of theirs. In this sense, it could be said that Nadia Boulanger's conformity with the expectation that a woman should not aim to become a professional composer worked, ironically, in her favour.

Although the ability and experience of Boulanger's students differed widely, her approach was fundamentally identical, whatever the level of tuition: she believed that aural training should be the foundation of musical appreciation and instruction. She said: 'The great privilege of teaching consists in bringing one's pupils to examine their thoughts in depth, to say what they truly want and to hear exactly what they hear; this is why a thorough and lifelong training in the language of music is

---

28 Montalais (1951): 'Elle affirme pourtant qu'elle n'a plus écrit parce qu'elle n'avait rien de neuf à dire.'

29 Monsaingeon (1980), p. 30: 'Comme j'accepte Dieu, j'accepte la beauté, j'accepte l'émotion, j'accepte aussi bien le chef d'oeuvre.'

30 Copland (1960).

31 D.F. Aitken (1936), untitled article in the *Radio Times* (13 November): 19.

essential.'[32] All her students were expected to have the same basic training in the language of Western classical music, because, in her words, 'unless he [the student] knows grammar, he cannot talk.'[33] Many former students have said that 'she taught music' rather than a particular musical sub-discipline, and her approaches to analysing and performing music were identical in the sense that she would always aim to project the structure of a piece.

Philip Glass began his studies with Boulanger at the age of 26; as Boulanger was uninterested in his music, she insisted he started by completing species counterpoint exercises.[34] In Glass's words:

> she had a variety of techniques that she was teaching. They included score reading, counterpoint, harmony, figured bass, and analysis. You spent the whole week preparing for that class. She had an assistant called Mademoiselle Dieudonné, a *répétiteuse*, who gave the other lesson. She did the ear training and the score reading. Between these two ladies, it was easy to spend six or eight hours a day doing basic music practice. With Boulanger, nothing was theoretical; it was all practical. The rules of harmony she could describe in a few sentences, but you could spend years writing it, because to her the difference between technique and theory was that technique is practice. Harmony is practice, counterpoint is practice – neither is theory. So, what she was interested in was harmonic practice of a certain period and contrapuntal practice of a certain period.[35]

David Diamond, in a letter to Roger Sessions and his wife written from Fontainebleau on 12 July 1937, goes into more detail about the content of his sessions with Boulanger. Besides looking at the compositions Diamond had been working on in New York, Diamond mentions that 'I am now working on 4 part counterpoint, 5th species, with two florid parts'.[36] But he was more excited by an invitation he received as a result of studying with Boulanger: 'Last Sunday, Stravinsky asked the advanced students of Nadia to his home with works. I was delighted that she asked me, and we played the *Psalm* for Stravinsky at one piano – 4 hands from score. I was so nervous with Stravinsky behind me all the time I could hardly play but I think we both gave a good impression of the work. After I left, Nadia said he thought the work the most mature and provoking, the orchestration very

---

[32] Monsaingeon (1980), p. 18: 'Le privilège très grand d'enseigner consiste à amener celui qu'on enseigne à regarder réellement ce qu'il pense, à dire réellement ce qu'il veut et à entendre nettement ce qu'il entend; d'où vient la nécessité d'un entraînement très grand dans la vie: la connaissance des mots.'

[33] Interview with Robert Layton, broadcast by the BBC on 30 September 1969; consulted at the National Sound Archive.

[34] Philip Glass, interview in 1989 with Ev Grimes; in Kostelanetz (1997), p. 30.

[35] Ibid.

[36] Olmstead (1987), p. 264.

original but *too dissonant!*'[37] – a criticism Boulanger also made of his music.

The values that she had imbibed from her traditional Conservatoire music education, with its emphasis on solfège, were thus transmitted to her students; the basic training that she herself had received became the basic training undertaken by her students. Moreover, much of the rigid Conservatoire curriculum formed the nucleus of her teaching. On the first page of some material produced for her elementary harmony class, now housed in the Lyon Conservatoire, she noted, with reference to a four-part harmony exercise: 'The student should study the progressions every day, working part by part, and transposing them. One should be able to write and play them by heart, and to analyse them by ear.' Hers was a quasi-religious approach to music: the students were expected to take in, memorize and interiorize a text.

The concept of harmony is introduced in this first lesson via the harmonic series, for Boulanger subscribed to the theory that tonal chords could be derived from this. More than once in her teaching material, Boulanger quotes Aristotle's dictum: 'Low notes contain high notes, but not vice versa.'[38] She stressed the importance of the fundamental note of any chord, and gave her students several basic exercises focusing on the recognition of chord inversions. In a nutshell, she impressed on her students that Western harmony had its basis in Nature, thereby implying that harmony is a given, something with which one should not tamper. No doubt, she resorted to this rationale to justify her distaste for serial music. Another expression she was fond of using – 'The history of music is the history of overtones' – likewise proceeded from the notion that music is an evolutionary art based on natural principles. Although the view that tonal chords can be derived from the harmonic series is not adhered to by all musicians who consider the question (it is particularly hard to explain the minor triad in this manner), its premise accords well with Nadia Boulanger's firm belief in the notion of hierarchy.

The small archive of teaching material preserved in the Boulanger Collection at the Conservatoire National Supérieur de Musique de Lyon – one of the few sources to reveal information about her teaching of non-expert musicians – offers some insight into her teaching methods and the content of some of her classes. One interesting document is the harmony exercise book of an American student, Kathleen Wolff, who studied with Boulanger in the mid-1920s. This material is dated 'Gargenville 1926'; Wolff was therefore one of a group of students invited to study with Boulanger over the summer vacation. In this exercise book, Wolff constructs triads and all types of seventh and ninth chords built on scales comprised of every

---

37 Ibid.

38 In Boulanger's words: 'le grave contient l'aigu, l'aigu ne contient pas le grave.'

interval, from a chromatic scale through to the whole-tone mode, and extending to scales consisting of perfect fifths. A beginner thus had to commence by writing down the basic building blocks of music. In Boulanger's harmony classes tonality could be stretched to its outer limits – but, equally importantly, these limits were never transgressed. A prime concern of Boulanger's was that students should realize that a single chord can appear in several different tonal contexts. She often required students to draw up a list of the possible functions of a single chord: a list that catalogued the different keys in which the chord could appear and specified, if necessary, the required resolution of the chord in a particular context. The harmonization of Bach chorales was a favourite exercise that Boulanger gave to students of all standards, although elementary-level students were expected to use only the tonic, dominant and subdominant chords in root position.

Boulanger's overview of her three-year-long harmony course as taught at the Ecole Normale de Musique reveals a similar approach. Students were provided with a handout detailing what they were expected to achieve by the end of each academic session, and all students were expected to recognize and use the full standard complement of figured bass symbols. The traditional French music education system requires students also to read and write in all clefs, four-part fugal exercises often being notated with a different clef for each voice (soprano, alto, tenor, bass). Lennox Berkeley recalls using these four clefs in the counterpoint exercises that he produced for Boulanger, although he also (privately) questioned whether this was a useful element of his training.[39]

Some future professional composers who studied with her, such as Berkeley, were noticeably less enthusiastic about her teaching methods. Berkeley's fellow Briton Nicholas Maw won a French government scholarship in 1958 to study with Boulanger, but they did not initially hit it off and Maw claims he learned little from her. He did, however, benefit from her submitting his music for a competition judged by Copland and Stravinsky, which he won, and enjoyed her reminiscences of Paris in the 1920s;[40] other experienced students, such as the British composer Edwin Roxburgh, were more enthusiastic about her methods.

Roxburgh, who describes her as 'no ordinary composition teacher', studied with Boulanger for two summers in Fontainebleau, and in Paris for several months. A Cambridge graduate who had also trained at the Royal College of Music with Herbert Howells, and in Italy with Luigi Dallapiccola, Roxburgh was already technically accomplished when he came to

---

[39] Interview with Bernard Keeffe, broadcast by the BBC in September 1973 and consulted at the National Sound Archive.

[40] Nicholas Wroe (2002), profile of Nicholas Maw in the *Guardian* Review (7 December): 26.

Boulanger. He recalls that 'The first thing I had to do for her was write a fugue, and she realised I could do that – otherwise, I would have had to go through her very rigorous training in harmony, counterpoint etc, but we got on to Stravinsky right away, which was nice. Not employing any analytical method, because in those days analysis was a separate subject at the Conservatoire, and anyone who wanted to study analysis went to Messiaen. So really, it was just a question of her tearing my pieces apart!'[41]

As far as composition was concerned, Roxburgh said that 'her teaching methods were very much based on her absolute knowledge of Stravinsky, of everything he wrote'. When I asked how Stravinsky was relevant to her criticisms of his pieces, Roxburgh replied: 'Pretty well every observation was related to Stravinsky. For instance, rhythmic characteristics – if you were going to write a pastiche, she would show how Stravinsky also committed the same sin, but the way he actually elaborated the music to such an extent moved the piece to a level above pastiche.' But Roxburgh also mentioned that she could be brisk with those who disagreed with her views; he recalls 'At one point, I expressed my lack of … understanding, I think, about the neoclassical phase – I couldn't see how anything "neo" could be productive, and she got quite abrasive about that, actually.'

Elliott Carter gave a precise example of Boulanger using a Stravinsky example to criticize a composition that he showed to her: 'I remember clearly that Mlle Boulanger, after seeing a passage I had written in bare parallel major sevenths, played from memory a passage with similar harmony from *The Rite of Spring*, in the "Cercles mystérieux des adolescentes" at rehearsal number 94, to show how Stravinsky had made this effect expressive and effective by adding rising tremolos in major seconds by the strings, producing various continually changing, richer harmonies.'[42]

Once Boulanger was assured that her students had a sufficiently good ear and a strong grasp of traditional harmony and counterpoint, her primary aim was to discover their opinions about music and to encourage them to develop an individual voice. Lennox Berkeley wrote: 'She was an inspiring force, and her inspiration consisted in making us aware of the necessity of acquiring the technique which is indispensable for a composer … Apart from that, she helped us to form our own tastes by insisting that we had to know music by composers of the past in depth; on this foundation she could help us too develop our sense of form.'[43] Berkeley added that in his

---

41 Interview with the author, 5 March 2001.

42 In Jonathan W. Bernard (1990), 'Interview with Elliott Carter', *Perspectives of New Music*, 28/2 (Summer): 199.

43 Monsaingeon (1980), 124: 'Elle était une inspiratrice, et l'inspiration consistait à nous faire prendre conscience de la nécessité d'acquérir la technique indispensable au compositeur … A part cela, elle nous aidait à former notre propre goût en insistant sur le nécessaire et profonde connaissance des

first year of study with Boulanger all he did was complete contrapuntal exercises, in which he was obliged to follow the rules of tonal harmony, however musical his alternative solutions may have been; Boulanger considered that he had a sufficiently sound grasp of harmony to be excused from her basic harmony course.

Those who merely parroted Boulanger's opinions did not win her approval; she once told a student who asked her if his harmonic language was what she required: 'Well, I have no idea, I don't know what you want. As long as I don't know what you want, you don't exist for me, musically speaking.'[44]

By the second year of his studies with Boulanger, Philip Glass was assigned harmony exercises which were really style composition exercises. A small group of students were invited to participate in a class they nicknamed 'Black Thursday', and the harmony solutions they found were measured against a Mozart or Beethoven original. In Glass's words: 'Basically all she had wanted us to do was simply the exact harmony that Beethoven had done. ... Well, of course, had we *known* that piece, we might have been able to do it; but she always picked a piece that no one knew or found something so obscure. It could be anything.'[45] Glass eventually realized the purpose of these lessons:

> I understood that she wasn't teaching technique, she was teaching style. ... It becomes clear that personal style is a special case of technique. So that, for example, if you take a passage of Rachmaninoff or a passage of Mozart, they sound very different within seconds. ... After you got through the first couple of years of Boulanger, then she got into this next stage where you were meant to find out for yourself that technique forms the basis of style ... From her point of view, there's no point in teaching style without a technical basis.[46]

The harmonization of given melodies (known as 'chants donnés') in a prescribed style, was another task often undertaken by Boulanger students; not only did the student have to harmonize the given melody, but he or she also had to explain the reasons why a particular harmonization was chosen. Some of these 'chants donnés' were clearly old favourites that had been used in many classes. Melodies by nineteenth-century composers such as Delibes and Dubois were frequently used, reflecting the French bias of the Paris Conservatoire curriculum. More interestingly, it seems that other melodies were composed especially for Boulanger's classes. The Lyon

compositeurs du passé, sur la base de laquelle elle était en mesure de nous aider à bâtir notre sens de la forme.'

[44] Ibid., p. 54: 'Mais je n'ai aucune idée, je ne sais pas ce que tu veux. Tant que je ne sais pas ce que tu veux, tu n'existes pas musicalement pour moi.'

[45] Ibid., p. 31.

[46] Ibid., p. 35.

Conservatoire archive contains two fugue subjects composed in 1947 by Henri Dutilleux and a two-page melody in the style of Gabriel Fauré composed by Olivier Messiaen.

An overview of the history of early music in thirteen lessons in Boulanger's hand is also preserved at Lyon Conservatoire. Dated 1932–33, an identical course exists in English translation; this material was used for classes that Boulanger took in Cambridge, Massachusetts, in 1941. As several dozen copies of most of these lessons survive in the Lyon archive, it may be presumed that they were used as lecture handouts. Most of Boulanger's French contemporaries ignored music composed before J. S. Bach, but her course starts from the Ancient Greek modal system (with a nod of acknowledgement to the Conservatoire professor of music history Maurice Emmanuel, a specialist in the field). Subsequent lessons cover such topics as the development of the Catholic liturgy, Gregorian chant, the troubadours and organum. Each class briefly surveys about a century, and the course illustrates the development of the musical language from monody to polyphony. It focuses on Boulanger's belief that 'the history of music is the history of overtones', since the teacher demonstrates that the earliest music was monodic and that composers gradually introduced the harmonization of this monody first at the octave and then at the fifth, adding more intervals progressively as and when these were considered consonant.

This history course emphasizes sacred music, partly because, as Boulanger stated, little was then known about secular music of the period, but also doubtless because religious belief was assumed to be shared by the teacher and her students. In this history class outline, Boulanger also briefly mentions contemporary historical events and artistic achievements (emphasizing contemporary cathedral construction) and suggests further reading. Music is therefore viewed within a historical context, and the teacher nods towards the notion of general culture. In her handouts Boulanger often praises symmetrical musical forms and shows a predilection for musical forms based on imitation and varied repetition rather than simple repetition.

I have already said that many of Nadia Boulanger's amateur students came from wealthy backgrounds. While the teacher appreciated the origins (and the money) of these students, the appreciation flowed in both directions. Many of her students were impressed by the supposedly aristocratic origins of Nadia Boulanger's domineering mother, who remained constantly at her side until her death in 1935. Mother and daughter even slept in the same bedroom.

Boulanger often told her friend Topazia Markevitch, the second wife of the conductor, that aristocrats were 'good and modest and serene', and she strongly objected when someone of that background was criticized in her presence.[47] It seems certain, therefore, that she herself refrained from criticizing her royal or aristocratic students, not only because of this deferential attitude but also because she never attempted to push those of her students who were wealthy but not necessarily gifted, since they were not working towards a professional career. She aimed to develop their love of music, and it is true that these students also inadvertently cross-subsidized her would-be 'professional' students, most of whom hailed from more modest backgrounds. The aspiring professionals were seeking a rigorous training from one of the most esteemed teachers of the time: a *curriculum vitae* bearing Boulanger's name and, even better, her seal of approval of the music composed by the student, could open many doors for the serious student composer. A small number of future professional performers (including Dinu Lipatti and Jeremy Menuhin) studied in the same classes as these student composers.

The students invited to her home – group classes for these students took place on Wednesdays at 3 p.m. – formed a select group on whose music she commented, and whom she led in discussions centring on set musical works ranging from Josquin to twentieth-century composers. Most of the students at these Wednesday afternoon classes were men, most had ambitions to become professional composers, and all had proven musical talent. The music of J. S. Bach was the one constant feature of her history and analysis classes, and Boulanger significantly said of Bach: 'I believe that a musician should know the two books of "The Well-Tempered Clavier" and, if possible, some cantatas, in depth. I try to give this daily bread to my pupils at all cost. It would seem odd to me if someone had never read the Bible.'[48] While Boulanger's amateur students were given a sound technical knowledge of the workings of music and a general knowledge of the history of Western music, her more advanced students were given extra challenges in the form of these analysis classes.

Joseph Horovitz recalls that all these students participated in a choral class in this Wednesday afternoon session; he started studying with her in 1949, and said that this was the only opportunity for her private and Conservatoire students to meet. Boulanger both directed the ensemble and accompanied the students at the piano if the work she had chosen required accompaniment. Horovitz specifically remembers singing Monteverdi contrapuntal works and reading Stravinsky's Mass from the original manuscript.[49]

---

[47] Rosenstiel (1998), p. 368.

[48] Monsaingeon (1980), p. 68: 'J'estime qu'un musicien doit connaître à fond les deux volumes de "Clavier Bien Tempéré" et si possible un bon nombre de cantates. J'essaie de les faire enfourner à mes élèves coûte que coûte. Il me paraîtrait un peu drôle que quelqu'un n'ait jamais lu la Bible'.

[49] Contribution to a round table session at the Royal Academy of Music study day on Nadia and Lili Boulanger, 19 October 2003.

Teaching schedules drawn up in the last five years of her life show that in these sessions Boulanger led discussions that concerned works by living composers, who included Olivier Messiaen, Henri Dutilleux, Maurice Ohana and Iannis Xenakis.[50] The Wednesday classes, which had started in 1921, continued almost until the end of her life. The official end of the class – two hours later – coincided with a weekly 'at home', offered by Boulanger's mother Raïssa until her death and continued by Boulanger afterwards. Selected students were invited to stay for this gathering, and other guests would include such eminent artists as Stravinsky and Paul Valéry. It is clear that introductions to the celebrated artists and society figures who attended these tea parties could be highly beneficial to the students.

The music from different epochs studied during the Wednesday classes mirrored Boulanger's own concert programmes; her conducting career resumed in the 1930s, initially in the salons of aristocratic patrons including the Princesse de Polignac, and most of her favoured performers were initially her students. Writing in the *Radio Times*, D. F. Aitken noted:

> Her method is summed up in the French word *rapprochement*. She will take several pieces of music from widely separate periods, in totally different styles. To the mere historian they will seem poles asunder. No one else would have thought of them in the same breath. Yet to her it is clear that each in its own way is saying the same kind of thing. And so she brings them suddenly together in one programme in the hope that her listeners may be able to appreciate for themselves the meaning that they have in common.[51]

This approach was seen as revolutionary at the time, although in a sense it was also an approach to programming that was very much of its time. Boulanger's belief that music from very different historical periods should be juxtaposed in concert programmes or classes fortuitously coincided with the neo-classical compositional movement that she favoured. Aitken pertinently observes: 'The nineteenth century, in Mademoiselle Boulanger's view, has been a dangerous influence. We are only now getting back to the great tradition of the past – a tradition of order and restraint and discipline, in fact of classicism.'[52]

I believe that behind this generalized view of nineteenth-century music lies, in part, a criticism by Nadia Boulanger of her own compositions, which are quintessentially late-Romantic in their harmonic progressions, stretching the frontiers of tonality without ever quite breaking through them. She rarely included Romantic music in concert programmes, though made an

---

[50] Document preserved in the Lyon Conservatoire.

[51] Aitken (1936).

[52] Ibid.

exception for Brahms's *Liebeslieder* waltzes and Schubert songs. And when Joseph Horovitz raised the topic of Wagner, Boulanger replied: 'If you want to talk about Wagner, you do it outside this room'![53]

Boulanger justified abandoning chronological order in many of her history classes and concert programmes on pedagogical grounds. She remarked: 'I think that styles differ only in appearance; people may be dressed differently, but in their thoughts, their reactions and their beliefs, they are similar. You will find, across the centuries, there are some masterpieces which are different on the surface, but whose thought processes are similar, and which evoke similar thoughts in the listener's mind.'[54] As an example of this, she cited Debussy's *Le Martyre de Saint Sébastien* and a thirteenth-century motet.

This juxtaposing of musical works from different periods led to stimulating discussions and discoveries. Boulanger's central belief was that student composers should be aware of their musical heritage, and should therefore understand how their own music fitted into that tradition. Her skill as a composition teacher lay not in inspiring her students through the example of her original creative work, but in teaching them to understand a wide variety of musical styles, one or more of which might prove stimulating to them in their creative work.

Nevertheless, from the 1930s Nadia Boulanger became associated with the neo-classical style of composition. She was not free from musical prejudices; students interested in the techniques of serial composition, in *musique concrète* or in electronic music would have been well advised to look elsewhere for a sympathetic teacher. Joseph Horovitz recalls that she did not discuss Boulez or Messiaen during their lessons in the early 1950s, and the composer Adrian Beaumont claims that she said Messiaen wrote 'too many notes'![55] Boulanger said that she rarely discussed the music of the Second Viennese School 'because other people talk about it so much and it's played so much that I think one should throw a bit of light on music in shadow. I prefer to choose works which are in the shadow, or which are unjustly neglected.'[56] While this appears to be a laudable reason for choosing certain pieces, Boulanger is not being open about her distaste for pre-

---

[53] Contribution to a round table session at the Royal Academy of Music study day on Nadia and Lili Boulanger, 19 October 2003.

[54] Monsaingeon (1980), p. 67: 'Je crois qu'il n'y a différence que d'apparence entre un style et un autre; les gens sont habillés autrement mais dans leurs pensées, dans leurs réactions, leur foi, ils se ressemblent. Vous trouverez à travers les siècles quelques chefs d'oeuvre qui sont différents dans leur accoutrement mais qui sont semblables par la pensée qu'ils dégagent, par la pensée qu'ils font surgir chez l'auditeur.'

[55] Contributions to a round table session at the Royal Academy of Music study day on Nadia and Lili Boulanger, 19 October 2003.

[56] Monsaingeon (1980), p. 68: 'parce qu'on en parle tellement par ailleurs et qu'on la joue tellement que je crois qu'il faut projeter un peu d'éclat sur l'ombre. Je sélectionne plus volontiers des oeuvres qui sont dans l'ombre, ou mal connues.'

Stravinskian serial music, which was surely her fundamental reason for not discussing it much in classes. Horovitz considers that she was 'tonality personified' in the early 1950s, though Edwin Roxburgh remarks that her tastes moved on; by the time he studied with her, from 1959, she was drawing comparisons between Stravinsky's *Movements* and Boulez's Second Piano Sonata. According to Roxburgh, 'she very much respected Boulez and understood him'.[57] It is also apparent that she revised her views on serialism following Stravinsky's change of heart regarding this method in the mid-1950s.

Her distaste for certain composers was obvious to her students. Elliott Carter recalls that, while he was studying with her,

> I used to write like Bartók, or like Varèse, and she didn't like that at all. ... She was in the same composition class with Varèse when she was young and she had a very low opinion of him as a composer. ... She said that Varèse would come into the class with one measure of a composition and explain to Widor, their teacher, how it was going to go on ... And then the next week he'd arrive with another measure, and another explanation, for a different piece. Finally Widor got angry at him, because he never brought in any more than a very few measures, with enormous explanations of what the pieces were going to be like! Nadia told us this story as a lesson to us students, that we mustn't do that.[58]

Carter even admitted that his Woodwind Quartet (1948), which he describes as 'like [my] Piano Sonata in that it wavers between two keys' is 'a retrogressive piece. In a sense, I wrote it for Nadia Boulanger' because 'I always thought of it as something that Nadia wished I had written when I was a student.'[59]

Aaron Copland felt that Boulanger's critical and analytical skills, combined with her exceptionally broad knowledge of music, rendered her comments particularly valuable. He wrote: 'I am convinced that it is Mademoiselle Boulanger's perceptivity as a musician that is at the core of her teaching. She is able to grasp the still uncertain contours of an incomplete sketch, examine it, and foretell the probable and possible ways in which it may be developed. She is expert in picking flaws in any work in progress, and knowing why they are flaws.'[60]

But, for a student composer, constant negative criticism could prove profoundly dispiriting, and it seems that praise from Boulanger was valued all the more because it was dispensed so rarely. Elliott Carter said:

---

[57] Interview with the author, 5 March 2001.
[58] Carter, interview with Jonathan W. Bernard (1990): 193–4.
[59] Ibid., 193.
[60] Copland (1960).

I think that Nadia Boulanger taught me, maybe more than anything else, about how concern for small details in music can make a great deal of difference in the total effect. It came out, obviously, in the study of counterpoint. We did counterpoint in up to eight parts with her, and she was always pointing out little things about how if you did it in another way, it would sound better, and she would take passages from Bach cantatas and show us how effectively the voices had been written.[61]

These Bach cantata sessions became a central part of her composition classes from 1931, and eventually led to the foundation of her own vocal ensemble, as we shall see in Chapter 6.

Boulanger said that all that a composition teacher can do is 'to develop in a pupil the faculties which will allow him to manipulate the tools of his trade. The teacher has no control over what he will do with this tool. I can't give someone the capacity to invent, no more than I can take that capacity from them; I can, however, give him the freedom – that's the right word – to read, to listen, to see, and to understand.' Composers need their own language and, according to her, 'within this established language, the freedom to be themselves ... The ability to be yourself is already a sign of genius.'[62]

Her approaches to harmony and the history of music were systematic and thorough, and her teaching materials for these disciplines could easily have been published. Many publishers suggested to her that she should collate her material and make it available to a wider public. Although Boulanger toyed with this idea on several occasions, she never followed it up. Léonie Rosenstiel claims that she was hurt when the New York publishing house, Schirmer, rejected a proposal (from her via Walter Damrosch) to publish a method and exercises for young children, and that she never forgot or forgave this rejection;[63] certainly, Boulanger bore several grudges. But her harmony and history course materials were clearly developed over a number of years, and are models of lucidity. Moreover, although she always took an interest in contemporary music, her teaching material did not substantially evolve over the years. Her belief that her system of training was the only one suitable for students of Western music was unshakeable.

If her material had been published, it is possible that some students would have regarded a book purchase as a cheaper and more practical option than coming to Paris to study with her. However, her elite students

---

61 Interview with Bernard (1990): 199.

62 Monsaingeon (1980), p. 52: 'Tout ce qu'un professeur peut faire consiste à développer chez l'élève les facultés qui lui permettent de manipuler des outils. Sur ce qu'il fera de l'outil, le professeur n'a pas d'action possible. Je ne peux pas donner d'invention à quelqu'un, je ne peux pas non plus la lui enlever; je peux lui donner la liberté, je dis bien, de lire, d'entendre, de voir, de comprendre ... Il faut un langage établi et puis, dans ce langage établi, la liberté d'être soi-même ... Etre soi-même, c'est déjà être génial.'

63 Rosenstiel (1998), p. 202.

undoubtedly valued her personal presence and criticism more than the rigorous aural training, harmony and counterpoint lessons, which could, arguably, have been disseminated as successfully via publication. Also, her amateur students would surely not have been dissuaded from the exciting prospect of studying in France with her by the easy availability of a book.

But I am sure the fundamental reason why Boulanger refused to publish her course materials was because she felt that personal contact between teacher and student was just as essential as the transmission of cultural information and values. She expounded her credo as a teacher to Bruno Monsaingeon: 'It's essential to tell the truth [to students] but with the aim of increasing self-confidence and developing individuality: it's very hard, and group classes do not allow for that. If I only deal with groups of students, I have to submit them to a discipline which is a form of blindness towards the individual. So, I believe it's always essential to have that face-to-face contact with someone.'[64] And we have seen that her concern for her students went far beyond musical matters.

Aaron Copland certainly believed that her magnetic personal presence played a significant role in her success as a teacher. He wrote: 'By a process of osmosis, one soaks up attitudes, principles, knowledge, reflections … Nadia Boulanger knew everything there was to know about music.'[65]

---

[64] Monsaingeon (1980), pp. 58–9; 'Il faut dire la vérité mais avec l'idée de susciter la confiance et de libérer le moi intérieur; c'est très difficile, et l'éducation collective ne le permet pas. Si je n'ai affaire qu'à des groupes d'élèves, je suis obligée de les soumettre à une discipline qui est quelque chose d'aveugle vis-à-vis d'eux. D'où, je crois, la nécessité d'avoir toujours un contact avec quelqu'un face à face, parce que celui-là n'est aucun autre. Il est un.'

[65] Copland (1960).

CHAPTER 6

Reputations

Although no longer active as a composer after 1923, Nadia Boulanger's achievements in other musical fields were astonishingly varied. In addition to her teaching and lecturing activity, she was one of the first female professional conductors, appeared in public as a solo pianist and accompanist, was warmly reviewed as an organist, edited early music for publication and performance and occasionally acted as a concert reviewer. She was also a strong supporter of those contemporary composers she admired, not only former students, and the principal guardian of the flame of Lili Boulanger's reputation, promoting it tirelessly until her own death in 1979.

During Nadia Boulanger's first concert tour of the USA, in January–February 1925, her sister's music appeared on the programme and was well received by critics. Boulanger was the soloist in Copland's Symphony for Organ and Orchestra – a part written for her – with the New York Symphony Society conducted by Walter Damrosch. On the same programme, she performed Handel's Organ Concerto in D minor, and Lili Boulanger's *Pour les funérailles d'un soldat* was given its American premiere. The programme was repeated on 20 February in Boston by that city's Symphony Orchestra conducted by Serge Koussevitzky. While reviews of Nadia Boulanger as an organist were good, she was not a dazzling virtuoso and she made at least as strong an impression as a lecturer, giving a lecture recital in New York Town Hall on 19 January 1925. During this lecture, she said: 'The experiments of Schoenberg, the Austrian, have given a new impetus to music all over the world.'[1] This was to be her last positive appraisal of Schoenberg, and indeed she rarely mentioned his name in later years. Rosenstiel speculates that this was because Stravinsky was also in the USA at this time and may well have seen reviews of Boulanger's lecture; as his animosity with Schoenberg was then at its height, he may have encouraged Boulanger to choose between them.[2]

Boulanger is generally associated with the neo-classical movement of the 1920s and 1930s and in particular with Stravinsky. She first came across his music in 1909, during the Ballets Russes' season in Paris; besides being a

---

[1] Léonie Rosenstiel (1998), *Nadia Boulanger* (New York and London: Norton), p. 185.
[2] Ibid.

great supporter of his music through all his apparent changes of style, she empathized with his Russian origins. She became a trusted friend and saw him often when both emigrated to the United States during the years of the Second World War. At Stravinsky's request, Boulanger conducted the first performance of his *Dumbarton Oaks* concerto on 8 May 1938, though the composer was undergoing a cure for tuberculosis at the time and was therefore unable to do the job himself and it was Stravinsky who conducted the public premiere on 4 June 1938 in Paris. Boulanger was also involved in the premiere of Stravinsky's Sonata for two pianos in July 1944 in Madison, Wisconsin, the other pianist being Richard Johnson, and it is partly thanks to Boulanger that Stravinsky was offered the chair of poetry at Harvard in 1939–40, as the original approach was made through her.[3] Many critics have drawn a parallel between Stravinsky's *Poetics of Music* – the book resulting from this lecture programme – and Valéry's *Poetics* (Valéry was a close friend of both musicians), and some have even claimed that Boulanger had a hand in writing the book. Given her antipathy to the written word, it is unlikely that she helped draft the book; however, their shared professorship at the Ecole Normale and their shared views on many topics make it likely that discussions with Boulanger may have helped Stravinsky to formulate some of his ideas. In particular, they had a horror of sentimentality in music and a shared love of Renaissance and Baroque masters.

Nadia Boulanger as conductor

As one of the first female professional conductors, Nadia Boulanger also promoted her sister's work in concerts and recordings. An article published in 1928 by Simone Ratel compared Boulanger the conductor to a celibate male (i.e. a priest), thus erasing her gender and sexuality. Ratel considered her conducting career as an extension of her teaching activities, a view which highlights Boulanger's activity in a traditional female occupation (teaching) rather than her pioneering work in the overwhelmingly male-dominated profession of orchestral conducting.

Although Boulanger made her debut as a conductor as early as 1912, conducting Pugno in a performance of her own *Rapsodie variée*, her conducting career was put on hold after his death, no doubt because a young woman would not have been taken seriously as a professional conductor without the protection and support of a celebrated older man. However, her later conducting activities grew out of her group classes. From 1931, Nadia Boulanger led her students in Bach cantata run-throughs

---

[3] Eric Walter White (2/1979), *Stravinsky: The Composer and his Works* (London: Faber), p. 112.

in her Wednesday classes and according to Doda Conrad, by June 1935 she had conceived the idea of forming a small vocal ensemble which would explore the madrigal repertoire. This embryonic ensemble performed works by Monteverdi as part of her class at the Ecole Normale, and according to Conrad, Alfred Cortot was impressed by the vocalists.[4]

Jeanice Brooks cites an interview Boulanger gave to the *Boston Evening Transcript* in 1939 which sheds light on how she perceived this turning point in her conducting career:

> 'Fifteen years ago', she says, 'I conceived the plan of making my pupils gather once a week and sing a Bach cantata. I think that there is nothing to equal singing for instilling into one a true sense of musical values, and I was convinced that such an exercise would vastly improve both their knowledge and execution. The enthusiasm with which they responded surprised even me. As their ability increased, so did their repertory and their numbers, until even well-known singers were asking to be admitted into the group.
>
> Even then I had no idea that we should become a professional company. However, I was offered a small engagement somewhere and accepted it chiefly to enable the young musicians to feel the sensations of performing in public. Our success was instantaneous, and engagement followed engagement ... This was really why I became a conductor. You cannot have a group of singers without one, and so I had to set to and learn this new department of my art.'[5]

Brooks rightly mentions that Boulanger has here erased from history her conducting debut with Pugno over twenty years earlier, and that she portrays herself here as being 'carried away by events rather than actively choosing to seek conducting engagements'.[6] Boulanger therefore adheres to a traditionally feminine, passive role here, not as a competitor of male colleagues in a male-dominated profession where charisma and power are normally considered essential attributes.

Indeed, Boulanger's conducting activities revived in the stereotypically 'feminine' environment of the aristocratic salon. By the 1930s, this world was very much in decline after its nineteenth-century heyday, but Boulanger had been a regular attender of Princesse Edmond de Polignac's splendid salon since the early 1920s.[7] The Princesse de Polignac, born Winnaretta Singer (the family fortune came from their sewing machine firm), lived in

---

[4] Doda Conrad (1995), *Grandeur et mystère d'un mythe: 44 ans d'amitié avec Nadia Boulanger* (Paris: Buchet/Chastel), p. 66.

[5] Cited in Jeanice Brooks (1996), '*Noble et grande servante de la musique*: Telling the Story of Nadia Boulanger's Conducting Career', *Journal of Musicology*, 14/1 (Winter): 98–9.

[6] Ibid., 99.

[7] According to Rosenstiel, she met the Princesse in 1922 after publishing an article on Fauré's sacred music for the *Revue musicale*, which was then edited by Henry Prunières, an associate of the Princesse who introduced the two women (Rosenstiel (1998), p. 193).

Paris from her late teens and twice married French princes, though her first marriage to the Prince de Scey-Montbéliard was later annulled due to non-consummation. Her second husband – thirty years her senior, a composer and a homosexual – proved a far more suitable companion. Nadia Boulanger and the Princesse became close from 1932; Boulanger invited her to one of her Bach cantata sessions, the Princesse attended for the first time on 13 December 1932 and persuaded her niece by marriage, the singer Marie-Blanche (Comtesse Jean de Polignac) to join her.[8]

Although the fabulously wealthy Princesse – who was also a notorious promiscuous lesbian – was never a close friend of Nadia Boulanger's, she came to trust her musical judgement, and her private concert hall on the rue Cortalembert, as well as her salon, was the venue of several premieres of works by Boulanger's favourite pupils, including Igor Markevitch and Jean Françaix. Boulanger and the Princesse de Polignac had in common a love of Fauré's music, Bach and music of the Renaissance, and both were organists. However, the Princesse's passion for Wagner was not shared by Boulanger. The Princesse was even the soloist (in Vivaldi's Organ Concerto in D minor) at the first concert to be entirely conducted by Boulanger.[9] This concert, which took place on 30 June 1933 at her rue Cortalembert concert hall, featured music by Bach and Vivaldi; Marie-Blanche de Polignac and the young soprano Maria Modrakowska were the vocal soloists in the Bach cantata extracts on the programme.[10] These two soloists also performed at Nadia Boulanger's public Paris debut as a conductor on 13 February 1934, when she directed the orchestra of the Ecole Normale, though this time Annette Dieudonné was the organist. While Boulanger had been associated with the Ecole Normale for a number of years as a teacher, Sylvia Kahan writes that the Princesse de Polignac was instrumental in Boulanger obtaining this conducting engagement: 'Winnaretta's connections with Alfred Cortot led him to incite Boulanger to conduct the orchestra of

---

8 Sylvia Kahan (2003), *Music's Modern Muse: A Life of Winnaretta Singer, Princesse de Polignac* (New York: University of Rochester Press), p. 296.

9 Kahan (2003), p. 304. Kahan writes: 'Boulanger had written out a version of the organ part suited to the Cavaillé-Coll and to her student's abilities, and reorchestrated the instrumental accompaniment to fit the acoustics of the space.'

10 Rosenstiel (1998), p. 245. Marie-Blanche, Comtesse Jean de Polignac (1895–1958) was the daughter of the couturier Jeanne Lanvin, the designer of Nadia Boulanger's concert dresses. Her second husband was the Princesse de Polignac's nephew. A gifted pianist and singer, she was the dedicatee of numerous Poulenc songs, including the *Trois poèmes de Louise de Vilmorin* which she premiered with the composer at the piano in 1938. Poulenc's *Elégie* for two pianos (1958) is dedicated to her memory. Poulenc described her as 'The very opposite of an amateur: a true musician, I would even say a professional. Blessed with an exquisite voice, as pure as crystal, her singing was ravishing. … Yes, she was music made female.' (Cited in Myriam Chimènes (ed.) (1994), *Francis Poulenc: Correspondance 1910–1963* (Paris: Fayard), p. 1043: 'Le contraire d'un amateur: une vraie musicienne, je dirais même, une professionnelle. Douée d'une voix exquise, pure comme le cristal, elle chantait d'une voix ravissante. … Oui, elle était la musique faite femme.')

the Ecole Normale, where she was on the music theory faculty.[11] From 1934, Boulanger was involved in performances under the auspices of the Cercle Interallié, 'an elite men's club whose founding committee included Prince Pierre de Monaco';[12] the Prince was another nephew of the Princesse de Polignac, who acceded to the Monaco throne when he married Princesse Charlotte Grimaldi. Boulanger was in charge of these performances from autumn 1934, and several of their concerts were broadcast. Her relationship with Prince Pierre, a music lover who instituted a prize bearing his name, was close, and in the late 1940s, Prince Pierre appointed her *maître de chapelle* of his household. She remained in this post when his son, Prince Rainier, ascended to the throne. Boulanger's connection with the royal family of Monaco raised her public profile when she organized and prepared the music for the marriage of Prince Rainier and Grace Kelly in 1956. She later taught music to their daughters, Princesses Caroline and Stéphanie, as children,[13] and often stayed with the Monaco royal family as a friend.

In 1936, Boulanger was offered another post conducting concerts for an elite audience. Daniel Crohn, the publicity director of the Hôtel Georges V (then and now one of the most luxurious Paris hotels) invited her to give a series of four morning concerts per season for a fee of 1000F per concert. Crohn had come across Boulanger at the salon of the Princesse de Polignac, a part-owner of the hotel. The idea of a concert series in a hotel was not new – indeed, several competitors of the Georges V already hosted similar events – but the concerts were a welcome opportunity for Boulanger and her ensemble to give public performances before their groundbreaking Monteverdi recordings of February 1937.[14]

Edwin Roxburgh stresses the novelty of Boulanger's performances of early music, and emphasizes that 'she was also a marvellous performer – a splendid organist – and I remember her performances of Brahms two-piano works with Dinu Lipatti, where you wouldn't know which pianist was Lipatti and which was Boulanger. And of course there was the monumental work she did on Monteverdi in the 20s and 30s, recording many of his works for the first time, with piano accompaniment of course, but that was the fashion in those days.'[15]

Typically, Nadia Boulanger did not want to draw attention to the pioneering nature of her Monteverdi recordings, instead insisting to Bruno Monsaingeon that the idea was 'in the air at that time'. She said: 'I would like to say it was I who rediscovered Monteverdi, but that would be

---

[11] Kahan (2003), p. 314.

[12] Ibid., p. 315.

[13] Unlike her other students, however, the two girls were spared the rigours of a traditional French solfège course.

[14] Rosenstiel (1998), pp. 264 and 270.

[15] Interview with the author, 5 March 2001.

claiming something of which I am unworthy. Vincent d'Indy and Charles Bordes did an extraordinary job in creating an edition, though they did make one mistake: they translated the texts into French.'[16] Her (Italian-language) recordings were made in 1937, and she was the editor of much of the Renaissance repertoire performed by her vocal ensemble. Alexandra Laederich notes that the 'core of the ensemble were the singers who participated in the London concerts in 1936: 3 sopranos (Marie-Blanche de Polignac, Gisèle Peyron and Irène Kédroff), 2 contraltos (Lucie Rauh and Nathalie Kédroff), 2 tenors (Hugues Cuénod and Paul Derenne), 2 basses (Doda Conrad and Nicolas Kiritchenko)'.[17] While several ensemble members were French, a significant number were of Eastern European origin; Boulanger had a lifelong attachment to Russian culture because of her mother's origins, and also had many Polish friends.

These London concerts – a series of five programmes, each about half an hour long, which were recorded for broadcast by the BBC – were given thanks to the financial support of the Princesse de Polignac. Anthony Lewis was responsible for the BBC broadcast in 1934; he had studied with Boulanger at Fontainebleau, and was one of the select number invited to Gargenville; he had started a series of programmes entitled *Foundations of Music* and wanted to invite Boulanger to give lectures and performances as part of this series.[18] The programmes focused on French vocal music from the French Renaissance to the present day, including two premieres by Poulenc: his *Litanies à la Vierge Noire* and 'Belle et ressemblante', the fifth of his *Sept chansons* (1936).[19] The *Litanies à la Vierge Noire*, written after a pilgrimage to Rocamadour that marked Poulenc's return to the Catholic faith and which was a crucial turning point in his life, were written for the ensemble. Poulenc wrote in a letter to Boulanger in September 1936 that the work was 'surely one of the two of three works by me that would be my "Desert Island Discs". It's written for female chorus in three parts and organ. I offer you the premiere whenever and wherever you wish. ... I'm relying on you to help me edit the organ part, which is rather straightforward.'[20] The work was first performed on 17 November 1936 in

---

16 Bruno Monsaingeon (1980), *Mademoiselle: Entretiens avec Nadia Boulanger* (Paris: Van de Velde), p. 95; 'Je veux bien avoir redécouvert Monteverdi, mais ce serait m'approprier un bien qui ne me revient pas. ... Vincent d'Indy et Charles Bordes avaient accompli un travail préparatoire d'édition extraordinaire avec toutefois une erreur: ils l'avaient traduit en français.'

17 Alexandra Laederich (2002), 'La première audition à Londres des *Litanies à la Vierge Noire*', in Alban Ramaut (ed.), *Francis Poulenc et la voix: texte et contexte* (Lyon: Symétrie), p. 160.

18 Rosenstiel (1998), p. 264.

19 Laederich provides complete programme lists in her 2002 article: pp. 166–7.

20 Chimènes (ed.) (1994), p. 428: 'sûrement une des deux ou trois oeuvres de moi que j'emporterais avec moi au jeu de l'île déserte. C'est écrit pour choeur de femmes à trois parties et orgue. Je vous en offre la première audition pour où et quand vous voudrez. ... Je compte absolument sur vous pour m'aider à mettre au point la partie d'orgue, très simple d'ailleurs.'

the company of works by French medieval and Renaissance composers including Pérotin and Josquin, usually in performing editions by Nadia Boulanger, and a short new work by her student Léo Préger. Boulanger accompanied the ensemble at the piano for several numbers, though Annette Dieudonné was the organist in the Poulenc premiere.

Laederich also notes that two works performed in London by the ensemble were edited by Fauré, who shared with Boulanger a love of Renaissance polyphony. Citing Jean-Michel Nectoux's biography of the composer, she mentions that 'it is little known that Fauré, in 1906, edited three chansons for the collection of Henry Expert (also a former pupil at the École Niedermeyer), titled *Masters of the French Renaissance*: "Mignonne allons voir si la rose" by Guillaume Costeley; and "Quand mon mary vient du dehors" and "Qui dort icy" by Roland de Lassus.'[21] The first two of these works were included in the BBC broadcasts.

In an introduction to these BBC broadcasts, Boulanger succinctly justified her choice of programmes: 'It is not to ensure diversity or contrast that Debussy, Ravel and Poulenc appear between the masters of the Renaissance, or that Poulenc's *Litanies* and Préger's *Motet* are surrounded by medieval music ... There is a reason for this coming together: works from the most striking periods [in French music] have been selected. The idea was to show that the past illuminates the present, but also that the present illuminates the past, and the five programmes therefore create new links between them.'[22]

The Princesse de Polignac also paid for the hire of the London Philharmonic Orchestra when Boulanger became their first female conductor. Her first public concert in London as a conductor took place in November 1936, when she conducted a work by Heinrich Schütz and the British premiere of Fauré's Requiem. Reviews of her conducting were uniformly favourable, and Fauré's work was also much appreciated, though the Schütz was considered to be a work of more limited appeal. In 1968, Boulanger recorded both the Fauré Requiem and her sister's three Psalm settings at Fairfield Hall in Croydon, recordings which are still available.

Nadia Boulanger's public reputation as a conductor thus flourished thanks to the support of a wealthy patron (who paid all expenses for these concerts) rather than through being invited to fulfil various engagements

---

21 Laederich (2002), p. 160; 'l'on ignore généralement que Fauré a établi, en 1906, l'édition de trois chansons pour la collection d'Henry Expert (élève lui aussi de l'Ecole Niedermeyer), intitulée "Les Maîtres de la Renaissance française": Guillaume de Costeley, *Mignonne allons voir si la rose*; Roland de Lassus, *Quand mon mary vient du dehors* et *Qui dort icy*.'

22 Ibid., p. 161; 'Ce n'est pas pour préserver la diversité ou le contraste que Debussy, Ravel et Poulenc sont insérés parmi les maîtres de la Renaissance, que les *Litanies* de Poulenc et le *Motet* de Préger sont entourés de musique médiévale ... Il y a dans le rapprochement une intention: des oeuvres des périodes les plus frappantes ont été choisies. L'idée était de démontrer que le passé éclaire le présent, mais également le présent le passé, et les cinq tableaux ont ainsi créé de nouveaux liens entre eux.'

with established professional ensembles. While this was no doubt the only way a woman could develop a conducting career in the 1930s, it again shows Boulanger's dependence on an essentially nineteenth-century privately financed salon environment. She was one of the last musical beneficiaries of this world; as James Ross has written, 'With the death of the Princesse de Polignac in 1943, exiled in London, it is not unreasonable to see the end of an era. She and her salon were irreplaceable.'[23]

Boulanger spent much of the Second World War in the United States, where she taught and gave a number of concerts. On 5 April 1941, she conducted a concert at Carnegie Hall in honour of the fiftieth anniversary of Ignace Jan Paderewski's debut at the hall, a concert arranged with the support of her many Polish friends and colleagues. The ensemble was comprised of 45 members of the New York Philharmonic Orchestra, and in Rosenstiel's words: 'At the first rehearsal, the instrumentalists not only ignored Nadia, they openly insulted her. While she tried to rehearse the orchestra, its concertmaster, Michel Plastro, fiddled a squaredance tune.' According to an eyewitness, 'She stopped the orchestra and she said: "Gentlemen, this is beautiful music. Let us work together!"' The orchestra later claimed that they were not used to being conducted by a woman, and suitably embarrassed at the end of the rehearsal, they applauded Boulanger.[24]

Nadia Boulanger's workaholism was noted by most people who came into contact with her. She slept as little as possible, and devoted her life to her students and colleagues, both as a teacher and by keeping up a vast correspondence. Paul Dukas, in a letter to Gustave Samazeuilh on 26 September 1924, ruefully commented on a request from Boulanger, who had just sent him a substantial questionnaire to fill in: 'She's going to do some lectures in American and thinks it is essential to inform herself about my "artistic theories." ... I have only been able to reply how overwhelmed I am in the fact of such a stern test, and that I need to think for several weeks about such important topics.'[25]

Even acquaintances could expect a letter from her on their birthday or other significant event, and Boulanger was particularly assiduous in offering her sympathy to the bereaved. Winifred Ferrier (whose sister, the contralto Kathleen Ferrier, once sang for Boulanger) was touched to receive a letter of sympathy following her sister's death from cancer at the age of 41. The letter was all the more appreciated because, as Winifred Ferrier wrote, Nadia

23 James Ross (2005), 'Music in the French Salon', in Richard Langham Smith and Caroline Potter (eds), *French music since Berlioz* (Aldershot: Ashgate, 2006), p. 113.

24 Rosenstiel (1998), pp. 318–19.

25 Autograph letter; sold in Hôtel Drouot sale on 20 October 2004 (Thierry Bodin, expert): 'Elle va faire des conférences en Amérique et juge indispensable de se documenter sur mes 'théories d'art'. ... Je n'ai pu lui répondre jusqu'ici que par l'expression de mon épouvante devant une épreuve aussi grave et la promesse de réfléchir pendant quelques semaines à tant de sujets importants.'

Boulanger knew exactly what it was like to lose a beloved sister at a young age. While one might presume that the correspondence between the two women would be limited to this single expression of sympathy, this was not Nadia Boulanger's style. For the 25 years until Winifred Ferrier's own death, Boulanger sent her a letter on the anniversary of her sister's death. Miss Ferrier replied conscientiously to each of these letters; on 10 October 1975, she wrote: 'Dear Mlle Boulanger, It is wonderful of you to remember the sad date of 8th October, although it is 22 years since Kathleen died.' Winifred Ferrier and Nadia Boulanger met on only one occasion, in 1950 at Nadia Boulanger's home. Miss Ferrier's surprise that Boulanger should continue the correspondence is apparent, though it is naturally expressed in a very British, reserved manner.[26]

Judging by the significant surviving correspondence to Nadia Boulanger housed in the Bibliothèque Nationale de France, only one person regretted not being in closer touch with her: Lili Boulanger's closest friend, Miki Piré. Miki Piré was clearly a sensitive and insecure young woman whose friendship with the sisters was central to her life. She never really got over Lili's death (she always refers to her in letters as 'Elle' with a capital E, as if she were a deity) and found it difficult to cope with the physical and emotional distance between herself and Nadia Boulanger in later years.

Although Nadia Boulanger was an exceptionally prolific correspondent, she was reluctant to publish any writings by herself; she grew to dislike reviewing concerts, no doubt because the short lapse of time between writing and publication was anathema to her perfectionist temperament. Also, she sometimes struggled with the written word, as she admitted in a letter to Poulenc written on 11 September 1931. Poulenc had recently sent her copies of his *Trois poèmes de Louise Lalanne* and *Quatre poèmes d'Apollinaire*, and she responded: 'If I was not so afraid of words, I would better be able to express how much I loved this work which is so profoundly musical, its intelligent declamation, its freshness and vitality, its feeling too – and then this "unique quality" which is yours alone (My God what appalling expression!). But I am afraid of words – and I simply thank you for being such a *musician*.'[27]

Nadia Boulanger's decline in health (and, some would say, influence) was painful for those close to her to witness. By the 1950s, the American

---

[26] In a letter written to Nadia Boulanger on 21 October 1952, Kathleen Ferrier expressed regret at being unable to accept an invitation to sing in a *De profundis* on 29 December that year – perhaps Lili Boulanger's setting of Psalm 130 – though she hoped it would be possible in the future to perform with her. Sadly, the contralto did not live long enough to follow up this intriguing offer (letter now housed in the BN).

[27] Chimènes (1994), p. 345; 'Si je n'avais pas si peur des mots, je vous dirais mieux combine j'ai aimé ces pages si réellement musicales, cette déclamation si intelligente, cette rapide et fraîche vitalité, l'émotion aussi – et puis ce "quelquechose de vous" qui n'est qu'à vous (Mon Dieu quel français!). Mais j'ai peur des mots – et je vous remercie tout simplement d'être un tel *musicien*.'

composer Ned Rorem thought that her former vigour had gone and her social behaviour was anachronistic; he wrote 'At her "Wednesdays", she moves like an automaton with still enough oil in its unreal veins to provide transfusions for certain human ladies. ... She *receives*, and in a manner unrivalled for quaintness.'[28]

Virgil Thomson wrote in 1962: 'America does not greatly need her now, though she remains our Alma Mater ... She loves us for old times' sake, as we love her; and she adores revisiting us. But her real work today is with students from the just now developing musical regions.'[29] He thereby implied that Nadia Boulanger's principal value was as a teacher of the fundamentals of Western musical culture to those who lack this foundation. Thomson's view supports Boulanger's own opinion that one can effectively teach only the basics of the musical language, and that only those students who have mastered these basics are capable of realizing their musical talent.

In 1978, Doda Conrad proposed to Emmanuel Bondeville, the 'Secrétaire Perpétuel de l'Académie des Beaux-Arts', to give him his impressive title, that Nadia Boulanger could be elected as the first female member of the Institut for her ninetieth birthday. The august body overseeing French cultural life (and, in the Boulanger sisters' student days, the Prix de Rome) decided to award her a gold medal and make Boulanger a Grand Officier of the Legion d'Honneur, the highest French civilian decoration, but Conrad 'had to realize that the idea [of a female member of the Institut] was impossible; the nomination of a female musician would create a precedent, and the members of all the other sections would then present their own female candidates!'[30] Clearly, this notion was beyond the pale, though the first woman member was elected only two years after Conrad's proposal, when the novelist Marguerite Yourcenar became a member in 1980.

Nadia Boulanger's impact on musical life of the twentieth century was huge: as the teacher of several prominent American composers, she was often viewed as the embodiment of French musical culture. As one of the first women conductors, she was an assiduous promoter of her sister's music

---

[28] Ned Rorem (1966), *The Paris Diary of Ned Rorem: With a Portrait of the Diarist by Robert Phelps* (New York: Brazillier), p. 20. Although Rorem was one of the most prominent American Francophile composers of his generation, he did not actually study with her, though he did win the Prix Lili Boulanger in 1950. He did, though, approach Nadia Boulanger as a potential student, but, in his words, 'She weighed the pros and cons but concluded that at twenty-four I was now formed – her nudging could only falsify what she termed my *nature bête*' (in Rorem (1983), *Setting the Tone: Essays and a Diary* (New York: Coward-McCann), p. 19).

[29] Virgil Thomson, article in *New York Times Magazine* (4 February 1962).

[30] Conrad (1995), 251; '[il] fut obligé de se rendre à l'évidence que la chose était infaisable; la nomination d'une musicienne ferait jurisprudence, et les membres des autres sections de l'Institut de France présenteraient tous des candidats!'

(though not of her own) and her innovative concert programmes introduced many to early music as well as contemporary works by her pupils. She moved in aristocratic as well as artistic circles and provided a valuable service by introducing pupils and other composers she admired, including Poulenc, to potential patrons and commissioners.

Her legacy as a composer, however, is more problematic. Nadia Boulanger's former pupil Georges Szipine, and others, believed that her failure to win first prize in the Prix de Rome could be ascribed to sexism.[31] Nadia Boulanger did not wish to discuss this possibility, refused to acknowledge that she could be seen as a role model for women composers and often said that women could not hope to combine an artistic career with family life. In an interview given in the year that she abandoned composition, she was asked about the principal concerns of young women of the time. She replied: 'Artists think only of their art, and they consider it is totally incompatible with the joys of family life. From the day a woman wants to play her one true role – that of mother and wife – it is impossible for her to be an artist as well.'[32] Her apparent lack of sympathy with the feminist movement is revealed by her oft-repeated belief that marriage and caring for children were the supreme female achievements. This view devalues Nadia Boulanger's own considerable professional success, since she never married and had no children.

Boulanger once described herself as 'a mere teacher',[33] again diminishing her own achievements. Whilst she is surely correct in implying that, in the musical world, teachers are rather less important than composers, it is also fair to say that teaching was the only branch of the musical profession in which she could have excelled. But by the end of her long life, women composers had become less of a novelty than they were in the early years of the twentieth century. It is depressing to note that critics of Boulanger's music almost invariably made reference to her gender, refusing to judge her music on its merits. Whatever obstacles Boulanger encountered in her teaching career, she was invariably taken seriously by her fellow professionals and gained a worldwide reputation that no woman composer of her generation achieved.

Boulanger's teaching career flourished largely thanks to private support. As we have seen, her talented but impecunious students were effectively cross-subsidized by aristocratic or wealthy but less talented individuals. Her performing ensemble similarly combined aristocratic performers with those

---

[31] Interview with Bernard Keeffe for the BBC programme *The Tender Tyrant* (first broadcast in September 1969), consulted at the National Sound Archive.

[32] Interview in *Femina* (1913): 647: 'Les artistes ne rêvent qu'à leur art et le jugent absolument incompatible avec les joies de l'existence familiale. Du jour où la femme veut tenir son rôle véritable de mère et d'épouse, il lui est impossible de tenir son rôle d'artiste, écrivain ou musicienne.'

[33] In an interview with the magazine *Minerva* (15 July 1928); cited in Rosenstiel (1998), p. 222.

of humbler origins, and several members (from both these social camps) were of non-French origin. Perhaps Boulanger could be seen as a mediator between these two universes: from a supposedly royal and exotic though not wealthy background on her mother's side, and descended from working musicians on her father's side, she fitted in with both camps and her wide-ranging musicianship and expertise guaranteed her position as the director of the ensemble.

The two sisters may have had several musical influences in common, and both benefited from the stimulus of a musical family and a Conservatoire education, but they have always been perceived quite differently as creative artists. There are factors besides the likely differences in their natural ability as composers which must be considered in this context. Firstly, female composers were very much in the minority in early twentieth-century Paris; although women composers are still a minority, it must be remembered that Nadia and Lili Boulanger were viewed as pioneers, and Nadia certainly prepared the ground for her younger sister's success in the Prix de Rome. Women composers in the decades preceding the sisters' emergence as composers (in Paris, these included Cécile Chaminade) tended to work in genres considered 'appropriate' for women: the solo song and piano piece. Such works could be performed in private homes; the woman's work was therefore safely contained within the domestic sphere. There was much resistance to women seeking a wider audience for their compositions, and it was expected that a woman would not seek to earn a living from her music.

If we compare the musical careers of the two sisters, some significant differences are apparent. As the catalogue of her works forming Appendix A demonstrates, the vast majority of Nadia Boulanger's works are solo songs, and her only significant large-scale pieces (other than works composed for Conservatoire competitions) are a *Rapsodie variée* for piano and orchestra, written for and premiered by Pugno, and the opera composed in collaboration with Pugno, *La ville morte*. As she composed no substantial works after his death, we may assume that she felt she could only succeed in the public genres of orchestral or operatic music with the support of this influential older man. As a composer, she therefore largely conformed to public expectations of the capabilities of a female composer, and many of her works were first tried out in the family home. The sentimental, second-rate verse she chose to set typifies the texts set by composers of salon music; the majority of these poems deal with the topics of love, romance and piety, and treat these topics in the superficial manner which was considered sufficiently inoffensive to be suited to a young female audience.[34] At the same time, Nadia Boulanger was obliged to earn her

---

[34] Simone de Beauvoir recalls in her *Mémoires d'une jeune fille rangée* that her unmarried aunt, even when in her twenties, was expected to read only books written for young girls.

living as a musician to support not only herself, but also her mother and ailing sister.

Lili Boulanger's death resulted in Nadia Boulanger taking charge of her younger sister's musical legacy. Only one work of Lili's was published in her lifetime (*Faust et Hélène*), which was published by Durand just before she signed an exclusive contract with Ricordi. Several works of hers appeared in print in 1918, and the song cycle *Clairières dans le ciel* was published the following year, with an attractive blue cover with silver lettering. Nadia Boulanger edited a revised version of *Clairières dans le ciel* in 1970 for Durand. It is interesting that many precise pedalling and dynamic indications in the Ricordi score are absent in this revised version; the Durand score invariably indicated where the pedal should be depressed and where a crescendo or diminuendo should begin, but it does not show where these markings end. While most of these differences are relatively trivial, one is important: at the end of the first song, the composer notes that the second should follow immediately afterwards. In the first, Ricordi, edition, this connection is made explicit by the pedalling indications: the pedal is to continue over the rests in the final bar and is not lifted until after the first chord of the second song. The Durand edition, however, simply notes that the pedal is to be depressed at the same point, but does not show where it should be lifted; as most performers would not choose to pedal over the rests, it is reasonable to interpret this as a notable difference between the two editions. Manuscript evidence shows that Lili Boulanger was a good deal more meticulous than her elder sister in the dating of her works and the inclusion of precise performing indications.

While Nadia Boulanger, as a composer, can be seen very much as a nineteenth-century figure in her choice of genres, texts and musical language, Lili Boulanger's style is more forward-looking, and her easy synthesis of tonal and modal harmony is very much typical of early twentieth-century French music. Her output is biased towards large-scale works suited to public rather than private performance, and even two of her songs, *Le retour* and *Dans l'immense tristesse*, push at the conventional boundaries of the *mélodie* in their length and quasi-orchestral piano accompaniments. While, of course, one can only speculate about the future development of Lili Boulanger's musical style had she lived, it is likely that her opera, *La princesse Maleine*, would have been completed and performed, thus further establishing her as a composer of significant works for substantial forces. One could even go further and surmise that she may have developed along the lines of Honegger or Florent Schmitt, for example, as the composer of orchestral psalms for concert rather than strictly liturgical use.

In April 1926, Nadia Boulanger published a series of lectures delivered at the Rice Institute. According to the title page, these were lavishly described as 'Lectures on Modern Music delivered, under the auspices of the Rice Institute Lectureship in Music, January 27, 28 and 29 1925 by Mlle Nadia Boulanger, Professor of Harmony at the American Conservatory at Fontainebleau, and of Organ, Harmony, Counterpoint and Fugue at the Paris Normal Music School'. The lectures were based on three topics: Modern French Music; Debussy's *Préludes*; and Stravinsky. Towards the end of the lecture on modern French music, Boulanger mentions her sister in the same breath as her former student Pierre Menu (1895–1919), describing them both as geniuses; it is clear that the two composers were bracketed together because they both died tragically young. She quotes from an article written by Camille Mauclair for the *Revue musicale* in 1921; he described Lili Boulanger as 'a woman who has divined all the tragedies of the human world and a child as innocent and bent by fate as the poor little princess Maleine whose destiny, a symbol of her own, she sought to interpret'. Significantly, Nadia Boulanger added: 'Even when Mlle [Lili] Boulanger is commenting on the verses of another, it seems as though the words were her own.'[35] The powerful image of Lili Boulanger as a frail and emotionally sensitive young composer who completely empathised with the characters in the works she set was therefore strongly encouraged by her most important supporter, and this image persists to the present day.

On 6 June 1924, a concert devoted to Lili Boulanger's works was given at the Salle Pleyel in Paris, an event preceded by a lecture on her music by Camille Mauclair. Mauclair's text was published in the *Revue musicale*, and the journal also featured a review of the concert. Mauclair describes the composer as 'a child' (une enfant) throughout, and highlights a supposed dichotomy in her life and works: 'There is the tale of a child who died at the age of 24, who was almost always in pain, and the tale of a genius which chose to manifest itself through this fragile and charming figure.'[36] Mauclair is highlighting the mysterious aspects of her composing career – why should such a young and fragile woman be the receptacle of such genius? – and also hinting that Lili Boulanger is not the agent of her own destiny but rather the passive recipient of an external force of genius. While he does guard against the popular interpretation of Boulanger's music as being connected to her life ('Lili Boulanger's music is not the lyrical and sentimental description of her short life: it utterly transcends it'[37]), he also views her as an isolated figure who (paradoxically) could belong to any age

---

35 Nadia Boulanger (1926), *The Rice Institute Pamphlets* (Houston), 13/2: 150–1.

36 Camille Mauclair (1924), 'Lili Boulanger', *Revue musicale*, 10: 147; 'Il y a l'histoire d'une enfant disparue à vingt-quatre ans sans avoir presque jamais cessé de souffrir, et l'histoire d'une génie qui, pour se révéler, choisit ce corps fragile et charmant.'

37 Mauclair (1924); 'La musique de Lili Boulanger n'est pas le testament lyrique et sentimental de sa courte vie: elle la dépasse de toutes parts.'

of French music rather than a composer who, like all other composers, is influenced by the past.

This concert featured a wide variety of her works: the *Vieille prière bouddhique* (called *Prière hindoue* by the reviewer, Georges Migot); *Clairières dans le ciel*; Psalm 129 (*Il m'a assez opprimé*); *Pour les funérailles d'un soldat*; *Pie Jesu*; the solo songs *Reflets* and *Dans l'immense tristesse*; and, intriguingly, two violin works in versions for soloist and orchestra, *Nocturne* and *D'un matin de printemps* (the *Nocturne* orchestral version seems not to have survived, though an orchestration in the hand of Nadia Boulanger is housed in the Bibliothèque Nationale de France). Georges Migot reviewed the concert for the *Revue musicale*, describing the song cycle as a masterpiece comparable with Schumann or Wolf's lieder. His critique of Psalm 129 reiterates the commonly held view of the composer: 'Its masculine and powerful chord progressions are expressive of the dull hatred and exasperation of an oppressed people. It is a forceful and powerful work which surpasses the fragile creature who felt and composed it.'[38] Again, the apparent paradox of a strong and powerful work composed by a sickly young woman is expressed. In an earlier article, the same author compared Boulanger to Pergolesi, Schubert, Chopin and Mozart – not because her music has anything in particular in common with these composers, but again because they all died young.

Some recent critics have reiterated this view. In 1982, René Huyghe wrote, using very French terms which do not easily translate into English: 'In eight years, this young girl, this child, whose fragile and pale figure, so flexible and so discreet, struck so many during the Prix de Rome competition, produced an important body of work.'[39] And Christopher Palmer, in one of the first British articles on the composer published some years earlier, is surprised to note that 'Lili Boulanger's music is by no means the effete, circumscribed, colourless affair such as might have been expected from a frail and sickly schoolgirl whose worldly experience was limited, to say the least'.[40]

It would be unwise to presume that Nadia Boulanger failed to write more large-scale musical works purely because societal attitudes dictated that substantial musical genres were inappropriate for female composers. Lili Boulanger's musical output is more varied in genre than her older sister's, and <u>Lili succeeded</u> in writing large works and, importantly, in securing

---

[38] Georges Migot (1924), 'Oeuvres de Lili Boulanger', *Revue musicale*, 10: 163–4; 'Les progressions mâles et puissantes expriment la haine sourde et la colère exaspérée d'un peuple opprimé. C'est une page pleine d'une force qui dépasse, en affirmant tout sa puissance, la nature fragile qui l'a ressentie et composée.'

[39] René Huyghe (1982), 'Lili Boulanger', *Revue musicale*, 353–4 [number devoted to Nadia and Lili Boulanger]: 11; 'En huit années, cette jeune fille, cette enfant, dont la minceur fragile et blanche, flexible et discrète, avait tant frappé, lors de l'épreuve du concours de Rome, a réalisé une oeuvre qui compte.'

[40] Christopher Palmer (1968), 'Lili Boulanger 1893–1918', *Musical Times*, 109: 228.

performances of them. Her victory in the Prix de Rome brought her much favourable press coverage and opened doors for her that remained closed to her sister. Most importantly, the publisher Ricordi offered her a monthly stipend so she could concentrate on composition, a privilege her sister never received; Tito Ricordi's letter to Nadia Boulanger on this subject must have been painful for the older sister to read.[41] It is hardly surprising that Lili appeared more confident as a composer than her elder sister. Was Lili 'allowed' to have a public career as a composer because her contemporaries knew her health was precarious, and therefore she was unlikely to be a professional rival in the long term?

It would be easy to conclude that Nadia Boulanger's musical style developed more slowly than that of her sister, and in a sense this is true; even her last known compositions, dating from the early 1920s, do not reveal an individual voice. But it would be more accurate to say that neither sister attained maturity as a composer, Lili because of her death at the age of 24, and Nadia because she gave up composing. Many writers have suggested that Nadia abandoned her creative work because she was badly affected by her sister's death, but there is no hard evidence to support this assertion; moreover, Nadia stopped composing some years after Lili's death in March 1918. What is certain is that her abandonment of creative work was due to several factors: the death of Raoul Pugno in 1914; that of her younger sister in 1918; and, perhaps most importantly, her highly self-critical attitude towards her own music.

The distinctly lukewarm critical reception that her music received is surely another factor that led her to stop composing. 'Here's a composer who didn't try to stun us', wrote the critic of the *Echo de Paris* after a performance of two of her songs, and *Le courrier musical* was, as we have seen, hardly more complimentary about her *Rapsodie variée*.[42] The latter critic only had words of praise for the soloist, Raoul Pugno, and his death on 3 January 1914 surely affected Nadia's composing career even more than Lili's death. In Pugno she had a collaborator and mentor who had a great deal of influence in the French musical scene; had he lived, he would no doubt have continued to give her the encouragement and support she needed. By early 1914, plans to stage *La ville morte* at the Opéra-Comique were well advanced, but the outbreak of the First World War as well as Pugno's untimely death resulted in the premiere being postponed – for good, as it turned out, as the opera has never been performed in its original version. This production would have brought Nadia Boulanger a good deal of publicity and would no doubt have led to other opportunities for her to compose substantial works.

---

[41] Fauser (1997): 71; the letter from Ricordi to Nadia Boulanger is dated 12 July 1913.

[42] Critiques both cited in Rosenstiel (1998), pp. 78 and 105.

But if Lili Boulanger is remembered as a composer, it is largely thanks to Nadia, who was a tireless and selfless advocate of her sister's music. Nadia Boulanger's decision to abandon composition meant that she held a unique and paradoxical position in twentieth-century musical life: although not active as a creative artist for almost all of her long teaching career, she was one of the most important composition teachers of her time.

APPENDIX A

Catalogue of Nadia Boulanger's Works

The date of composition appears in the left-hand column (dates in quotation marks are precise dates taken from the manuscript), and the right-hand column details, where possible, the location of the manuscript(s). Abbreviations are as in *The New Grove Dictionary of Music and Musicians*, 2nd edition, with the exception of those listed in the prelims.

'le 16 septembre 1901 Paris' [her 14th birthday]
Extase, v/pf
Text by Victor Hugo
MS: BN Ms 19512 (1), 4 pp.
Inc. 'J'étais seul près des flots par une nuit d'étoiles'

'1er avril 1902'
Aubade, v/pf
Text by L. Tiercelin
MS: BN Ms 19512 (2), 3 pp.
Inc. 'Le printemps fleurit les buissons'

'14 avril 1902'
Désespérance, v/pf
Text by Paul Verlaine
MS: BN Ms 19502, 3 pp.
Inc. 'Un grand sommeil noir' [text also set by NB in 1906]

'17 Jan 1905'
Allegro, orch
MSS: BN Vma.ms.1152, 82 pp.; orchestral parts: CNSM de Lyon

'28 fév 1905'
Allons voir sur le lac d'argent, 2 vv/pf
Text by Armand Silvestre
MS: BN Ms 19505, 5 pp.

'18 avril 1905'
Les sirènes, SSAA/orch
Text by Charles Grandmougin, also set by Lili Boulanger in 1910
MSS: BN Ms 19530 (unfinished, 17 pp., and

unfinished vv/pf reduction); CNSM de Lyon (choral parts)
Inc. 'Nous sommes la beauté qui charme les plus forts'

'Paris, Décembre 1905'

Ecoutez la chanson bien douce, v/pf or orch
Text by Paul Verlaine (from *Sagesse*)
MSS: BN Ms 19506 (piano version, 4 pp.) and CNSM de Lyon; BN Ms 19507 (orchestrated version, 33 pp.); CNSM de Lyon (orchestral parts)
pubd: Hanneucourt, 1905

1906

A l'aube, SATB chorus/orch (written for Prix de Rome preliminary round)
Text by Armand Silvestre
MSS: BN Ms 19494, 36 pp.; MS and parts: CNSM de Lyon
Inc. 'C'est le réveil des fleurs des grands bois, c'est l'heure où s'argentent de feux pâles encore'

'Gargenville, 21 avril 1906'

Élégie, v/pf
Text by Albert Samain
MSS: BN Ms 19508, 3 pp.; orchestral parts: CNSM de Lyon
pubd: Hamelle 1909
Inc. 'Une douceur splendide et sombre'
prem. (public): 21 March 1907, Fernande Reboul (S), Salle Pleyel, Paris

'Gargenville, Août 1906'

Ilda, v/pf
Text by Albert Samain
MS: BN Ms 19510, 5 pp.
Inc. 'Pâle comme un matin de septembre en Norvège'

'Gargenville, 12 août 1906'

Mon coeur, v/pf
Text by Albert Samain
MS: BN Ms 19514, 4 pp.
Inc. 'Mon coeur tremblant des lendemains'

'Gargenville, 1er sept. 1906'

Désespérance, v/pf
Text by Paul Verlaine
MS: BN Ms 19503, 4 pp.
Inc. 'Un grand sommeil noir'

1906/7?	**Soleils couchants**, v/pf Text by Paul Verlaine MS: CNSM de Lyon (orchestral material) Inc. 'Une aube affaiblie verse par les champs' prem. 21 March 1907, Fernande Reboul (S) Salle Pleyel, Paris
1907	**Soleils de Septembre**, W/orch (written for Prix de Rome preliminary round)
1907	**Selma**, 3 vv/pf Text by G. Spitzmuller (Prix de Rome cantata) MS: CNSM de Lyon
'26 sept. 1907, Gargenville'	**Poème d'amour**, v/pf Text by Armand Silvestre MS: BN Ms 19520, 6 pp. Inc. 'Je veux que mon sang goutte à goutte'
'Paris, 15 mars 1908'	**[Choeurs pour 4 voix de femmes sans accompagnement]** 2 titles: 'Die blauen feilchender Augelein' and 'Sie liebten sich beide' Texts by Heinrich Heine MS: BN Ms 19501, 7 pp.
'3-7 mai 1908 Compiègne'	**A l'hirondelle**, 4 vv/orch (written for Prix de Rome preliminary round) Text by Sully-Prudhomme MS: BN Ms 19495, 21 pp.; pf reduction, Ms 19496, 11 pp. Inc. 'Toi qui peut monter solitaire'
'30 juin 1908'	**La sirène**, 3 vv/orch Text by Eugène Adenis and Gustave Desveaux-Vérité (Prix de Rome cantata) MSS: BN Ms 19527 (incomplete; pp. 1–25 and 44–86 only); CNSM de Lyon (orchestral parts only) Inc. 'Vierge Marie, vois mes larmes' Extract *A la mer*, T/pf, from the second scene pubd in *Revue musicale* in 1908 (its MS: BN Ms 19528, inc. 'Mer perfide et que pourtant j'aimais')

'Gargenville,   **Was will die einsäme Thräne**, v/pf
1er août 1908'   Text by Heinrich Heine (plus French version, entitled
                           Larme solitaire)
                           MS: BN Ms 19534, 3 pp.
                           Inc. 'Réponds, ô larme furtive'

'Gargenville,   **Ach die Augen sind es wieder**, v/pf
11 septembre 1908'   Text by Heinrich Heine
                           MS: BN Ms 19497, 3 pp.
                           Inc. 'Ach, die Augen sind es wieder'

'Compiègne 1909'   **Soir d'été**, SATB/orch
                           Written as *essai* for Prix de Rome
                           MS: BN Ms 19531, 17 pp.
                           Inc. 'Vers le ciel étoilé montent comme un encens'

'4 juin 1909'   **Roussalka**, 3 vv/orch (later performed as
                           Dnégouchka)
                           Text by Georges Delaquys (Prix de Rome cantata)
                           MSS: BN Ms 19526, 34 pp. (incomplete vv/pf
                           version of *Roussalka*); Ms 19504, 91 pp. (incomplete
                           vv/orch version of *Dnégouchka*); orchestral parts:
                           CNSM de Lyon
                           Inc. 'La pâle nuit semble bercer'
                           prem. (*Dnégouchka*): 13 March 1910, Concerts
                           Colonne, 13 May 1909
                           pubd (*Roussalka*): Hamelle 1909

'Gargenville,   **Les heures claires**, 8 songs for v/pf written in
13 août 1909'   collaboration with Raoul Pugno
                           1 Le ciel en nuit s'est déplié
                           2 Avec mes sens, avec mon coeur
                           3 Vous m'avez dit
                           4 Que tes yeux clairs, tes yeux d'été
                           5 C'était en juin
                           6 Ta bonté
                           7 Roses de juin
                           8 S'il arrive jamais
                           Texts by Emile Verhaeren
                           MS: BN Ms 19673, 52 plus 3 pp.
                           pubd: Heugel 1910

1906/14   **Douze mélodies**, v/pf
1. Soleils couchants
Text by Paul Verlaine
Inc. 'Une aube affaiblie verse par les champs'
prem. 21 March 1907, Fernande Reboul (S), Salle
Pleyel, Paris
2. Elégie (also orchestrated)
Text by Albert Samain
MSS: BN Ms 19508, dated 'Gargenville 21 avril 1906';
orchestral parts, CNSM de Lyon
Inc. 'Une douceur splendide et sombre'
prem. 21 March 1907, Fernande Reboul (S), Salle
Pleyel, Paris
3. Ne jure pas! ('O schwöre nicht!')
Text by Heinrich Heine, plus Fr trans. by Michel
Delines
MS: BN Ms 19515, 6 pp. dated '1908 Paris'
Inc. 'O schwöre nicht und küsse nur'
4. Larme solitaire (translation of 'Was will der
       einsame Thräne')
Text by Heinrich Heine, trans. Michel Delines
Inc. 'Que veut la larme solitaire?'
5. Prière (also orchestrated)
Text by Henry Bataille
MS: BN Ms 19525, 7 pp., dated '22 Janvier 1909,
Paris'; orch version, BN Vma.ms. 1154, 11 pp.; orch
parts, CNSM de Lyon
Inc. 'O Marie! soyez Marie et mon coeur vivra'
prem. (v/pf): 13 February 1910, Rodolphe
Plamondon (T), Grands Concerts Symphonia, Paris
6. Cantique [de soeur Béatrice] (also orchestrated)
Text by Maurice Maeterlinck
MS: CNSM de Lyon (orchestral parts)
Inc. 'A toute âme qui pleure'
prem. (v/pf): 13 February 1910, Rodolphe
Plamondon (T), Grands Concerts Symphonia, Paris
7. Mélancolie
8. Versailles
Text by Albert Samain
MSS: CNSM de Lyon (first version and corrected
proof copy); BN Ms 19533, dated '17–21 avril 1906',
5 pp.
Inc. 'O Versailles, par cette après-midi fanée'

prem. 30 October 1906, Jane Bathori (S), Nadia
Boulanger (pf), Grand Palais des Champs-Elysées,
Paris
9. La mer
Text by Paul Verlaine
MSS: BN Vma.ms.1149, 4 pp.dated '29 déc 1910';
corrected proof copy in CNSM de Lyon
Inc. 'La mer est plus belle que les cathédrales'
10. Le beau navire
Text by Georges Delaquys
MS: BN Ms 19499, dated '21 mars 1910', 4 pp.
Inc. 'Si lourd, si tranquille et si brave, le beau navire
aux rêves clairs'
prem. April 1910, Salle Pleyel, Nadia Boulanger (pf)
11. Heures ternes
Text by Maurice Maeterlinck
MSS: CNSM de Lyon (2 copies; one neat)
Inc. 'Voici d'anciens désirs qui passent'
prem. April 1910, Salle Pleyel, Nadia Boulanger (pf)
12. Chanson
Text by Georges Delaquys
MSS: CNSM de Lyon (corrected proof copy)
Inc. 'Les lilas sont en folie, cache-cache, et les roses
sont jolies'
pubd: Heugel, 1909 (1–7); 1914 (1–12)

c. 1909–13   **La ville morte**, opera in 4 acts composed in
collaboration with Raoul Pugno
MSS: BN Ms 19674 (complete vocal score in both
NB and RP's hands, *c.* 300 pp.); BN Ms 19675 (full
score of Act III in both hands, 126 pp.); BN Ms
19676 (sketches for Act I in both hands, 31 pp., and
Prelude, dated 'novembre 1913', in NB's hand);
Heugel, Montrouge (Act I OS in NB's hand, dated
'septembre 1923' and Prelude (reduction for 2 pianos)
in NB's hand)
Libretto: MS BN Th.B.4929 (1–3); vol. 1 61 pp; vol.
2 32 pp; vol. 3 7 pp. Volumes 1 and 2 feature notes
in Pugno's hand, volume 3 has annotations by
D'Annunzio
pubd: VS, Heugel 1914

1910   **Pour toi**, v/pf

Text by Heinrich Heine
Prem. Dec 1910, Boulanger family home

'25 avril 1910'	**Pièces pour 2 pianos** (only sketches survive) MS: BN Ms 19516, 14 pp.
'Septembre 1911. Gargenville'	**Improvisation**, org MS: BN Ms 19522, 7 pp.
'Septembre 1911. Gargenville'	**Petit canon**, org MS: BN Ms 19523, 3 pp.
'Septembre 1911. Gargenville'	**Prélude**, org MS: BN Ms 19521, 6 pp. pubd: Ricordi 1912 (with Improvisation and Petit canon, above)
c. 1912	**Rapsodie variée**, pf/orch (written for Pugno) MSS: BN Ms 19509 (reduction for 2 pf, 62 pp.); full score in copyist's hand with NB's annotations in CNSM de Lyon (originally titled 'Fantaisie'); orchestral parts: CNSM de Lyon
1914	**Trois pièces**, vc/pf (in E flat minor, A minor and C sharp minor) MS: BN Vma.ms. 1150 (1–3), 4, 3 and 6 pp. respectively pubd: Heugel 1919. Boulanger subsequently withdrew the second piece and presented the works in E flat minor and C sharp minor as a *Diptyque*
1914	**Trois pièces pour piano**, pf No. 1 dated '5 juin 1914' MS: BN Ms 19517 (1–3), 2 pp. each
1914–15	**Soir d'hiver**, v/pf or orch Text by Nadia Boulanger MSS: BN Ms 19532 (orchestrated version, dated 1915, 10 pp.); CNSM de Lyon (unfinished voice/piano version) Inc. 'Une jeune femme berce son enfant' pubd: Heugel 1916 prem. 29 December 1915, Théâtre Sarah-Bernhardt

1915   **Pièce pour orgue sur des airs populaires flamands**, org
            MS: BN Ms 19519, 7 pp.
            pubd: Ricordi 1919
            prem. 22 March 1915, Nadia Boulanger, at concert arranged by Union des Femmes Professeurs et Compositeurs de Musique, 27 rue Blanche, Paris

1917   **Vers la vie nouvelle**, pf
            Commissioned by Mme Rivachovsky of La Société Régénératrice, an organization dedicated to improving the lot of children by founding schools
            pubd: Ricordi 1919
            prem. March or April 1917, Paris, Nadia Boulanger

1922   **Au bord de la route**, v/pf
            Text by Camille Mauclair
            Inc. 'Cet homme ne voulait plus vivre'
            pubd: Ricordi 1922

1922   **Chanson**, v/pf
            Text by Camille Mauclair
            Inc. 'Elle a vendu mon coeur'
            pubd: Ricordi 1922

1922   **Le couteau**, v/pf
            Text by Camille Mauclair, adapted from popular source
            Inc. 'J'ai un couteau dans l'coeur'
            pubd: Ricordi 1922

1922   **Doute**, v/pf
            Text by Camille Mauclair
            Inc. 'Il y a si longtemps que ton âme'
            pubd: Ricordi 1922

1922   **L'échange**, v/pf
            Text by Camille Mauclair
            Inc. 'Lorsqu'il fut ivre et désolé'
            pubd: Ricordi 1922

1922   **J'ai frappé**, v/pf
            Text by François Bourguignon [pseudonym of Renée

de Marquein]
Inc. 'Ma main a frappé les portes closes'
pubd: Ricordi 1922

Transcriptions

'Paris, 2 octobre 1904'

Messidor (Alfred Bruneau), entr'acte symphonique of opera
transcr for org
MS: BN Ms 19535, 6 pp.

c. 1922

Fantaisie dans l'ambiance espagnole (Pierre Menu), pf/orch transcr by Nadia Boulanger for 2 pf
MS: BN Ms Vma.ms.1083, 24 pp.
Durand

c. 1924

Psaume CCXXVIII (Lili Boulanger); is actually Psalm 129 transcr for unison male chorus and orchestra
MS: BN Ms 19474, 16 pp.
Durand 1924

c. 1924

Psaume XXIV (Lili Boulanger), version for orchestra without the organ part
Durand 1924

c. 1940

Symphony in C (Igor Stravinsky), transcr for pf duet
MS: BN Rés.Vma.ms.1029, 22 pp.
Unfinished. The BN also possesses some notes by NB for analysis of this work (Rés.Vma.ms.984, 8 pp.) which are undated and unfinished

c. 1950

Sonata for flute, violin and harpsichord (J.S. Bach, BWV 1079), realization of figured bass by Dinu Lipatti (pp. 1–6) and NB (pp. 7–12)
MS: BN Rés.Vma.ms. 1033

Undated

Dans l'immense tristesse (Lili Boulanger), transcr for v/str qt/hp
MS and parts: BN Ms 19445

APPENDIX B

Catalogue of Lili Boulanger's Works

1910

[untitled piece], could be for violin or flute and piano
MS: BN Ms 19456, 3 pp., dated 'Mercredi 6 juillet 1910'

1911

Nocturne, fl (or vn)/pf
Originally titled 'Pièce courte pour flûte et piano' (title added by publisher)
MS: BN Ms 19457, 3 pp., dated 'Vendredi 27 octobre 1911'
Orchestration in the hand of Nadia Boulanger (2 flutes, 2 clarinets, harp, violin or flute solo, strings), c. 1950
ded. 'à ma chère Marie-Danielle Parenteau'
pubd: Ricordi 1918

1911

Renouveau, vv/pf (or orch)
Text by Armand Silvestre
MS: BN Ms 19483 (incomplete; 3 pp.); BN Vma.ms.1147 (dated 'Octobre 1912'); orchestral version: BN Ms 19481, 34 pp., dated '20 janvier 1913'
ded. 'à mon cher Maître et Ami Paul Vidal en respectueuse gratitude et sincère admiration'
Inc. 'Mesdames et messieurs, c'est moi, moi, le printemps'
pubd: Ricordi 1919
prem. March 1912, Boulanger home; 9 November 1913, Palais d'Orsay (Prix de Rome winner's concert)

1911

Les sirènes, Mez/female vv/pf
Text by Charles Grandmougin
MS: BN Ms 19486, 11 pp., dated 'Vendredi 15 déc. 1911'; BN Ms 19485 (incomplete sketches for orchestral version, 15 pp.)
ded. 'à Madame Engel Bathori'

Inc: 'Nous sommes la beauté qui charme les plus
forts'
pubd: Ricordi 1918
prem. March 1912, Boulanger home

1911   **[Prélude en ré bémol]**, pf
              MS (untitled): BN Ms 19467, 3 pp., dated 'Dimanche
              12 mars 1911'
              Unfinished?

1911   **[Prélude en si]**, orchestral piece in short score form
              (misleadingly titled by the BN; the piece is not, apart
              from the final six bars, in B)
              MS (untitled): BN Ms 19465, 3 pp., and BN Ms
              19466, 8 pp., dated 'Dimanche 12 mars 1911.' Titled
              'Prélude pour orchestre' in Nadia Boulanger's hand

1911   **Reflets**, v/pf (also orchestrated)
              Text by Maurice Maeterlinck
              MS: BN Ms 19480, 8 pp. (orchestral version in Nadia
              Boulanger's hand), not dated
              ded. 'à M. et Mme Paul Gentien'
              Inc. 'Sous l'eau du songe qui s'élève'
              pubd: Ricordi 1919
              prem. 10 December 1913, Salle Pleyel, David Devriès
              (T)/Lili Boulanger (pf)

1911   **Maïa**, 'cantate no. 1', 3 vv/pf
              Text by Fernand Beissier (Prix de Rome cantata text
              for 1905)
              MS: BN Ms 19454, 32 pp. Dated: 'Prélude avril mai
              1911, St. Raphaël. La suite en 1911 à Paris et à
              Gargenville.'
              Inc. 'Puisque tu dois demain pour toujours me laisser'

Aug.–Sept. 1911   **Sous-bois**, SATB/pf
              Text by Philippe Gille, extract of *L'Herbier, Fleurs et
              feuilles* (1890)
              MS: BN Ms 19491, 9 pp., dated 'Gargenville. Copie
              la 23 sept. 1911.' Sketches: BN Ms 19490, 14 pp.,
              dated '25 au 30 août 1911'
              Inc. 'Marchons devant nous, bien douce est la pente'
              pubd: Durand 2000

1911   **Frédégonde**, vv/pf (dummy run for Prix de Rome cantata)
Text by Charles Morel (Prix de Rome cantata text for 1897)
MS: BN Ms 19449, 18 pp., dated '1ère scène faite du 17 sept. au Samedi 23... 1911'; BN Ms 19448 (first scene and beginning of second)
Inc. 'Malgré notre promesse'

1912   **Attente**, v/pf (or orch)
Text by Maurice Maeterlinck
MS: BN Ms 19434, 3 pp. (copy?, includes some sketches by Nadia Boulanger)
ded. 'à Mme J. Montjovet'
Inc. 'Mon âme a joint ses mains étranges'
pubd: Ricordi 1919

1912   **Hymne au soleil**, Mez/SATB chorus/pf
Text by Casimir Delavigne, extract of *Paria*
MS: BN Ms 19452, 10 pp.; unfinished orchestral version, BN Ms 19453
ded. 'à Comte H. de San Martino e Valperga'
Inc. 'Du soleil qui renaît bénissons la puissance'
pubd: Ricordi 1918
prem. 9 November 1913, Palais d'Orsay (Prix de Rome winner's concert)

1912   **Le retour**, Mez/pf
Text by Georges Delaquys (also text *La nef légère*)
MS: BN Ms 19484, 7 pp.
ded. 'à Hector Dufranne'
Inc. 'Ulysse part la voile au vent' (and 'La nef légère a pris l'essor')
pubd: Ricordi 1919
prem. 9 November 1913, Palais d'Orsay (Prix de Rome winner's concert)

1912   **La source**, SATB/pf or orch
Text by Leconte de Lisle, from collection *Poèmes antiques* (1852)
MS: BN Vma.ms.1151, 27 pp.; pf reduction: BN Ms 19489, 8 pp. (accompaniment in Lili Boulanger's hand, rest in Nadia Boulanger's hand)

Inc. 'Une eau vive étincelle en la forêt muette'
pubd (vv/pf version): Durand 2000

April 1912

[Pendant] la tempête, TBarB/pf
Text by Théophile Gautier, extract of poem from
collection *Poésies nouvelles, España* (1844)
MS: BN Ms 19492, 8 pp. (titled *La tempête*)
Inc. 'La barque est petite et la mer immense'
pubd: Durand 2000

1912

Fugue, SATB
MS: BN Ms 19450, 7 pp., titled *Fugue. Concours de
Rome. Essai 1912* and dated 'Mardi 14 mai 1912 au
Conservatoire'

1912–13

Pour les funérailles d'un soldat, Bar/SATB/pf or
orch
Text by Alfred de Musset
MS: BN Ms 19464, 14 pp., dated 'Dimanche 13
octobre 1912'; orchestral version: BN Ms 19463, 28
pp., dated '30 janvier 1913'
ded. 'à mon cher Maître et Ami Georges Caussade en
profonde reconnaissance et sincère attachement'
Inc. 'Qu'on voile les tambours. Que le prêtre
s'avance'
pubd: Ricordi 1919
prem. 7 November 1915, Concerts Colonne-
Lamoureux, cond. Gabriel Pierné

1913

Fugue, SATB
Written for Prix de Rome
MS: BN Ms 19541, 7 pp., dated 'Mai 13. Compiègne'

1913

Soir sur la plaine, S/T/SATB chorus/pf (or orch)
Text by Albert Samain
MS: BN Vma.ms.1148 ('état préorchestral')
ded. 'à la mémoire de mon grand ami Raoul Pugno'
Inc. 'Vers l'Occident, là-bas, le ciel est tout en or'
pubd: Ricordi 1918

1913

Faust et Hélène, Mez/T/Bar/orch (also exists in pf
reduction)
Text by Eugène Adenis

ded. 'à ma soeur Nadia Boulanger'
MS: BN Ms 19446, 115 pp.; vocal score, BN Ms 19447, 52 pp.
Inc. 'Esprits qui voltigez dans l'ombre du soir calme'
pubd: Ricordi 1918; Durand 1970 (ed. Nadia Boulanger)
prem. 5 July 1913, Institut de France (Prix de Rome judging); Claire Croiza (Hélène), David Devriès (Faust), Henri Albers (Mephistophélès), Nadia Boulanger (pf), Lili Boulanger (cond)

1913–14   **Clairières dans le ciel**, T/pf
Text by Francis Jammes
MS: BN Ms 19438, 96 pp.; sketches in BN Ms 19436; orchestral score (in Nadia Boulanger's hand) BN Ms 19437, 84 pp. (songs 1, 7, 10, 6, 5, 11, 12, 13)

1   'Elle était descendue': ded. 'au Maître Gabriel Fauré'; prem. 6 June 1919, SMI concert at Salle Gaveau, David Devriès (T), Nadia Boulanger (pf)
2   'Elle est gravement gaie': ded. 'à ma petite Miki [Piré]'
3   'Parfois, je suis triste': ded. 'à Fernand Francell'; prem. 6 June 1919, SMI concert at Salle Gaveau, David Devriès (T), Nadia Boulanger (pf)
4   'Un poète disait': ded. 'à Yvonne Brothier'
5   'Au pied de mon lit': ded. 'à ma chère Maman'
6   'Si tout ceci n'est qu'un pauvre rêve': ded. 'à mon grand ami Monsieur Tito Ricordi'
7   'Nous nous aimerons tant': ded. 'à Henri Albers'
8   'Vous m'avez regardé'
9   'Les lilas qui avaient fleuri': ded. 'à R[odolphe] Plamondon'
10 'Deux ancolies': ded. 'à mes chers Marthe et Richard Bouwens van der Boijen'
11 'Par ce que j'ai souffert': ded. 'à David Devriès'
12 'Je garde une médaille d'elle'
13 'Demain fera un an': ded. 'à mon cher ami Roger Ducasse'; prem. 6 June 1919, SMI concert at Salle Gaveau, David Devriès (T), Nadia Boulanger (pf)
Nos. 1, 5, 6, 7, 12 and 13 were orchestrated in 1914
pubd: Ricordi 1919; Durand 1970
complete prem. 9 June 1921, Salle Pleyel (Concerts Dandelot)

1914 **Thème et variations**, pf
Titled 'Morceau de piano … thème et variations' on
the MS
MS: BN Ms 19493, 10 pp.; sketches (various dates in
1914) BN Ms 19438

1914 **D'un jardin clair**, pf
Titled 'Morceau pour piano no. 4' on the MS
MS: BN Ms 19441, 4 pp., dated 'Vendredi 19 juin
1914'
ded. 'à Ninette Salles'
pubd: Ricordi 1918

1914 **D'un vieux jardin**, pf
Title in another hand on MS
MS: BN Ms 19442, 4 pp., dated '3 juin 1914'
ded. 'à Lily Jumel'
pubd: Ricordi 1918

1914 **Cortège**, pf (later arranged for vn or fl and pf)
Title in another hand on MS
MS: BN Ms 19439, 4 pp., dated 'Jeudi, Vendredi 4, 5
juin 1914'; transcription BN Ms 19440 in Nadia
Boulanger's hand
ded. 'à Yvonne Astruc'
pubd: Ricordi 1919

1914–17 **Psaume CXXX**, Mez/SATB/orch
MS: BN Vma.ms.1145, 69 pp.; reduction by Nadia
Boulanger for voices and 2 pianos, BN Ms 19477, 48
pp.; various sketches in Ms 19435 and Ms 19438
(dated 1914)
ded. 'à la mémoire de mon cher Papa'
Inc. 'Du fond de l'abîme'
pubd: Durand 1925 (reduction published by Durand
in 1924)

1914–17 **Vieille prière bouddhique**, T/SATB chorus/orch
Text: translated by Suzanne Karpelès
MS: BN Vma.ms.1143, *c.* 1920 (reduction for voices
and piano); preliminary sketches (dated 1914) in Ms.
19438
Inc. 'Que toute chose qui respire'

pubd: Durand 1921/25
prem. 9 June 1921, Salle Pleyel (Concerts Dandelot),
cond. Henri Busser

1916

Psaume XXIV, vv/org/orch; also transcr. vv/pf
MS: BN Ms 19471, 8 pp., in Nadia Boulanger's hand,
dated 'Rome 1916'; piano reduction, BN Ms 19472,
12 pp., in Nadia Boulanger's hand
ded. 'à M. Jules Griset'
Inc. 'La terre appartient à l'Eternel'
pubd: Durand 1924

1916

Psaume CXXIX, Bar/vv/orch
MS: BN Ms 19475, 6 pp., in Nadia Boulanger's hand.
NB also adapted work for male voices in unison and
orchestra *c.* 1924 (BN Ms 19474, 16 pp.)
Inc. 'Ils m'ont assez opprimé dès ma jeunesse'
pubd: Durand 1924
prem. 9 June 1921, Salle Pleyel (Concerts Dandelot),
cond. Henri Busser

1916

Dans l'immense tristesse, v/pf
Text by Bertha Galeron de Calonne
MS: BN Ms 19443, 6 pp., dated 'Gargenville 24 août
1916'; BN Ms 19444, 4 pp., in Nadia Boulanger's
hand; transcription for voice, string quartet and harp:
BN Ms 19445, in Nadia Boulanger's hand
ded. 'à ma chère Claire Croiza'
Inc. 'Dans l'immense tristesse et dans le lourd silence'
pubd: Ricordi 1919

1917–18

La princesse Maleine, unfinished opera
Text by Maurice Maeterlinck, adapted from his play
(1890)
MS: BN Ms 19470, 44 pp. (various sketches, dated 13
February 1917 to 18 January 1918); Ms 19469, 9 pp.
(Act I, scene ii)

1917–18

D'un matin de printemps, vn (or fl)/pf or
vn/vc/pf or orch
MS: BN Ms 19458, 24 pp. (with *D'un soir triste*, jointly
titled 'Pièces en trio'); BN Ms 19460, 14 pp. (version
for violin or flute and piano in Nadia Boulanger's

hand); orchestral version (NB's hand), BN Ms 19459, 16 pp. Transcribed for two pianos by Jean Françaix *c.* 1935
pubd (flute/violin and piano version): Durand 1922
prem. June 1922, Conservatoire de Paris (Prix de Rome *envois* concert)

1917–18   **D'un soir triste**, vn or vc/pf, vn/vc/pf or orch
MS: BN Ms 19458, 24 pp. (with 'D'un matin de printemps' above; jointly titled 'Pièces en trio'); Ms 19461, 18 pp. (orchestral version, in Nadia Boulanger's hand); Ms 19462, 3 pp., incomplete cello and piano version in Nadia Boulanger's hand
prem. June 1922, Conservatoire de Paris (Prix de Rome *envois* concert)

1918   **Pie Jesu**, v/str qt/hp/org (also transcr for v/org and v/orch)
MS: BN Ms 19455, 6 pp., in Nadia Boulanger's hand; orchestrated by NB *c.* 1960, BN Ms 19478, 14 pp.
pubd: Durand 1922

Lost or destroyed works, and projects

La lettre de mort, v/pf
Text by E. Manuel
Lost

Psaumes 131, 137, vv/orch
Projects?

Ave Maria, v/org
Lost

Apocalypse, solo vv/orch
Only opening survives

Psaumes 1, 119, ch/orch
Projects?

Trois études, pf
Possibly the pieces now in the BN

Deux études, pf duet
Lost or destroyed

Alyssa, cantata, STB/orch
Lost

Pièce, ob/pf
Lost

Pièce, vc/pf
Lost

Pièce, tpt/small orch
Lost

Poème symphonique, orch
Project?

Marche funèbre et Marche gaie, small orch
Lost

Sicilienne, small orch
Lost

Undated: **Les pauvres**, v/pf (Verhaeren), only opening survives; **Psaume 126**, ch/orch, only opening survives

Select Bibliography

On the two sisters

Nadia et Lili Boulanger: special number of *Revue musicale* (no. 353–4, 1982).

Fauser, Annegret (1998), '"La guerre en dentelles": Women and the Prix de Rome in French Cultural Politics', *Journal of the American Musicological Society*, 51/1: 83–130.

Potter, Caroline (1999), 'Nadia and Lili Boulanger: Sister Composers', *Musical Quarterly*, 83/4: 536–56.

On Lili Boulanger

Dratwicki, Alexandre (2005), 'Les "Envois de Rome" des compositeurs pensionnnaires de la Villa Médicis (1804–1914)', *Revue de musicologie*, 91/1: 99–193.

Dumesnil, René (1938), *Portraits de musiciens français* (Paris: Plon), pp.11–23.

Fauser, Annegret (1997), 'Lili Boulanger's *La princesse Maleine*: A Composer and her Heroine as Literary Icons', *Journal of the Royal Musical Association*, 122: 68–108.

—— (2001), 'Boulanger, (Marie-Juliette Olga) Lili' in *The New Grove Dictionary of Music and Musicians*, ed. Stanley Sadie (London: Macmillan), vol. 4, pp. 95–6.

Gallo, Paola (1996), *Lili Boulanger, l'innocenza del songo simbolista* (Treviso: Canova).

Landormy, Paul (1930), 'Lili Boulanger', *Musical Quarterly*, 16 (October): 510–15.

Mauclair, Camille (1921), 'La vie et l'oeuvre de Lili Boulanger', *Revue musicale*, 10: 147–55.

Orledge, Robert, and Fauser, Annegret (1995), 'Boulanger, (Marie-Juliette Olga) Lili' in *The New Grove Dictionary of Women Composers*, ed. Rhian Samuel and Julie Anne Sadie (London: Macmillan), pp. 77–9.

Palmer, Christopher (1968), 'Lili Boulanger, 1893–1918', *Musical Times*, 109: 227–8.

Rosenstiel, Léonie (1978), *The Life and Works of Lili Boulanger* (Cranbury, NJ: Associated University Presses).

Spycket, Jérôme (2004), *A la recherche de Lili Boulanger* (Paris: Fayard).
Stièvenard-Salomon, Birgit (1993), *Lili Boulanger: l'oeuvre retrouvée* (catalogue for exhibition in Issy-les-Moulineaux).

On Nadia Boulanger

Brooks, Jeanice (1993), 'Nadia Boulanger and the Salon of the Princesse de Polignac' *Journal of the American Musicological Society*, 46/3: 415–68.
—— (1995), 'The Fonds Boulanger at the Bibliothèque Nationale', *Notes*, 51/4: 1227–37.
—— (1996), '"Noble et grande servante de la musique": Telling the Story of Nadia Boulanger's Conducting Career', *Journal of Musicology*, 14/1: 92–116.
Campbell, Don G. (1984), *Master Teacher: Nadia Boulanger* (Washington: Pastoral Press).
Conrad, Doda (1995), *Grandeur et mystère d'une mythe: 44 ans d'amitié avec Nadia Boulanger* (Paris: Buchet/Chastel).
Depaulis, Jacques (1999), *Roger-Ducasse: Lettres à Nadia Boulanger* (Sprimont (Belgium): Mardaga).
Kendall, Alan (1976), *The Tender Tyrant. Nadia Boulanger, a Life Devoted to Music: A Biography* (London: Macdonald and Jones).
Laederich, Alexandra (2002), 'La première audition à Londres des *Litanies à la Vierge Noire* par Nadia Boulanger', in Alban Ramaut (ed.), *Francis Poulenc et la voix: texte et contexte* (Lyon: Symétrie), pp. 153–67.
Locke, Ralph and Barr, Cyrilla (eds) (1997), 'Mildred Bliss Tells Nadia Boulanger to Think of Herself for Once' (annotated by Jeanice Brooks), in *Cultivating Music in America: Women Patrons and Activists since 1860* (Berkeley: University of California Press), pp. 209–13.
Monsaingeon, Bruno (1980), *Mademoiselle: Entretiens avec Nadia Boulanger* (Paris: Van de Velde).
Orr, Robin (1979), 'A Note on Nadia Boulanger', *Musical Times*, 999.
Perlis, Vivian and Rosenstiel, Léonie (1995), 'Boulanger, Nadia (Juliette)', in *The New Grove Dictionary of Women Composers*, ed. Rhian Samuel and Julie Anne Sadie (London: Macmillan), pp. 79–80.
Potter, Caroline (2000), 'Nadia Boulanger's and Raoul Pugno's *La ville morte*', *Opera Quarterly*, 16/3: 397–406.
—— (2001), 'Nadia Boulanger', in *The New Grove Dictionary of Music and Musicians*, ed. Stanley Sadie (London: Macmillan), vol. 4, pp. 96–8.
—— (2002), 'Nadia Boulanger (1887–1979): The Teacher in the Marketplace', in *The Business of Music*, ed. Michael Talbot (Liverpool: University of Liverpool Press), 152–70.
Rosenstiel, Léonie (1982, reprinted in paperback 1998), *Nadia Boulanger: A*

Life in Music (New York and London: Norton).

Simeone, Nigel (2001), 'Offrandes oubliées 2: Messiaen, Boulanger and José Bruyr', *Musical Times* (Spring): 17–22.

Spycket, Jérôme (1987), *Nadia Boulanger* (Lausanne: Payot).

Sources mentioning Nadia Boulanger

Bernard, Jonathan W. (1990), 'An interview with Elliott Carter', *Perspectives of New Music*, 28/2 (Summer): 180–215.

Copland, Aaron and Perlis, Vivian (1984), *Copland*, vol. 1: *1900–1942* (London: Faber).

Craft, Robert (ed.) (1982), *Stravinsky: Selected Correspondence,* vol. 1 (London: Faber), pp. 235–62.

Kahan, Sylvia (2003), *Music's Modern Muse: A Life of Winnaretta Singer, Princesse de Polignac* (New York: University of Rochester Press).

Kostelanetz, Richard (ed.) (1997), *Writings on Glass* (New York: Schirmer).

Li-Koechlin, Madeleine (ed.) (1982), *Charles Koechlin (1967–1950): Correspondance,* triple number of *Revue musicale* (348–50).

Olmstead, Andrea (1987), *Conversations with Roger Sessions* (Boston: Northeastern University Press).

—— (ed.) (1992), *The Correspondence of Roger Sessions* (Boston: Northeastern University Press).

Index